WELL FED, FLAT BROKE

EMILY WIGHT

WELL FED FED FLAT BROKE

RECIPES FOR
MODEST BUDGETS
AND
MESSY KITCHENS

ARSENAL PULP PRESS • VANCOUVER

ARSENAL PULP PRESS
Suite 202–211 East Georgia St.
Vancouver, BC V6A 1Z6
Canada
arsenalpulp.com

The publisher gratefully acknowledges the support of the Government of Canada
(through the Canada Book Fund) and the Government of British Columbia
(through the Book Publishing Tax Credit Program) for its publishing activities.

The author and publisher assert that the information contained in this book is
true and complete to the best of their knowledge. All recommendations are made
without the guarantee on the part of the author and publisher. The author and
publisher disclaim any liability in connection with the use of this information. For
more information, contact the publisher.

Note for our UK readers: measurements for non-liquids are for volume, not weight.

Design by Gerilee McBride
All photographs and food styling by Tracey Kusiewicz/Foodie Photography except
for the following: Emily Wight (pp. 2, 5, 21, 29, 81, 117, 119, 134–135, 174,
184–185, 205–207, 247; Bethany Schiedel (p. 11); Jordan Mitchell (p. 47);
Gerilee McBride (p. 65); Grace Yaginuma (p. 133)
Editing by Susan Safyan

Printed and bound in Canada

Library and Archives Canada Cataloguing in Publication:

Wight, Emily, 1983–, author
Well fed, flat broke : recipes for modest budgets and
messy kitchens / Emily Wight.

Includes index.
Issued in print and electronic formats.
ISBN 978-1-55152-579-2 (pbk.).—ISBN 978-1-55152-580-8 (epub)

1. Low budget cooking. 2. Cookbooks. I. Title.

TX714.W547 2015   641.5'52   C2015-900397-0
                                           C2015-900398-9

TO NICK AND HUNTER.

SORRY FOR LEAVING THE KITCHEN SUCH A MESS, AND SO STICKY.

CONTENTS

INTRODUCTION

I like to believe that the best cooks are the messiest cooks because they are so focused on the masterful preparation of a meal that things like spilled liquids and crumbs are secondary or irrelevant. However unfounded that idea might be, I've put my faith in it—I need to believe that what I am doing is worthwhile, even if it is only in the moment. I need Nick to believe that too, because I need him to wash the floor.

Nick and I live in an apartment in East Vancouver, and it is wonderful and terrible and expensive and perfect and dusty. We have a two-year-old, Hunter, and when people come over and step in something sticky, I blame him. Our couch smells like yogurt and peanut butter, and I pretend it's all his fault—a toddler is a scapegoat, which makes up for so many of the other things a toddler is. We also have a cat and a lot of cat hair everywhere.

Nick and I have creative writing degrees—we met in poetry class—so we've never been wealthy. We're not even economical with our words. But we're better with money now than we have been, out of necessity—Vancouver can be a hard place to live, especially for low-income people and young families. Daycare for a single child can cost as much per month as rent. It's not impossible to make it work here, but it's not always easy; here, as elsewhere, what you save in money you often lose in time.

We are all doing our best, recognizing that "our best" is measured on a sliding scale. Some days, my best is a lovingly prepared meal with wine and pleasantries; other days, my best is an egg cracked into a bowl of instant ramen and a series of indecipherable grunts. Some days I cook because I have to, and other days I cook because I love to. It's the love that makes the have-to's worthwhile.

I don't remember a time when I wasn't so busy or so tired, and some days the world feels very small. At the end of any weekday, I get an hour and forty minutes with Hunter. Most days, I leave for work before or just after he wakes up in the morning, and he eats breakfast at daycare. When he gets home in the evening, he needs to be fed and usually bathed and read to and played with and tickled and to have his constant stream of questions responded to thoughtfully and in oddly specific detail. Most days, most of my time belongs to other people.

Nick also has type 1 diabetes, so just having popcorn for dinner is not really an option for him, to my dismay. We also need lunches for work the next day, and I don't like doing any more than I have to. So I cook almost every day but Friday, unless we're having company. On Fridays we get pizza or sushi or pho, or Nick fries some frozen pierogies in bacon fat with onions and we eat that while we vegetate on the couch after Hunter's gone to bed. I watched most of *Twin Peaks* with a bowl of pho balanced on a throw pillow on my lap. I watched all of *30 Rock* covered in nacho grease. Some weeks, I live for Friday.

I used to feel guilty about what I wasn't doing, or what I wasn't doing "right," but life is short. If you're a mom on Facebook (or if you know moms on Facebook), you've doubtless read that "the days are long but the years are short" at least three times just this week, probably superimposed in calligraphy over a silhouette of a family against a pink and orange sunset, but it's not true, at least for me. The days are short too. There is never enough time to do everything, but everything somehow still needs to get done. And dinner can be a hassle, but it needs to keep happening, every single day.

We do our best. To be honest, most of the time when I bake it's because my apartment smells bad because no one's remembered to run the dishwasher lately and everything in it has turned to reeking rot. Once a realtor friend told me that the aroma of baking cookies makes a place smell like home for potential home-buyers, and I took to that bit of advice in earnest. If a home is fragrant, its secrets are safe. My life smells like cookies, even if it sometimes looks like a pile of dirty flatware.

The best advice I can give you about cooking is to just rethink what dinner, or a meal in general, means. Think of a balanced diet in weekly terms—you'll get everything you need in seven days, so don't spend every day trying to fit everything in, and let yourself be okay with taking short-cuts here and there. And let yourself dawdle over a pot of braising meat for hours and hours, if that's what moves you and makes you happy. Cooking is about generosity, but before you can take care of everyone else, first you have to do what's best for you. Sometimes what's best for me is a scrambled egg and some mashed avocado on toast; that's something that's not bad for anyone (and if it is a problem, there is no lock on the refrigerator or any great mystery about how the stove works). Square meals night after night are for people who can consistently do three things at once. I like dinner to be a single dish whenever possible, though if time allows, a salad is nice too. I don't like washing dishes, and because I cook with cast iron (which can't go in the dishwasher), I like to get away with using just one pan.

Please do take shortcuts. Research supports the notion that a diet rich in whole foods is important, not just for your health but for your budget as well, but that doesn't mean you have to rely on fresh produce all the time. Fresh produce, especially out of season, can be expensive, and in many places not readily available. In my kitchen, canned beans and tomatoes and frozen vegetables and fruit are essential, and are often the difference between a scratch-made meal and a jar of peanut butter for dinner. You do what you can with what you have, including your time. Even Ina Garten is not above store-bought time-savers and canned beans, and she is the fanciest home-cook there is. Good cooking is not about perfection, and it need not be expensive or time-consuming.

Whether you intend to or not, you tell the story of your life in every meal that you serve to other people. My life is messy and calamitous and boozy, and a meal at my table tends to reflect that. I feel trapped and anxious when life falls too much into a routine, so to keep things interesting we eat eclectically, choosing Salisbury Steak (p. 168) one day and bright Rice Noodle Salad with All the Veggies (p. 190) the next. Travel is expensive and rare, so we try to bring as much of the world into our home as we can; the nice thing about where we live is that so much is available to us. Vancouver is home to a diverse immigrant population, many of whom come from Asia, so Nick and I have grown up in an environment where Asian ingredients are essential to the food we've always eaten. It has never been hard for us to come by Indian spices, big jars of kimchi, or Chinese sauces, and so our family's culinary culture has evolved distinct from our cultural backgrounds. We like a little of everything. It all feels like home.

Everything is better if you can find the joy in it, and even though I love cooking, I don't always like it. I'm busy. I'm tired. The little one will just throw most of it on the floor anyway. But even when the week's been a slog and all that's left over after paying the bills is a pocketful of errand money, a warm, nourishing meal is a salve that makes the other stuff easier to take. When work is annoying and the bus smells like a damp sheep's crotch and my bra is particularly oppressive, a warm bowl of veggies and dumplings (p. 201) or a plate of fish cakes (p. 125) is the difference between hopelessness and optimism. If there's joy to be found in cooking, even if you don't particularly enjoy cooking, it's in the eating. That moment when Nick and I finally get to sit down together with dinner is the moment we drag ourselves toward all day long. The weight of our bodies finally off our feet, the warmth in our bellies replaces the dull ache that's been there since three o'clock. When we don't have much else, we have food. Really good and pretty healthy food,

most of the time, and our lives are better because of the simple dishes that we look so forward to.

Even at our worst, we are well fed. It is what keeps us together and keeps us going. It is the reason our floors are sticky and why our friends come over to share meals with us, even on weeknights. The days are short, and you can't do everything. I hope that sometimes you can leave the chores undone and take a little longer over dinner instead. I hope that, in all the mess of life and living, you find yourself and your loved ones well-fed too.

♡ EMILY

KITCHEN EQUIPMENT ✳

I'm cheap, and I only have a couple of cupboards and one drawer in my kitchen, so I don't buy anything that isn't useful for at least two things. However, there are a few essentials I can't do without. Some things you can save money on (almost everything), and some things you should splurge on (a decent knife). Here's what I have, and what I recommend you use.

THE BASICS

Knives

Buy one good knife, then buy one pretty good paring knife, preferably something you'd spend less than twenty dollars on, because if your partner is like mine, eventually the tip of that paring knife is going to end up bent or broken, and you will never get a satisfactory explanation as to why. Buy a good, all-purpose chef's knife that's comfortable to hold and a good weight in your hand. And then make sure you sharpen it at least once a year. A good knife will last forever. A partner who mangles your paring knife? Re-evaluate at the end of each quarter.

Scissors

You need a good pair of kitchen scissors, something that can cut through string and scallions and spatchcock a chicken if you need to; I lucked out and was able to steal a pair from my parents when I left home. They either didn't notice or have grown weary of me. Either way, I have pretty good scissors.

Pans

Buy cast iron, but don't spend a lot. My best-used pan is from the camping section of the local Army & Navy store. I have one 9-in (23-cm) pan and one 12-in (31-cm) pan, and they work pretty well, most of the time, for most things. Cast iron is great because it's durable and it transfers well from the stove to the oven; I don't like dirtying more than one pan if I can get away with it. Once you get into the habit of using it, it works as well as non-stick pans do, and it lasts forever. I also use my smaller cast-iron pan to bake things (see Skillet Cornbread with Blueberries, p. 222, and Orange Upside-down Cake, p. 241)—it's been seasoned so thoroughly at this point that it works better for me than a baking dish in many cases. I'll let you know as we go when a recipe will work in your pan.

Pots

Most of my pots are pretty cheap—I won them in a raffle at my high school graduation—but they're also decent quality; they're heavy on the bottom and they don't incinerate everything I cook in them. I have received a couple of enameled cast-iron Dutch ovens over the years as gifts, and they are what I use most. If you have a small saucepan, a pot big enough to boil pasta or potatoes, and a good, sturdy Dutch oven that you can use on the stove or in the oven, then you're basically set. A stock pot is nice to have. You don't need to spend much on these, but whatever you do buy, make sure that the lids fit snugly.

Things for stirring

I like wooden spoons, and use about four—one long, one short, one for sweet stuff, and the other one (which is who knows how old but I just can't throw it out). You'll also need a rubber spatula and a sturdy whisk. That's all. I don't know why my utensil drawer won't close.

The usual gadgets

A good quality vegetable peeler, a can opener that doesn't mangle cans, and a reliable set of measuring spoons will make cooking more pleasant and efficient.

Thermometer

Get a thermometer, the probe kind you stick into a cut of meat to see if it's cooked inside. This need not be expensive. You should not have to spend more than five or six dollars for an analog thermometer; a digital probe thermometer may cost around ten dollars. You won't need a fancy one. If you're like me, you'll forget to turn it off and let it sit in a puddle of gravy until company leaves and you get down to finally cleaning up.

Tongs

Tongs are the reason I still have skin on my fingers. I have two pairs, both long enough to reach into a canning pot and pull a jar out, and they are metal with silicone ends. I always have a pair in use and another in the dishwasher. They're good for everything from salad-tossing to hot-potato-transport to gently moving a piece of roasted meat onto a platter or cutting board. Get good, springy tongs.

Rolling pin

You should own a rolling pin, or at least something with which to comfortably roll out dough. Mine is absolutely terrible; it wobbled on its axis so I took it apart, and now I have half a rolling pin, but it works and I won't replace it until it cracks or Nick uses it as kindling after finally giving up listening to me complain about it.

Bowls

In the recipes that follow, I usually specify whether you'll need a small, medium, or large bowl. A small bowl is just a soup bowl, a medium bowl will hold about 2½ qt/L, and a large bowl will hold about 5 qt/L. I use just three bowls for most of my cooking, and while I'm sure it would be nice to have more, I'd have to store them and wash them, and neither of those to-dos is very appealing at the moment.

Dishes, platters, and casseroles

Thrift stores are your best friend for things like this—there are always stacks of dishes and bakeware when I visit mine, and they cost almost nothing (which makes forgetting them at that friend's house who never returns anything a lot easier to take). You can also find bakeware on clearance after the holidays—pick up boxed sets then when they're priced to clear. Another cheaterly way to avoid paying too much? Buy seasonal versions of things, if you're not bothered by serving summer vegetables in Christmas-themed Corningware or holiday dinner on a platter painted with lobsters. In summary? Never pay full price.

SMALL APPLIANCES

Immersion blender

When Nick's mom bought me one, I wasn't sure I'd use it, but now I've burned through three of them. I use this all the time. I use the Cuisinart immersion blender with the mini food processor attachment and the whisk attachment, and it's served me well—I like it for soups and making jam. Don't buy a plastic model—let's just say I lost a boiling pot of homemade raspberry jam to a blade that detached itself and its accompanying parts mid-blend.

Food mill

I held out on a food mill for a long time because I already had an immersion blender and couldn't see the point. Well. Let me tell you, for mashed potatoes alone it was worth it, but it's also great for tomato sauces and salsas, and fruit purées. I got mine on clearance for eight dollars, and it's by far one of my most useful kitchen tools. The handle broke, but I still use it at least twice a week.

Slow cooker

I have a Crock-Pot, and it gets me through those weeks when I have to be everywhere for everyone; I also use it to make stock, so it comes in handy when I don't have time to let a pot simmer on the stove for two hours. It's also great for large volumes of stuff you can freeze for later meals—I like making a huge pot of chili or stew and then portioning it into containers to be frozen and then reheated for lunch at work. The only time I use dried beans is when I use my slow cooker.

Kitchen scale

I don't have a fancy kitchen scale; it's not even digital. But it's very helpful, especially for fruits and vegetables, which vary a lot in size—I measure most veggies by weight. This is another thing I found cheap—mine's from a thrift store. I think it was six dollars. Anything you think you'll need but aren't sure how often you'll really use it? Buy it from a thrift store first. If it breaks and you loved it, replace it with a new model (but never pay full retail).

NUTRITION ✳

I don't think there's a single family anywhere anymore who's not dealing with a mess of nutritional requirements and allergies and autoimmune disorders. What a time to be alive! Nick's got type 1 diabetes and is insulin-dependent. On Nick's side of the family, food allergies and Celiac disease run rampant; on mine, heart disease and type 2 diabetes are concerns I should probably pay more attention to.

Also, there are the vegans and the vegetarians and the folks who avoid dairy or gluten (for non-Celiac reasons) or carbs or food that cavemen probably didn't eat. Has it ever been more complicated to try and feed people?

If you are coming for dinner, I will accommodate your allergies and your sensitivities and your weird issues if you give me sufficient notice. I kind of like dietary concerns and affectations; I find them challenging. Cooking for someone with cancer or Celiac disease or a CrossFit membership invigorates me the same way that sports riles fit people up. Special diets are my time to shine! (I don't have enough hobbies.)

That said, the day-to-day of feeding someone with challenging dietary needs is at best something to adapt to, and in general kind of a pain. For us, that pain is carb counting.

Carbohydrate foods raise blood glucose levels the most. In order to balance blood sugar and take the right amount of insulin, many people with type 1

diabetes will estimate the carbohydrate levels in a given meal and calculate their insulin dose accordingly. Those with type 2 diabetes who use pills or fixed doses of insulin to manage their blood glucose also adhere to a carbohydrate "budget"—often referred to as basic carb counting—in order to control their blood sugar and tailor their meals and snacks around a set goal of carbohydrate grams.

Carb counting is an imperfect science, and many people have trouble estimating carbs versus insulin. It's particularly difficult to calculate the carbohydrate load of combined ingredients, especially when dining out or eating meals that deviate from the whole-plate meat, starch, and vegetable model, such as curries, stews, and most pasta dishes. It can also be hard to know intuitively what is a small, medium, or large serving, especially on plates that aren't your own. The easiest way to practice carb counting well is to be able to read and understand nutrition labels. This doesn't mean you should increase your processed food intake in order to make carb-counting easier, because it's also important to avoid excess sodium and hidden sugars, which many packaged foods are packed with.

On the one hand, carb counting makes it easier to control your blood sugar; on the other hand, even people who do it well can find it a burden. Fruit is the trickiest—measuring fruit portions can be challenging, because one serving of fruit is not necessarily the same thing as one whole fruit. I make us smoothies in the morning when we're running behind, and if Nick misjudges how much insulin to take based on what I guess I've thrown into the blender, it can throw off his workday considerably. We'll get to this topic a few times in this book, but there are some foods that your guts will convert into glucose pretty quickly, which will cause your blood sugar to spike and then drop. Ideally, your digestive system will have to work a little harder to do this, which is why whole grains are better than refined grains, including flour and instant rice and oats.

THE DASH DIET

The DASH diet was developed by North American researchers with sponsorship from the National Institutes of Health. DASH stands for "Dietary Approaches to Stop Hypertension," and the diet is meant to be a simple, healthy way to reduce your blood pressure. In a clinical study, patients who followed the DASH diet were able to decrease their blood pressure considerably in as little as two weeks. The diet worked for those with and without hypertension, men and women, and for people from different ethnic groups.

DASH involves eating four to five servings of fruit and four to five servings of vegetables per day, and includes whole grains, poultry, fish, and nuts. It strives to reduce your intake of cholesterol and total fat, particularly saturated fats like those found in meat and dairy products. Adherents to DASH consume little or no sweeteners—artificial or otherwise—or sugary drinks, including pop and juice. As a result, the diet is high in potassium, calcium, magnesium, and dietary fiber, and low in sodium.

So basically, that makes it the most sensible diet ever. It's not one we adhere to most of the time, but it can be a great way to repent after the holidays, or any particularly hedonistic period during which many pounds of meat and cheese and Doritos are eaten. And while the diet is designed to prevent hypertension, lowering blood pressure is good for most of us. A welcome side effect of following the diet even casually has been a reduction in how much salt we use. For that reason, I am fairly liberal in my instructions to "adjust seasonings to taste," as you get different mileage out of sodium depending on how freely you use it.

ON SALT

People have a lot of ideas about what salt you should use and for what. I use Windsor-brand coarse salt for most things, because it produces consistent results. Windsor is a Canadian brand, so it's reasonably priced here; find a brand of coarse or kosher salt that you like and stick with it. I put iodized table salt in my salt shakers (and therefore on my popcorn, which I eat too much of), because a little iodine here and there is a good thing, especially if you're concerned about your thyroid, and especially if you're not getting it from other sources. The World Health Organization recommends that you use iodized salt as a way to meet your daily requirements; however, if you suffer from hyperthyroidism, check with your doctor.

I bought some fleur de sel as a souvenir in France and can confirm that it is wonderful; if you buy it, use it sparingly—it's expensive and most foods are simply not worthy of it. I like just a whisper of it sprinkled on desserts—try it sprinkled atop peanut butter cookies or a slice of watermelon at the peak of summer.

ON FAT

Fat is awesome as part of a healthy diet. Don't fear it in moderation—where there's nonfat (in processed foods, that is), there's sugar and artificial sweeteners and an abject lack of satisfaction. If you're going to eat something, really eat it; you'll get more joy out of the fatty stuff, but you'll most likely eat less (unless we're talking about doughnuts and then maybe *you'd* eat less, but I wouldn't). What kind of fat should you use? There are so many options. I asked a dietitian and was pleased to hear that in her own kitchen, she uses butter, bacon fat, olive oil, and canola—there's no need to get into fancy oils (flax, rice bran, grape seed, and nut oils) unless you like the taste of them.

Butter

In small amounts it's magical and cannot be replaced. It is a saturated fat, so use it sparingly, but when you do use it make sure you really, really enjoy it.

Bacon fat

You're going to end up with bacon fat if you cook any bacon at all, so save it. This is another fat where a little goes a long way—try it in Peanut Butter Bacon Fat Cookies (p. 220), or just use it to fry onions or sear a steak. Again, sparingly.

Olive oil

Get plain old olive oil for cooking, and extra-virgin olive oil for salads. Olive oil is one of those good fats—it's a heart-healthy source of omega-3 fatty acids, which are beneficial for growth, development, and mental acuity. Olive oil will make you smarter, probably.

Canola oil

Use canola oil for everyday cooking, as it's cheap, and a source of omega-3s.

Sesame oil

Use this to taste; I like a few drops of sesame oil in salads, fried rice dishes, or in soups because it's nutty and strong-flavored—it really doesn't take much. Look for toasted sesame oil that's 100 percent sesame; some companies cut their sesame oil with soy oil. Don't bother with that stuff.

Peanut oil

If you're going to fry something at high temperatures, like chicken, use peanut oil. It's a little more expensive, but you can strain it through a filter-lined sieve and use it multiple times. Find the cost of peanut oil a little prohibitive? You can fry with canola, but some people think it imparts a fishy taste when heated.

What should you stay away from? Avoid soy oils, vegetable and safflower oils, which are high in omega-6 fatty acids, something we get a lot of by eating commercially prepared foods. If you use a lot of oil (maybe don't do that?), stay away from soy.

What about the current fad-nutrition darling coconut oil? Well, if you like it, go ahead and use it. Just don't eat an inordinate amount. Is it good for you? That's debatable; it does make your hair shiny…when you apply it directly to your hair. There is no magic oil that's going to make you super healthy and change your life; save your money if that's what you're hoping for with coconut oil. A quarter cup a day may change your life, though not the way you might hope. But that goes for everything.

PICKY EATERS ✳

Before Hunter, I was, theoretically, a great parent. I had such good ideas! "Oh, I'd never hide vegetables in other foods," I'd say. "Kids should just learn to appreciate the taste and texture of vegetables from the start," and "I'd never make a second meal just for a kid—he'll eat what we're eating, and that's that." I was convinced that picky eating was the parents' fault, and that by introducing a diverse array of homemade, delicately spiced vegetables, stewed meats, and fruit, I'd have a champion eater and the smug satisfaction I've always longed for.

So I worked hard, sourcing the very best ingredients and lovingly preparing individual portions of homemade food, offering a different taste at every meal. And at first, he loved it! I was on my way to being smugly satisfied, occasionally dropping totally reassuring truth bombs like, "Oh, I just mush up a little bit of what we're eating, and he eats that right up—I don't make a big fuss, so he doesn't either" to other mothers, as if I'd figured it all out like a damn food genie. Unfortunately, and I didn't realize this at the time, when you get too comfortable with something, or when you think you've achieved some level of success as a parent, kids can sense it, and they'll abandon their course just as easily as they picked it up. Somewhere around eighteen months, he decided that all food is poison and henceforth has primarily eaten peanut butter toast ever since. I have come to understand that I don't know shit. I'm so much better with cats.

Research suggests that half of all parents describe their young children as "picky eaters"; it also suggests that it may take up to fifteen attempts to expose a child to a new flavor before he'll be willing to try it. I think that may be an average—Hunter will refuse things twice that many times, at least. He's an overachiever when it comes to stubbornness. I'm so proud.

Children are naturally averse to foods with bitter or strong tastes (brassicas, root vegetables) or foods with challenging textures, such as meat. In the English-speaking western world, it's common practice to start kids out with plain and bland foods, such as Pablum and unseasoned grains and starches. I haven't met a kids' menu yet that didn't offer buttered noodles as an entrée. As a child-free person, I remember scoffing at this; as someone who is toddler-encumbered, I look at this and hope he'll try at least one noodle, maybe dipped in ketchup, and do consider begging him to do so.

The context for my assumption that Hunter is picky has been that he doesn't want to eat what we eat. This is annoying, but according to Kelly Mulder, registered dietitian and PhD candidate in human nutrition at the University of British Columbia, picky eating is one thing, but particular eating is another. A kid who will eat five or six different kinds of foods, and who will occasionally try something new, is pretty normal. A picky eater is a kid who will only eat one or two things, like plain white buns or one particular kind of soup (no variation allowed). If your little one is excluding entire food groups, and continues to do so for a long time, it may be worth a visit to a registered dietitian or a pediatrician to ensure he's growing and developing as he should. Another thing to think about? Kids don't eat like we do, and the number of calories they need depends on a multitude of factors, including their age, where they are developmentally, and their activity level (an active kid is a hungry kid!). As a result, yours may not eat the same amount every day—some days she may eat everything in your pantry, and other days—or for many days on end—she'll seem to live on air and water. Hunter is like this—he's a binge-and-coast kind of kid, eating a tub of yogurt, half a loaf of bread, and a jar of peanut butter one day, and practically nothing for three or four days following. He's also tall for his age, and solid. So if your child is eating with some degree of variety and appears to be growing and energetic, then just slip him a multivitamin and hope for the best. You'll get through this. So will they.

Have a picky eater? Take heart:

- It's up to you to offer healthy food, but up to them to eat it. Start by offering small amounts of a variety of foods. Small portions may be less intimidating; kids will ask for more if they're still hungry.

- Avoid grazing. Kids need to learn the difference between feelings of hunger and fullness, and frequent snacking may keep them always sort-of-satisfied, so that they'll eat less at meal times. Meals should be large enough that children will still be hungry for their next meal, but not so small that they require snacks in the meantime.

- Milk is not food. Hunter would beg to differ, but it's not. Children between the ages of two and eight should have two servings of milk or milk alternatives (like cheese and yogurt) per day. Let water be their main drink, and offer milk at the end of a meal. They are sneaky buggers and will fill up on liquids if you let them.

- Don't bribe them. Lead by example, be the change … just don't reward them with candy for eating a piece of broccoli. Teach them—by showing them—that eating is fun. Enjoy sitting down together and make conversation that is not about the food; a relaxed child is a child who may be open to trying something new.

- Involve kids in shopping, cooking, and gardening. Make food fun by teaching kids where it comes from. Let them help, even when doing so is not particularly helpful in getting dinner on the table. Involve them in preparing lunch or snacks on the weekends if you're pressed for time during the week.

- Don't restrict certain foods. Limit junk food, but don't make a big fuss about sugar or junk food—restricted food is more attractive because it's harder to come by. Remember all that Green Apple Sour Puss you drank in your teens? Same idea. Let them have treats, and they will learn to self-regulate. Unless they are fifteen. Then I have no ideas for you, except to hide your pink wine and discourage them from hot tubs.

- Get into spices. Introduce herbs and spices to expand their palates. All they want is plain rice? Jazz it up with a bit of cinnamon. Plain, buttered pasta? Try a few flecks of dried basil. All they like is (insert vegetable here)? Liven it up with a little garam masala or mild Madras curry powder.

- Give them a choice. Hunter, for one, is fiercely independent and requires the illusion of control. They're going to have to eat a vegetable, so let them pick which one. Do they like cucumbers? Then always make sure there are cucumbers. Let them feel like their opinion matters by letting them have limited input about what ends up on the table.

- Let them play with their food. You know how they're always licking everything? They use their tactile senses to understand their world. By letting them touch, taste, smell, and play with their food, you let them get comfortable with the food and enable them to approach their meals more confidently.

- Hide stuff in other stuff. It's not ideal, but it will make you feel better. Does hiding spaghetti squash in a muffin mean the kid'll eat spaghetti squash? Then, whatever. Just do it. Yes, he's got to learn to eat; but you also have to get through the week without worrying constantly that he'll get scurvy or rickets.

Even if these aren't perfect solutions, they can be perfectly good coping mechanisms. Here I am, feeling as though I've offered you some real solutions to your potential picky-eater problems, and just as I've hit "return" on the last bit of advice, Hunter has removed his pants and is shouting about his imminent starvation and how just one jar of Nutella could fix it all. Do what feels right, and rest reasonably assured that there are very few thirty-year-olds who subsist primarily on peanut butter toast (or applesauce, or granola bars, or chicken nuggets, as the case may be).

STOCKING YOUR PANTRY ✳

My first apartment was a dank two-bedroom basement suite in East Vancouver, a cheaper part of the city that is well-served by public transit and local businesses. My friend Theresa and I wanted to live near trendy Commercial Drive, but couldn't really afford to live too close. We spent much of our year together covered in sparkly makeup, on a perpetual mission to find the cheapest drinks and late-night snacks. I put on ten pounds that year, most of it from the beef and blue cheese pizza at Uncle Fatih's.

During that time, I started to see cooking as more than a fun way to use up my parents' groceries. I had a full course load and tuition, but (as I am perennially bad at paperwork) filled out my student loan application wrong and somehow didn't qualify for free money. (Years later, I would finally be forced to understand that it was not free money, and then I would experience deep, deep regret.) I had to work more than I had time for, and as I wasn't prepared to trim my beer budget, food was a reasonable place to begin cutting back. Theresa, a semi-vegetarian ("except for fish and pepperoni"), already ate cheaply. But she cooked without necessarily caring a lot about what the result was, as long as it kind of resembled food. I wanted to do better.

One day, Theresa and I will share a two-bedroom condo overlooking some tropical sea, and we will do all the things we do now—no-pants mid-day cocktail parties where we consume lavish, cheese-based feasts—but with less shame and more caftans. We were perfect roommates, compatible in our varying degrees of carelessness and disarray; Theresa is the only person I travel almost effortlessly with, because neither of us cares where we end up, as long as there is beer along the way. We're not "make and follow an itinerary or budget" kind of people, and though this approach can have drawbacks in travel as well as life, it has occasionally served us well. We will be very happy together as Golden Girls, because I will be doing the cooking. We'll hire a financial advisor.

Theresa's signature dish is Fart Stew. In case it wasn't obvious, Fart Stew gets its name from its smell. It smells like a cat's ass, and the smell sticks to all your fabrics (clothing, furniture, curtains, carpet) for the rest of the evening (or week—who can tell when you live in it?). But its ingredients cost little and it takes only ten minutes to make, so Theresa would make it a few times a week. Fart Stew is a combination of whatever packaged side-dish is on sale, a can of (what I assume was) cat food-grade tuna, a handful of bean sprouts, some chopped cucumber, and a bunch of frozen peas, corn, and carrots. There might have been hot sauce in there too. Not that it would have improved anything. "It's so cheap!" she would say in its defense, as if that is the single most important thing about a meal.

I want to assure you that just because you're broke, you don't have to eat Fart Stew. Yes, food can be expensive, and things certainly aren't getting any cheaper, but if you can be strategic in your shopping and open-minded about what constitutes a meal, there are a lot of ways to cut your costs down. For too long we've operated under the assumption that a meal has component parts and each part must be represented in order to achieve meal squareness. Meat and two vegetables, or meat with potatoes and salad, is how I was raised, and it took a long time to break out of the mentality that that's how a meal, especially dinner, should look.

I like Mark Bittman's philosophy of "vegan before 6:00 p.m.," which can be a good way to keep your costs down on breakfast and lunch. If you are disciplined, it's a good approach to meals (and probably life too). I think the problem with defining this approach as a sort of modified veganism is that it can be alienating to some people. It's just food—when we start labeling stuff as vegetarian or vegan, for a lot of people this implies that something is missing or that the dish lacks some essential component. The fact is, there are no essential components; a meal is whatever you're eating. A good meal is whatever you're eating, but with company. A great meal is whatever you're eating, and there's company, and there's wine.

The last time Nick went hunting, he was gone for a week, and I was free to eat whatever I wanted. The meal I enjoyed the most during that week? A small cauliflower, roasted, and three eggs softly scrambled in a little too much butter. With a glass of very cold wine and a magazine, it was one of those dinners that's totally blissful—the cauliflower was a little salty, a little crunchy, and just tender enough that it still had a little chew to it. The eggs were creamy and smooth, with just a sprinkling of finely sliced scallions on top. There was no meat, no cheese, and no bread, but I didn't miss them, or even notice they weren't there.

A meal is anything that will satisfy and sustain you. Whether that's soup and a grilled cheese sandwich, a rack of lamb and roast potatoes, or a sloppy little pile of eggs, if you feel good eating it, it counts. This is how I justify eating a big bowl of over-buttered, over-salted popcorn for dinner at least once a month.

STRATEGIC GROCERY SHOPPING TIPS

1. Don't buy everything in one store.
This is by far my most annoying tip, and it will require you to budget your time a bit. I generally do a big shop every six weeks or so for staples and condiments, and then shop weekly for things like produce, eggs, and milk. I buy my staples (beans, flour, canned goods, and cheese) at a big supermarket that sells a generic brand that's reliably good and affordable. I get my milk, eggs, peanut butter, and toilet paper at the drugstore near my apartment that offers points you can redeem for discounts on future purchases. I get my produce at farms and farmer's markets depending on the season. Sauces and condiments most often come from our local Asian supermarket chain or the little Korean grocer a few blocks from our building. This place also makes their own organic tofu and probably not-organic kimchi—this saves us even more, and the quality is better here than anywhere else. Items we use in large quantities (Sriracha, cooking oils) come from Costco. I also check local flyers for sales on things I use often, and I pick up ingredients like avocados or lemons on a day-to-day/as-needed basis.

2. Buy meat in bulk.

This one requires a bit of budgeting, but you end up saving a lot of money over the rest of the year. Nick hunts, so we get a lot of our protein in the form of wild deer or moose, but if he doesn't get anything in a given year we buy half a cow and store it in the freezer. This might be implausible if you don't have room for a deep-freeze; we don't, really, because we live in an apartment, but I'm not the best parent so we store it in Toddler's bedroom and hope he doesn't wonder what would happen if he put the cat in there.

If a whole or half of a cow or pig is too much to store or too much to afford all in one go, find a butcher you like who prices stuff reasonably. In my experience, a good butcher is cheaper and sells better quality meat than what you'll get in the supermarket. Of course, this takes a little more time. If you can find the time, it's worth it.

Buying better quality meat and less of it in general has improved our lives, because all our meat tastes better and we enjoy it more. It also means we eat less of it, which is never a bad thing. We appreciate it more when we have it.

It can be a stretch for some people, but offal meats are another way to get more out of your meat budget; heart and tongue are muscles and taste like the fleshy bits people usually eat—these can be easily disguised and no one you're serving them to will have any idea. I like cooking tongue in the Crock-Pot with onions, garlic, and spices like cumin and paprika, then shredding it and serving it in soft corn tortillas with cilantro—it's tender, like pulled pork, and meaty. I marinate chopped venison or beef heart in soy sauce, olive oil, garlic, and fresh rosemary and sauté it to medium-rare, and it's outstanding, like a really lean, tender steak. Liver and kidneys can take getting used to; I don't like cow's liver, but we always have chicken livers in the freezer. You can make a pretty amazing Bolognese-style pasta sauce out of mostly vegetables and a half-pound of mashed chicken livers—it's rich and meaty, makes enough for eight people, and costs less than twenty cents per serving of protein, using meat that often just gets thrown away.

3. Buy local, in-season produce.

This means that you don't get to have strawberries in December if you live anywhere but California, but it's actually kind of okay. You will eat a wider variety of fruits and vegetables, and when June finally arrives you will be so beside yourself with anticipation that the payoff will be sheer, unbridled joy when you get to the market and see those fresh berries for the first time in ten months. I'm not kidding. By the first week of July, I've already been picking berries and buying up ten-pound crates every time I pass a farm market. And they freeze well.

I cannot overstate the benefits of a deep-freeze. Find a used one on Craigslist, if you can afford to. They don't cost much, and sometimes they're free. Mine certainly wasn't new when I got it.

Part of eating seasonally is learning to make do with what's available. I'll admit that before I started to really look at my food costs, I only ate a few main veggies, mostly out of habit and because I was comfortable cooking them. I rarely had beets or turnips or cabbage, and never kale or kohlrabi or any kind of squash but spaghetti. I wouldn't have known what to do with them, for the most part. When you make do with what's available, you'll be surprised to discover a whole bunch of unfamiliar foods, and you'll force yourself to adapt with new recipes. Do a little bit of research—maybe what's in season features prominently in another culture's cuisine, and you have an opportunity to try a new dish. The benefit to eating seasonally, aside from the cost-savings, is that you have almost limitless options for potential meals, so you never get bored.

Of course, there are exceptions to this rule. We don't grow a lot of citrus in Canada, for example, and I use a lot of lemon and lime juice in my cooking. And Nick requires avocados to be happy, and his unhappiness is not something he suppresses or endures quietly. If I can't find something local or seasonal, I'll look for an organic option; if there's no organic option available, or it is too expensive, conventional is acceptable (any produce is better than no produce at all)—and don't let anyone tell you otherwise.

4. Can your excess.
The other side of eating seasonally is that late summer and fall are seasons of abundance, and you can get too much of a good thing, especially if you have more produce than you know what to do with. Canning is not terribly complicated, and it's a good way to stretch the joy of summer into those dark, gray months. You can start with simple water-bath canning—the supplies will cost you around fifty dollars to get started (you'll need a canning pot, some canning tongs, jars, lids, funnels, etc.), but then you're pretty much set for the next several years. Pressure canning will cost more, but you can preserve a bigger variety of foods, including low-acid foods (beans, carrots, etc.) and meats, which means you can put up a lot more. You can use a pressure canner for acidic things like tomatoes, pickles, peaches, and jams too, so if you're serious about stocking your pantry for the winter, a pressure canner might be your best option. A good one will run you between $100 and $300; watch for sales.

Canning is also a great way to save money on things you might ordinarily buy but that you can make pretty easily, like salsas, hot sauces, and relishes. If there's a condiment you use a lot, there's a pretty good chance you can make it at home. I will never buy salsa again (which is important, because I eat a lot of nachos).

Canning pro tip: Summer is hot, and canning food in a sweltering, window-less kitchen may not be the most comfortable way to spend a weekend. Freeze things like berries, chopped tomatoes and peppers, and corn, then make your jams, jellies, and salsas when the weather cools down. It'll work just fine.

5. Shop for points.

I don't just shop anywhere and will often go a little out of my way to frequent a place that offers me points on my purchases. But be warned—all points programs are not equal. A program where they are not redeemable for grocery discounts is a pointless points program and not worth your dollars.

Sometimes a bank will have a relationship with a supermarket, awarding you bonus points when you use your store's credit or debit card for in-store purchases. If you aren't able or don't want to do all your banking at your store's bank, set up a savings account or open a store credit card account that you can funnel your grocery money into. For my every-six-weeks shopping trip to the supermarket for my staple purchases (and clothes—I'm not totally unembarrassed to admit I buy my clothes where I buy my cheese), I put a portion of what I usually spend into my grocery account, building it up over a period of weeks. That way, the grocery money is spoken for and I can't spend it on wine, but it also doesn't come out of a single paycheck.

Get as many freebies as you can. Often, when the price is right, I'll buy a bit more than what I need to get the points, and I donate the excess to the food bank using the bins the store places conveniently on my way out the door.

Finally, if it's plausible, grow as much of your own food as you can. If you don't have a yard, plant a container of herbs on your balcony or windowsill; those little plastic clamshell packages of herbs in the grocery stores can run as high as three dollars apiece; that is too much when you just need a bunch of parsley here and there. Grow what you can! It's not only cost-saving, it's tremendously satisfying to tell everyone at the dinner table about your efforts. Who cares if they call you smug?! If you're like me, you'll get used to it.

THE WELL-STOCKED PANTRY

Stocking your pantry is critical, as there are plenty of days you won't feel like going to the store. Most of my non-working hours are spent in a battle against my inner sloth over whether to go out or stay home. The invention of yoga pants made it a little more likely that I'd leave my apartment sometimes, but it's still a battle every time it comes down to my fatigue versus Nick's and Toddler's increasingly vocal dinner-related demands.

Stocking a pantry can be a pricey up-front investment. It won't cost much to maintain, but it's building up your supplies that'll ding you in the beginning. To remedy this, buy in bulk. Spices in particular should never be bought at the supermarket unless from the bulk bins. Those jars you see in the baking section? Way over-priced, and the packaging is annoying (most of them you can't even get a teaspoon into), and chances are they've been sitting around a while, losing their flavor and potency. Buy in bulk from a place with good turnover (one that's busy and refills their bins regularly), then store spices in old jam or condiment jars with tight-fitting lids or small Mason jars.

You can also buy things like chocolate chips, nuts, dried fruit, flours, and grains (and even pasta) in bulk, which will save you a fair bit up front.

When buying ingredients like condiments and sauces, check local flyers. Most people hate junk mail—sure, it's a waste of paper and we get too much of it—but flyers are how I watch prices. ("Junk mail," like flyers and coupons, also keeps your mail carrier on the job!) I need to know when a huge jar of mustard is two dollars, or when mayonnaise is two for four dollars, because that's when I buy. Never pay full price if you can avoid it! And you can almost always avoid it.

Finally, for ingredients that play an important role in the cuisines of other cultures, like soy sauce or sambal oelek or dried chili peppers, visit a local Asian or Latin American grocer where such ingredients will be considerably cheaper and taste a lot better. There's a dish I make a fair bit called Nasi Goreng (p. 39), a Dutch-Indonesian dish of fried rice with ketjap manis, a sweet, thick soy sauce, as a central ingredient. The Dutch brand of ketjap manis, which is the brand you get at the supermarket, costs six dollars for a tiny bottle and it tastes like sadness, but the Indonesian brand I buy at my local Chinese grocer costs $2.49 is three times the size, and delicious.

Feeding yourself on a limited budget isn't hard; with just a little bit of time and energy, you can do it very well. It's hard to raise a family in an expensive city when you live paycheck to paycheck. It's demoralizing to eagerly anticipate payday only to realize that you have just a few dollars left after you've paid all your bills. But a meal should never make you feel poor, even when it's made of simple things. (No Fart Stew for you!) It's a lot easier to handle the indignities of just or not quite getting by when you know you've got a good meal to look forward to. You may occasionally be flat broke, but you should always be well fed.

SPECIAL INGREDIENTS

Annatto (also known as "achiote") is a seed most often used as a natural food dye. It does not have a strong flavor, but lends a red or yellow hue to dishes, including some cheeses. It is sold both whole and ground; the seeds do not soften when cooked, so if you want to use them whole, be sure to strain them out before serving.

Garam masala is an Indian ground spice mixture that generally contains black peppercorns, cumin, coriander, cinnamon, cloves, brown cardamom, nutmeg, and green cardamom. However, the spices used in the mixture vary widely; either find a brand you like, or blend your own mixture to taste.

Gochujang (also "kochujang") is a thick, sticky, dark-red paste typically made with red chilies, glutinous rice, fermented soybeans, and salt. It is pungent and flavorful and can be used in recipes, as a condiment, and as a substitute for other chili sauces when a richer, deeper flavor is desired. Allergen note: gochujang contains soy and can also contain wheat. Check ingredient labels before buying if gluten is a concern.

Ketjap manis (also "kecap manis") is an Indonesian soy-based sauce sweetened with palm sugar. It is thick, sweet, and dark and is useful in marinades, spice pastes, and sauces. Allergen note: ketjap manis contains wheat and soy.

Kimchi is a spicy, lacto-fermented vegetable side dish or condiment, similar to sauerkraut in principle. Commercially available kimchis are most often made with napa cabbage; sometimes it is possible to find daikon, cucumber, or mustard greens kimchi as well. It is spicy and pungent and very high in fibre. Kimchi can be eaten cold as a side dish or used as an ingredient in cooked dishes, but cooking reduces its probiotic benefits. Allergen note: kimchi can contain seafood (including shellfish), wheat, and/or soy.

Madras curry powder is a mix of cardamom, chilies, cinnamon, cloves, coriander, cumin, fennel, fenugreek, mace, nutmeg, pepper, saffron, tamarind, and turmeric. As with garam masala, the spices can vary widely, though Madras curry powder is recognizable for its yellow color. Madras curry paste is also available; in addition to dry spices, it commonly contains ginger, garlic, chilies, and onions.

Sambal oelek (also "sambal ulek") is an Indonesian ground chili paste that's used in recipes and as a condiment. Most commercial varieties are primarily a mix of ground chilies and vinegar, though traditional recipes can contain a range of complementary ingredients. Sambal oelek is made with ground whole chilies, seeds included, so if you're sensitive to spice, use it sparingly.

Sriracha is a smooth, thick hot sauce comprised of chilies, vinegar, garlic, sugar, and salt. It's based on a Thai hot sauce, and is commonly used both in recipes and as a condiment; though there are many variations and different brands, the most often used version in North America comes from Huy Fong Foods in the United States, and is known as Rooster Sauce because of the rooster logo on the bottle.

RICE AND GRAINS

The best thing in the world is when you order Thai food and they send more rice than you could possibly eat and you end up with enough to make a whole other dinner the next day. I know it's technically not a freebie, but it sure feels like one, especially on a weeknight. While it's true that you can get the same convenience from just making a bunch of rice ahead of time, the joy of take-out extras is not having to think ahead. I love it. I love not-thinking so much.

Fried rice is comfort food for a number of reasons—it's easy on the belly, you can make it with stuff you have in your cupboards already (I love not going to the store almost as much as I love not being required to think), and it's so stretchy. The more you add to it, the more meals it makes. If you're not a leftovers-y person, you can freeze it in lunch-sized containers and then take it to work where it'll taste as good as it did the day it was made, even after a spin in that fusty microwave no one in the office will clean.

For Nick, fried rice represents a celebration of all the things he likes—usually, salty meat, strong flavors, and an excess of chili paste. For me, it's about cleaning out the refrigerator, making a one-pot meal, and getting dinner on the table fast. It's basically comfort food for our relationship. Fried rice is one of those things I've always eaten in one form or another—pantry kedgeree, for example, has been a staple food since I left home and needed to stretch a tin of fish over three meals. A little rice and egg and fried Spam has cured what's ailed me for years now—but it wasn't until I met Nick's family that I really got the concept of fried rice as a real, intentional dish.

Nick's family is Dutch-oriented, his paternal grandparents having emigrated from the Netherlands to Canada in the 1950s. The Dutch, like so many colonial nations, left their tulip-addled homeland during the age of exploration for a taste of the spice. A side effect of 350-ish years of Dutch occupation of Indonesia is the influence of Asian flavors on what would otherwise be some bland-ass food. They really needed that spice.

There are a lot of Dutch immigrant communities in the suburbs surrounding Vancouver, and it seems like every Dutch (or Dutch-ish) mom has a recipe for nasi goreng, an Indonesian-inspired fried-rice dish made with a variety of seasonings ranging from a pre-packaged mix to a slop of sweet soy and sambal oelek. The dish is made with whatever you've got—after Christmas, our version often contains leftover ham; when times are tight, we use a little bit of bacon and some mushrooms instead. We've used Spam, ground pork, and even fish. The whole thing is traditionally topped with banana goop and fried eggs, but bananas are *the worst*, so we use sliced avocado instead. Fried rice gets us through, no matter what the times are like.

There's a reason so much of the world subsists on white rice—it's inexpensive, it cooks quickly, and it's delicious, especially topped or tossed with spicy stuff and maybe a bit of salty meat or fish. It's not as nutritious as brown rice, which retains its hull and bran; brown rice is a whole grain, and it takes longer to digest, which means it won't cause your blood sugar to spike and then fall quickly. I love its chewy texture and subtle nuttiness. It's the healthier choice, certainly; it also takes twice as long to cook, so sometimes I use white rice for dinner instead.

I cook a big batch of rice when I'm not too busy and then stick it in the refrigerator (in the pot) once it's cool, and it's there to save me when I need it, usually on a Tuesday when I have nothing left to give to the world or my family. Is the idea of dinner a huge and terrible effort? Fry some rice. Just heard a friend's in town, but you can't afford to go out? Have them over for tea and rice pudding. Feeling fancy? Risotto.

As white rices go, there are degrees of blood sugar-spikiness; the more refined the product, such as microwave or minute-rice, the less worthwhile nutritionally. Long grain white rice, such as basmati, is your best option—it's not too far from brown rice on the glycemic index. They're both somewhere in the middle. Depending on where you live, basmati is also very reasonably priced; in Vancouver, there's a large East Indian population, so I get my rice in big bags at Fruiticana, a local Indo-Canadian grocery chain, for not much money. Even the organic stuff isn't out of reach. There's also a brand of lower-GI "diabetes friendly" basmati rice; if you can't find it in your local store, you can buy it online for about $1.70 per pound. Rice is another product that's often available in bulk; I find it's best to buy brown rice this way as it can go rancid (you'll know it's off when it starts to smell like Play Doh).

Risotto is a dish that I really, really like, but Arborio rice is problematic both in that it can cost a bit more than regular long-grain rice, and that it's a short-grain rice, so it's higher on the glycemic index. One way that I stretch the (usually limited) amount of Arborio rice I have on hand and balance out the simple-carb numbers is to cut the amount of rice in half and make up the difference with pearl barley. Barley costs somewhere around $1.50 for a one pound (500 g) bag, and it's a great source of fiber. The best thing about it is that it's very forgiving—if you overcook a pot of risotto, it tastes like mush and disappointment. If you overcook a pot of risotto split with barley, you'll hardly know it, and this, as the parent of a toddler, has been my saving grace on many an evening. You can even make a barley version of risotto, a barlotto (p. 36). Barley retains its toothiness and chew a long way into the cooking process—you really have to boil it to death to have it puff into mush, and even then…

You can replace a portion of rice in almost any dish and supplement with another grain. Quinoa steams at the same rate as long-grain white rice, and barley or bulgur wheat, which are lower on the glycemic index than both white and brown rice, also work well combined with rice. Try cooking farro or spelt grains with brown rice. Whole grains like these are lower on the glycemic index, but they're also an easy way to eat a more diverse diet. I like these simple switches because they make me feel like I'm doing a little better and meeting a few more of my nutritional requirements. Whole grains are good sources of soluble and insoluble fiber; soluble fiber is, perhaps obviously, water soluble—it's the stuff that's converted to sugars to feed your cells and helps maintain your blood glucose levels. Insoluble fiber doesn't break down the same way, but the great thing about it is it helps you poop, and therefore keeps you regular. Nick won't talk to me about his bowel movements for whatever reason (i.e., because he is unreasonable and withholding), so including a mix of whole grains in his diet means I can just know he's doing well, digestively. It helps me to sleep better, knowing everyone's doing well, gut-wise. (Maybe I don't have enough going on right now?)

Anyway, what's important is that rice is easy.

As it turns out, it may have additional benefits for people with diabetes. A recent Korean study showed that rice consumption may, over time, improve insulin sensitivity in mice, especially those fed a high-fat diet. It's still a bit of a leap to say that the same thing works for humans, but it does seem promising that diets containing rice may improve cells' sensitivity to insulin in the long term; as far as white carbohydrates go, rice is starting to sound pretty good.

How to cook rice without a rice cooker

LONG GRAIN WHITE RICE NEEDS A RATIO OF ONE PART RICE TO TWO PARTS LIQUID. BROWN RICE NEEDS A RATIO OF ONE PART RICE TO ONE-AND-A-HALF PARTS LIQUID. RINSE THE RICE UNDER COLD TAP WATER BEFORE PUTTING IT IN THE PAN WITH THE COOKING LIQUID. WHETHER THE LIQUID IS LOW-SODIUM STOCK OR WATER DOESN'T MATTER, BUT EITHER WAY, MAKE SURE YOU ADD UP TO 1 TSP SALT PER 1 CUP (250 ML) RICE. RICE THAT IS SALTED DURING COOKING NEEDS LESS SEASONING IF USED FOR RECIPES; IF YOU'RE WATCHING YOUR SODIUM, YOU CAN COOK RICE WITHOUT ADDING SALT, BUT BE MINDFUL OF HOW MUCH YOU ADD TO SEASON IT LATER. IN A STURDY PAN WITH A TIGHT-FITTING LID, BRING RICE AND WATER TO A BOIL. ONCE IT'S BOILING, SLAP THE LID ON, REDUCE HEAT TO LOW, AND STEAM UNTIL RICE IS DONE: 20 MINUTES FOR WHITE RICE, 50 MINUTES FOR BROWN. REMOVE FROM HEAT, FLUFF WITH A FORK, AND EITHER SERVE OR TRANSFER TO A CONTAINER TO COOL, THEN REFRIGERATE UNTIL YOU'RE READY TO USE IT.

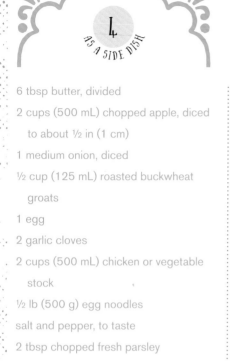

4
AS A SIDE DISH

KASHA & EGG NOODLES

6 tbsp butter, divided

2 cups (500 mL) chopped apple, diced to about ½ in (1 cm)

1 medium onion, diced

½ cup (125 mL) roasted buckwheat groats

1 egg

2 garlic cloves

2 cups (500 mL) chicken or vegetable stock

½ lb (500 g) egg noodles

salt and pepper, to taste

2 tbsp chopped fresh parsley

This is an unassuming side dish, a little beige but deceptively delicious. It's based on a recipe I came across a few years ago for kasha varnishkes, which traditionally uses schmaltz (chicken fat) and bowtie pasta. My version evolved because we never had either of those things on hand. It goes fabulously with roasted meats. You may want a bright burst of color to go alongside it—I recommend a bowl of Peas and Carrots (p. 187).

In a large, heavy-bottomed pot on medium-high heat, melt 2 tbsp butter and stir in apples and onions. Cover, cook for 10 minutes, then remove lid and reduce heat to medium. Stir frequently for 20 to 30 minutes, until apples and onions have caramelized and shrunk.

Meanwhile, in a pot on medium-high, heat 3 tbsp butter. In a bowl, stir buckwheat and egg until thoroughly combined. Pour into pot, stirring to keep groats from sticking together. Keep stirring until egg is cooked and appears dry. Add garlic, then chicken stock. Reduce heat to medium, and simmer until liquid is absorbed and groats are fluffy, about 15 minutes.

Bring a large pot of salted water to a rolling boil. Add noodles, and cook until just al dente. Drain.

Stir cooked groats and drained pasta into apple and onion mixture, and add an additional tbsp butter, stirring to coat. Taste and adjust seasonings. Stir in parsley and serve immediately.

KASHA, OR TOASTED BUCKWHEAT GROATS, IS A GRAIN THAT'S NOT A GRAIN—IT'S ACTUALLY A SEED, AND IT'S RELATED TO RHUBARB. NEVERTHELESS, IT'S VERY GOOD FOR YOU—A GREAT SOURCE OF PROTEIN AND SOLUBLE FIBER, IF EATEN REGULARLY, IT CAN CONTRIBUTE TO LOWER CHOLESTEROL. IT'S ALSO LOW ON THE GLYCEMIC INDEX. TRY IT IN OVERNIGHT BREAKFAST GRAINS (P. 40) FOR A FILLING, HEALTHY START TO YOUR DAY.

KIMCHI-FRIED RICE

I first discovered kimchi one summer when my parents hosted a couple of homestay students from Korea. Their English wasn't clear enough to explain what it was, but it smelled really good; I was sold, and they were so excited to share it. We get our kimchi—a spicy, fermented cabbage not unlike sauerkraut or curtido—from a place down the street that makes it fresh and with just the right amount of kick to it. Look for kimchi in Asian markets or the produce section of better supermarkets—you'll find it near the refrigerated salad dressings and wonton wrappers. You can find gochujang at Asian markets.

6 strips bacon, chopped

2 tsp sesame oil

1 onion, diced

4 garlic cloves, minced

2 cups (500 mL) cabbage kimchi, roughly chopped

2 tbsp soy sauce

1 tbsp gochujang

3 cups (750 mL) cooked rice

salt, to taste

4 scallions, finely chopped

4 eggs, fried over-easy (optional)

In a large pan, cook bacon on medium-high heat until crisp. Spoon bacon out of pan and onto a plate lined with a paper towel, and set aside. If bacon has released a lot of fat during cooking, drain off all but 2 tbsp.

Add sesame oil to pan. Add onions and sauté until browned around edges, 5 or 6 minutes. Add garlic, kimchi, soy sauce, and gochujang, and stir to combine. When kimchi begins to release its juices, after about a minute, add cooked rice. Stir, stir, stir.

Sauté rice for about 3 minutes, until it's broken apart and well coated by the flavors in the pan. Return bacon to pan, and stir again. Taste and add salt as needed. Sprinkle rice with scallions and serve as-is or topped with a fried egg.

4 SERVINGS

LEEK & BACON BARLOTTO

Barlotto is lovely because it's everything that's great about regular old risotto, but cheaper and slightly better for you. A 1 lb (500 g) bag of pearl barley will run you about $1.50, depending on where you shop. Nick likes this dish in particular because it's primarily a vehicle for cheese and bacon, but you feel good after eating it. Serve with crusty bread and a bit of steamed broccoli for a hearty, satisfying meal.

4 slices bacon, finely chopped

1 tbsp olive oil

1 cup (250 mL) chopped leeks (white and light-green part only)

3 garlic cloves, minced

1½ cups (375 mL) pearl barley

1 cup (250 mL) dry white wine

4 cups (1 L) warmed chicken stock

½ cup (125 mL) grated Parmesan cheese

1 tbsp butter

salt and pepper, to taste

In a large, heavy-bottomed pan on medium-high heat, sauté bacon until crisp. Remove bacon from pan to a plate lined with a paper towel. Drain off all but about 1 tbsp bacon fat, and reserve for another use.

Add olive oil to pan. Stir in leeks and sauté until glistening, 1 to 2 minutes. Stir in garlic and sauté 1 to 2 minutes. Add barley, stirring to coat in fat, and cook until barley smells toasted, about 1 minute. Stir in wine, scraping bottom of pan, and reduce heat to medium.

Once wine is absorbed, pour in 1 cup (250 mL) stock. Stir frequently until stock is absorbed. Repeat 2 to 3 more times, over 30 to 40 minutes, until barley has puffed and softened; texture should resemble al dente rice, slightly chewy but pleasing to the bite.

When almost all liquid is absorbed, return bacon to pan, and cook with barley until liquid has almost completely disappeared. Remove from heat.

Stir in Parmesan cheese and butter and season to taste.

4 SERVINGS

MUSHROOM RISOTTO

2 tbsp butter

1 onion, diced

2 garlic cloves, minced

1 cup (250 mL) Arborio rice

1½ tsp chopped fresh rosemary

½ cup (125 mL) dry white wine

4 cups (1 L) warmed chicken or
vegetable stock

½ lb (500 g) white button or crimini
mushrooms, chopped

¼ tsp ground nutmeg

1 tbsp butter

½ cup (125 mL) freshly grated
Parmesan cheese

salt and pepper, to taste

This is a warming, fragrant dish that's surprisingly weeknight-friendly; people seem to think that risotto is a lot of work and very time-consuming, but it comes together in about half an hour. It's is great on its own, with a side of green salad, or as a side dish to roasted meats. To lower the amount of simple carbohydrates, you can replace half the rice with pearl barley. Use a wine you enjoy drinking, but not one that's expensive—a dry white wine, such as chardonnay, would be fine.

In a heavy-bottomed pan on medium-high heat, melt 2 tbsp butter. Add onions and garlic, and cook for 2 to 3 minutes, until onions are translucent. Add rice to pan, stirring for about a minute, or until rice grains turn opaque. Add rosemary.

Pour in wine, and scrape bottom of the pan to ensure nothing has stuck. Reduce heat to medium. Cook until wine has been completely absorbed by rice.

Add 1 cup (250 mL) warm chicken stock, stirring frequently until liquid is mostly absorbed. Repeat with an additional 1 cup stock.

Add remainder of stock and cook, stirring frequently, until liquid is absorbed. When there's just a bit of liquid in pan, add mushrooms. Test rice for tenderness—if al dente, you're awesome and good work. If it isn't, it's probably the rice's fault, so just pour in a little bit more stock, as needed. Keep in mind that the mushrooms are going to sweat and release their own moisture.

When rice is ready, stir in nutmeg, butter, and Parmesan. Taste and adjust seasonings.

NASI GORENG

4-6 SERVINGS

I inherited this dish from Nick's family; it's one of their favorites. It evolved in an effort to re-create the taste of the package mix Nick is fond of, but which requires a special trip to a store 40 minutes away. "It's not the same," Nick says, "but I think I might like it better." If you can't find ketjap manis (also sold as ABC Sweet Soy Sauce), use 2 tbsp soy sauce and 1 tbsp brown sugar. This is great with Cucumber Salad (p. 179) and a spicy red wine. Serve hot, topped with a sprinkle of cilantro, some scallions, and an egg fried over-easy, so that the edges of the white are crisp but the yolk is still runny.

In a large pan on medium-high heat, sauté garlic in oil until it is golden and crispy but not burned (1 to 2 minutes—any longer and it will become too bitter). Remove garlic from pan with a slotted spoon, and drain garlic on a plate lined with a paper towel. Set aside.

In a blender or food processor, purée shallots with sambal oelek, ketjap manis, fish sauce, sesame oil, lime juice, and cumin. Set aside.

Add ground beef to the now garlic-infused cooking oil in hot pan. Continue cooking on medium-high heat until meat has browned and is cooked through. Add cooked rice and grated carrots and kohlrabi. Pour shallot mixture over pan contents and stir to coat. Cook for an additional 3 to 5 minutes. If rice appears dry, add ½ cup (125 mL) warm tap water to the pan and stir.

Stir crispy garlic into rice mixture. Taste and adjust seasonings with salt and pepper, to taste.

6–9 garlic cloves, sliced

3 tbsp canola oil

1 shallot, roughly chopped

2 tbsp sambal oelek

2 tbsp ketjap manis

2 tbsp fish sauce

1 tbsp sesame oil

2 tsp lime juice

¾ tsp ground cumin

1 lb (500 g) lean ground beef

6 cups (1.5 L) cooked rice

2 cups (500 mL) grated carrots

1 kohlrabi (or 2–3 broccoli stalks), peeled and grated

salt, to taste

½ tsp ground black pepper

ACCOMPANIMENTS

1 sliced avocado

1 fried egg per serving

cilantro, for garnish

chopped scallions, for garnish

additional sambal oelek

2-4 SERVINGS

OVERNIGHT BREAKFAST GRAINS

⅓ cup (80 mL) pearl barley

⅓ cup (80 mL) kasha (toasted buckwheat groats)

⅓ cup (80 mL) rolled oats (not instant or quick-cooking)

½ cup (125 mL) currants or raisins

pinch salt

½ cup (125 mL) applesauce

½ tsp vanilla extract

Everyone seems to love steel cut oats. Unfortunately, they can be expensive—$7 to $8 for just a few cups. I always have just a few grains left over, and this recipe, inspired by a recipe for steel cut oats that Mark Bittman posted on his blog a few years ago, provided the perfect solution. Use any combination of whatever grains you have. I've done this with bulgur, rice, quinoa—all kinds of things. The key here is variety—it makes for better texture. Rolled oats can clump and turn lumpy; if that bothers you, use steel cut oats or a smaller amount of rolled oats. Serve with milk and brown sugar, yogurt and berries, or sliced fresh fruit.

In a medium saucepan with a tight-fitting lid on medium-high heat, combine grains, 3 cups (750 mL) water, currants, and salt. Bring to a rolling boil, about 8 minutes. Boil for 1 to 2 minutes, then slap lid on top, turn off stove, and go to bed.

In the morning, warm mixture on medium-high heat. Stir well, breaking apart any lumps. When mixture begins to burble, stir in applesauce and vanilla.

Bring mixture back up to a burble, then spoon into bowls.

PANTRY KEDGEREE

This is one of those weird English dishes that, at first glance, doesn't make a whole lot of sense. It's not until you eat it that you get it—it's a simple fried rice with bright flavors and an interesting variety of textures, which doesn't look like much, but tastes fantastic. I've been eating this since I was a poor student who had spent her entire student loan; it's as comforting now as it was then. Best eaten on rainy nights while reading M.F.K. Fisher.

In a large pan on medium-high heat, melt butter with oil. Add onions, garlic, and ginger, and cook until onions have softened, about 2 minutes. Add salt, cumin and mustard seeds, garam masala, turmeric, and black pepper. Cook for another minute, until spices are toasted and fragrant.

Add rice, and toss to coat in spices and oil. Add ½ cup (125 mL) water to pan to refresh and re-steam rice. Cook until heated through, about 3 minutes. Add herring in pieces, then add peas. Cook until peas are cooked through, another 3 minutes. Taste and adjust seasonings as needed.

Add eggs, stir again, and serve sprinkled with fresh chopped scallions.

2 tbsp butter

1 tbsp canola oil

1 onion, diced

4 garlic cloves, minced

1 tsp minced fresh ginger

1 tsp coarse salt

1 tsp cumin seeds

1 tsp mustard seeds

1 tsp garam masala

½ tsp ground turmeric

½ tsp ground black pepper

3 cups (750 mL) cooked rice

3-oz (85-g) can smoked herring, drained

1 cup (250 mL) frozen peas

salt, to taste

4 hardboiled eggs, peeled and roughly chopped

4 scallions, finely chopped

RICE & LENTILS

This one's a bit time consuming, but if you've got the time, it's worth it. Somewhat similar to mujadara, a Lebanese rice and lentil dish, it's great as a main course or a base for a simple curry, such as Tomato Chicken Curry (p. 115). Serve with pink wine or hot, strong tea.

In a medium pot on medium-high heat, combine rice, lentils, bay leaf, 1 tbsp olive oil, and 1 tsp salt with 4 cups (1 L) cold water. Bring to a boil, then reduce heat to low, cover, and cook for 20 minutes. Remove from heat and keep covered.

Meanwhile, in a large pan on medium-high, heat 3 tbsp olive oil. Add onions, carrots, celery, and apple, and cook until onions are translucent. Reduce heat to medium and cook slowly, stirring occasionally for 30 to 60 minutes—however long it takes ingredients to turn golden and soft. Add remaining salt once veggies begin to brown. I let mine go until they're barely recognizable as their former selves and they smell sweet and faintly smoky.

Add garlic and tomato paste, allowing paste to dry but not to burn. Keep it moving, tossing veggies to coat in sauce.

When bottom of pan looks pretty dry, add rice and lentil mixture (first remove bay leaf). Pour about 1 cup (250 mL) water into pan to deglaze, and stir to quickly re-steam rice and redistribute flavors. Taste and adjust seasonings as needed. Serve sprinkled with fresh parsley.

1½ cups (125 mL) basmati rice

½ cup (125 mL) green lentils

1 bay leaf

4 tbsp olive oil, divided

1½ tsp salt, divided

2 cups (500 mL) diced onions

1 cup (250 mL) diced carrots

1 cup (250 mL) diced celery

1 Granny Smith or other tart, firm-fleshed apple, peeled, cored, and diced

4 garlic cloves, minced

3 tbsp tomato paste

salt and pepper, to taste

handful fresh parsley, for garnish

SPAM-FRIED RICE

2 tbsp canola oil, divided

1 tbsp sesame oil

12-oz (340-g) container regular Spam, diced

6 garlic cloves, roughly chopped

6 cups (1.5 L) cooked rice

1 tbsp fish sauce

2–4 tbsp sambal oelek

6 scallions, chopped

4 eggs, beaten

salt, to taste

2–3 scallions, chopped, for garnish

This dish is a treat—we don't eat it very often; twice a year, maybe, as a lazy date-night indulgence. If you want to make it healthier, use brown rice. But Spam is what makes this magic; don't sub it out for ham or bacon. If you haven't eaten Spam in a while, try it again, and don't let the smell of it right out of the can put you off—this dish is tasty, I promise.

In a pan on medium-high, heat 1 tbsp canola and sesame oil. Add Spam and cook until browned, 3 to 5 minutes. Add garlic, and cook until just golden, another 3 minutes or so.

Add rice, fish sauce, sambal oelek, and scallions. Stir to integrate Spam and garlic into rice and to coat the rice in fat and sambal.

Make a well in center of rice and add remaining 1 tbsp canola oil. Pour eggs into well, and, stirring rapidly, cook eggs until scrambled. Once cooked, stir to mix rice with eggs. Taste and adjust seasonings as needed. Garnish with scallions.

PASTA

In many ways, Nick and I are big, incompetent children, and this is never more apparent than when we're both too tired to figure out dinner. And it's not as if this hardly ever happens—we're both there in front of the refrigerator, exasperating one another at least three nights a week. Add to that the fact that we're chronically broke in the week leading up to payday (so just getting take-out is not really an option), and we have to figure out how to stretch a meal into lunch for work the next day too.

For those of us who are fundamentally lazy, pasta is kind of ideal—it's usually fast to prepare, you can load it up with whatever you've got and save a trip to the store, and if you make enough of it, you don't have to make lunch for the next day. Pasta is also one of those things that folks are prickly about—it's a "bad carb" in that it's pretty much white bread in noodle form, and it seems everyone's against that now.

But here is the thing: There are no bad foods, really. Carbs fuel our bodies and feed our cells. If you eat only simple carbohydrates, you'll survive although you won't be at your best—but that's true of anything. (You can turn orange from eating too many carrots, for example, or inflate and float away like a balloon from eating too many chickpeas. I love excess as much as the next person, but you *can* have too much of a good thing.) If you're choosing pasta as a budget-friendly item, try a bit of variety—many brands make a whole wheat version for the same price (or priced not too much higher); watch for sales on alternative grain and gluten-free pastas, like those made with corn, spelt, or brown rice.

In many places in the world, wheat flour is fortified with things like folic acid and iron, as well as thiamin, riboflavin, and niacin. Sometimes additional nutrients are added as well, at the discretion of government and industry. Now this is in no way a substitute for a well-balanced (plant-heavy) diet, but it does ensure that the general population is benefiting from the enrichment of foods they consume regularly—fortification prevents nutrient deficiencies, especially in vulnerable populations including young children and low-income families for whom a diverse diet may be less feasible.

For all my talk of "eat more vegetables! Kale for everyone!" I understand that it's not always easy to integrate hearty piles of root veggies and leafy greens into one's daily diet—for those with demanding work schedules (and multiple jobs), the endless busyness of young children or aging parents, or those with low incomes (or middle incomes plus crippling student debt), buying and preparing a wide variety of interesting produce can feel like a big ask, if not an impossibility. Pasta goes a long way, especially between paydays or opportunities to get to a store, and with a few simple ingredients it can nourish a family of four for not much money.

And while it's true that you should choose whole grains whenever possible, if all you can afford is an eighty-nine-cent bag of penne on sale, you don't have to feel bad about it. Make something delicious and feel sated by it, and revel in that satiety because many people lack it. Just as there are no superfoods, there are no food villains either—it's how you eat that matters, and the balance in your approach. White pasta today, brown bread tomorrow, and everyone should eat salad as much as possible, but sometimes you can skip salad and just have another bowl of macaroni and cheese if you want because this is life, not boot camp.

We'd all benefit from worrying less about "bad carbs" or carbs in general. Our attitude toward food in much of the English-speaking world is dysfunctional; it doesn't help that our culture is so uncomfortable with fat and sugar and flour. I mean, we love the stuff, but we hate ourselves for eating it. We treat flour like a bad habit. We overthink it, and we pit ourselves against it. Can we not eat a plate of spaghetti and just experience joy? There's a reason why we talk so much about carbs—they are delicious, and we miss them.

Pasta will fill your belly for not many dollars and, for many people, that's the most important thing. As a kid I ate a lot of pasta, most often with a simple sauce of ground beef, canned tomatoes, and chopped onions, carrots, and celery. The seasonings were simple—garlic, dried oregano, black pepper—but the result was always comforting and delicious. As a picky eater, this was a dish I could enjoy—there was no pleading or bargaining over how little I could get away with eating on pasta night. Because I grew up in the 1980s and early '90s, fettuccine Alfredo was a popular dish, sometimes with chunks of chicken. I also recall pasta primavera with baby carrots, red bell peppers, and snow peas, which my parents celebrated with gusto for a few years and then never spoke of again. If they were feeling fancy, sometimes my mom or dad would use smoked salmon to stretch a bit of white sauce—if it was a very good day, we'd get garlic bread (the good kind in the foil bag from the grocery store) and maybe Caesar salad too.

Another reason to love pasta is that it's an easy way to go meatless. While the existence of cheese means that pasta dishes from my kitchen are rarely totally vegan, most of the time they are vegetable-based. Occasionally I'll use bacon, but only as an herb—it's there for flavor but doesn't play a starring role in the dish. According to the folks at Meatless Monday, "Going meatless once a week

How to cook pasta

TO COOK PASTA WELL, ALWAYS BOIL IT IN GENEROUSLY SALTED WATER. COOK ONE LB (500 G) PASTA IN ABOUT 1 GALLON (4 L) WATER SALTED WITH 1 ROUNDED TBSP SALT. DON'T BOTHER WITH FANCY SEA SALT—IODIZED TABLE SALT IS FINE.

SOME RECIPES SUGGEST YOU ADD OIL TO THE POT, BUT THIS ISN'T NECESSARY—IF YOU USE A BIG POT AND ENOUGH WATER, AND STIR THE POT REGULARLY, YOUR PASTA WILL HAVE ROOM TO COOK AND WON'T CLUMP TOGETHER.

WHEN NOODLES HAVE REACHED THE AL DENTE STAGE—WHICH IS TO SAY, THEY ARE COOKED, BUT THERE'S A LITTLE BITE TO THEM (THEY'RE NOT MUSHY)— SCOOP OUT ABOUT 1 CUP (250 ML) COOKING WATER AND SET IT ASIDE. DRAIN PASTA, BUT DO NOT RINSE IT.

ADD PASTA TO SAUCE, AND ADD A PORTION OF PASTA WATER AS WELL (I USUALLY END UP USING ONLY ½ CUP [125 ML]). ADDING WATER TO SAUCE WILL THIN IT OUT A BIT, MAKING IT STICK BETTER TO THE PASTA. IT WILL ALSO HELP THE PASTA ABSORB SOME OF THE SAUCE, WHICH MAKES EVERYTHING TASTIER.

may reduce your risk of chronic preventable conditions like cancer, cardiovascular disease, diabetes and obesity." It's also gentler on the environment.

Pasta does, admittedly, veer higher on the glycemic index, which can be problematic for those trying to regulate their blood sugar. One thing I look for when I'm choosing pasta is a lower number of grams of carbohydrates per serving—once you start comparing nutrition labels, you'll see significant differences across brands and types of pasta. Spelt pasta in particular has been a great alternative for us, as it's a more complex carbohydrate, and also quite filling, so we use a lot less. I've been able to find it in bulk, which is great because "alternative" pastas can be costly. Note, this is not no-carb—this is just lower carb and higher fiber.

Choosing lower carb pastas is not always possible, for reasons ranging from limited availability on store shelves to it just being December, which is always financially dreary. That's why if I can't find lower-carb pastas, I'll just use whatever I've got

but add more other stuff, whether that's canned beans and legumes or more vegetables; this both stretches the pasta further and is easier on Nick's blood glucose levels. I prefer short, shaped pastas because they're easy to reheat the next day and eat at my desk.

The thing I like best about pasta is that it's endlessly adaptable and forgiving. A way to use up whatever's left in the crisper at the end of the week, it's a vehicle for repurposing leftover meat or hiding organ meats so nothing goes to waste. It's also perfect for weeknight entertaining, which is my favorite way to have a social life; guests on weekends can be a more costly endeavor, because I think people have loftier expectations for dinner on Saturday or Sunday nights. If you have friends over after work on a Tuesday, I guarantee they'll be thrilled to eat a big plate of spaghetti and meat sauce. Ask them to bring the garlic bread. The good kind, from the grocery store, in the foil bag.

BEEF STROGANOFF

4 SERVINGS

Beef stroganoff was a quick weeknight meal at the Wight house, and it was almost always made with ground beef, occasionally with meatballs. Traditionally this is served with a sprinkling of minced chives; I like it with fresh dill. Serve with Cucumber Salad (p. 179) and Honey-Mustard Beets (p. 183).

2 tbsp butter, divided

½ lb (250 g) button mushrooms, quartered

1 onion, diced

2 garlic cloves, minced

1 lb (500 g) lean ground beef

2 tbsp all-purpose flour

1 tsp ground black pepper

½ tsp coarse salt

½ lb (250 g) dried penne

½ cup (125 mL) dry white wine

2 cups (500 mL) low-sodium or homemade beef stock

1 tsp Worcestershire sauce

½ cup (125 mL) full-fat sour cream

3 tbsp chopped fresh dill

In a large pan on medium-high heat, melt butter. Add mushrooms and cook for 3 to 5 minutes, until they've lost some moisture and started to brown.

Meanwhile, bring a large pot of salted water to a boil.

Scoop mushrooms out of pan, and set aside.

Add 1 tbsp butter to pan, and let it melt. Stir in onions and garlic until onions are translucent and have begun to brown, another 2 to 3 minutes.

Crumble ground beef into pan, and cook until browned. Add flour, pepper, and salt, and stir until flour has been mostly absorbed by beef and onion mixture. Return mushrooms to pan.

When pot of water has come to a boil, add pasta. Cook until pasta is al dente, about 9 minutes or according to package instructions.

Meanwhile, add wine to beef mixture, scraping bottom of pan to loosen any browned bits. Add stock, then reduce heat to medium. Stir in Worcestershire sauce. Simmer for 8 to 10 minutes, until thickened and reduced slightly.

When pasta is ready, drain. Add sour cream to meat sauce and stir to combine. Taste and adjust seasonings as needed.

Add pasta to sauce, and stir to coat. Serve sprinkled with fresh dill.

4-6 SERVINGS

CAULIFLOWER MACARONI & CHEESE

3 lb (1.5 kg) cauliflower, chopped into florets

2 cups (500 mL) dried macaroni

3 tbsp butter, divided

3 minced garlic cloves, divided

3 tbsp flour

2 tsp grainy Dijon mustard

2 cups (500 mL) milk

½ tsp ground pepper

¼ tsp cayenne pepper

¼ tsp ground nutmeg

about 4 cups (1 L) grated aged cheddar cheese

salt, to taste

⅓ cup (80 mL) whole hazelnuts, toasted and then chopped

1 cup (250 mL) bread crumbs

This is a dish that's mostly made up of cauliflower and cheese; to be honest, the pasta's only here because I didn't think I should eat three pounds of cauliflower in a single sitting. This mac and cheese is creamy, rich, and crunchy, thanks to the nuts and crumb topping. It's a good dish to make when you've got friends coming over for dinner on a weeknight. Serve with lightly dressed greens and a lot of not-fancy white wine. If you've got room after, Grandpa's Radio Pudding (p. 214) makes a nice, warming conclusion to the feast.

Preheat oven to 375°F (190°C). Grease a 9x13-in (3.5-L) baking dish, and set it aside.

Place cauliflower in a large pot, fill to just over top of cauliflower with salted water, and bring to a boil on high heat. Boil for 5 minutes, drain, then set aside.

Meanwhile, to a large pot of water on high heat, add macaroni and bring to a boil. Cook until almost al dente, 5 or 6 minutes. Drain and add noodles to drained cauliflower.

In a medium saucepan on medium-high heat, melt 2 tbsp butter with 2 minced garlic cloves. When bubbling, add flour and mustard, and stir until a paste forms. Add milk, and whisk to combine. Reduce heat to medium. Add black and cayenne pepper and nutmeg. Simmer until thickened, stirring occasionally, for about 5 minutes.

Add most of the cheese, save for a handful. Taste and season with salt as needed. Stir sauce, then pour over macaroni and cauliflower. Add hazelnuts, and stir mixture to coat cauliflower and pasta in sauce.

Pour into prepared baking dish. Sprinkle with remaining cheese.

Meanwhile, in a small pot on medium-high heat, melt 1 tbsp butter with 1 garlic clove. When butter has foamed, add bread crumbs and stir to coat. Cook until butter is absorbed and pan looks dry, about 2 minutes. Pour over macaroni mixture.

Bake for 30 to 35 minutes, until sauce is bubbly and crumbs have turned golden. Serve, basking in the praise and admiration you so obviously deserve.

Don't buy breadcrumbs!

BREADCRUMBS COST WAY TOO MUCH, AND YOU PROBABLY HAVE STALE BREAD KICKING AROUND ANYWAY.

TOAST SLICES OF STALE BREAD IN OVEN AT 300°F (150°C) FOR 5 TO 10 MINUTES, UNTIL BREAD IS CRISP AND GOLDEN. LET BREAD COOL, THEN GRATE EACH SLICE ON THE DIAGONAL USING A CHEESE GRATER (LARGER HOLES). IF YOU HAVE A FOOD PROCESSOR, THAT'LL WORK EVEN BETTER.

NO BREAD ON HAND? SALTINES WILL DO IN A PINCH. TWENTY-EIGHT TO 30 SALTINES, OR ABOUT THREE-QUARTERS OF A STANDARD SLEEVE OF SALTINES, WILL EQUAL 1 CUP (250 ML) CRUMBS WHEN CRUSHED. YOU CAN DO THIS IN A BLENDER OR FOOD PROCESSOR, OR BY PUTTING THEM INTO A SEALED FREEZER BAG AND ROLLING WITH A ROLLING PIN TO DESIRED FINENESS. BE MINDFUL THAT IF YOU'RE USING SALTINES WITH SALTED TOPS, YOU MAY WANT TO CUT BACK ON SALT IN THE RECIPE.

CAULIFLOWER *with* ORECCHIETTE & ALMONDS

Cuddles, my grandmother, used to make a side dish of steamed whole cauliflower covered in drawn butter sauce and studded with toasted, slivered almonds. It was my favorite part of the meal—to the point where I would eat the entire dish just so no one else (my Uncle Tim in particular) could have any. Then it occurred to me that I could eat this dish a lot more often if I combined it with pasta, so I upgraded it with a pinch of cayenne pepper and some chili flakes, but the overall taste is about the same. Make it, and don't feel like you have to share it, especially not with relatives named Tim.

½ lb (250 g) dried orecchiette

½ cup (125 mL) butter

1 garlic clove, smashed

¼ cup (60 mL) all-purpose flour

1 lemon, zest and juice

½ tsp ground black pepper

½ tsp chili flakes + additional to taste, for garnish

¼ tsp salt

⅛ tsp cayenne pepper

1 lb (250 g) cauliflower, chopped into bite-sized florets, stems diced

½ cup (125 mL) slivered almonds, toasted and divided

salt and pepper, to taste

Bring a pot of salted water to a boil on high heat. Add orecchiette, and cook until al dente, as per package directions.

Meanwhile, in a heavy-bottomed pot on medium heat, melt butter with garlic. Let butter become foamy, then let foam subside before whisking in flour. Scoop out garlic clove, then add 1½ cups (375 mL) water, lemon zest and juice, pepper, chili flakes, salt, and cayenne pepper. Reduce heat to medium-low and cook, whisking often, until thick.

Two to 3 minutes before you expect pasta to be done, add cauliflower to pot of pasta.

Stir half of almonds into sauce, and continue to stir. Taste and adjust seasonings as needed.

When pasta is ready, scoop out about ½ cup (125 mL) cooking water. Drain, then add pasta and cauliflower to sauce. Stir, adding pasta water as needed to thin sauce so it coats noodles.

Serve sprinkled with remaining almonds and chili flakes.

4
SERVINGS

LINGUINE with TUNA & CAPERS

6-oz (170-g) can tuna, packed in oil

2 hardboiled eggs, peeled, yolks and
   whites separated

1 garlic clove, minced

1 large lemon, zest and juice

1 tbsp capers, rinsed and roughly
   chopped

1 tbsp chopped fresh dill

¼ cup (60 mL) dry white wine

¼ cup (60 mL) extra-virgin olive oil

1 tbsp fish sauce

1 tsp ground black pepper

salt, to taste

16-oz (480-g) pkg dried linguine

I don't know what it is about this dish, because even though it's made almost entirely of stuff I scavenge out of my refrigerator and pantry two days after the rent has been paid and we're totally broke, it feels fancy— the kind of thing you'd almost think of putting pants on to eat, the sort of thing you could serve to a date or a special friend or your mother. It is more than the sum of its parts, and it's delicious. Serve with a simple salad and the rest of the white wine.

In a medium-size bowl, mash together tuna (including its juices) and egg yolks, until the yolks have all but disappeared.

Chop egg whites, then stir into mixture. Stir in garlic, lemon zest and juice, capers, dill, wine, olive oil, fish sauce, pepper and salt.

Cover bowl with plastic wrap and let sit at room temperature for 30 minutes.

Meanwhile, in a large pot on high heat, boil pasta in salted water until al dente, following package instructions, then drain. Toss immediately with a third of tuna mixture, then pour into a serving dish and top with remainder of mixture.

ONE-POT PASTA WITH MEAT SAUCE

6-8 SERVINGS

Ordinarily I like to dawdle over a meat sauce. In the pre-toddler era, I would cook a rich, meaty Bolognese sauce for a couple of hours, pausing while occasionally passing through the kitchen to stir and inhale. In the current era, a meaty pasta is a weeknight dish, one I make while a tiny naked person shouts orders and causes a general ruckus. The one consolation? This one-pot dish tastes like a sauce you dawdled over, but you can make it while you try to prevent your tiny naked person from trying to climb into the dryer.

In a large pot with a tight-fitting lid on medium, heat 1 tbsp olive oil. Add mushrooms and ½ tsp salt. Cook until mushrooms have released their liquid and it has evaporated, 4 to 5 minutes.

Add 1 tbsp olive oil and crumble beef into pot. Stir and cook until browned, about 5 minutes. Remove contents of pot onto a plate and set aside.

Add 1 tbsp olive oil to same pot and return to medium heat. Add onions, celery, and carrots, and cook until the onions are translucent, about 3 minutes. Add garlic, give it 1 minute, then add wine, scraping bottom of pan. Add chicken stock, Worcestershire sauce, tomatoes (crushing them individually into pot), basil, oregano, chili flakes, and pepper. Simmer for 10 minutes, until sauce has reduced slightly.

Add pasta to mixture in pot, add 4 cups (1 L) water, and stir to distribute noodles throughout sauce. Bring to a boil, then simmer for 15 minutes, until pasta is cooked through and sauce is mostly absorbed. Let sit 5 minutes before serving.

3 tbsp olive oil, divided

1 lb (500 g) mushrooms, finely chopped

1 tsp coarse salt, divided

1 lb (500 g) lean ground beef

1 onion, diced

2 cups (500 mL) celery, diced

2 cups (500 mL) carrot, diced

4 garlic cloves, minced

½ cup (125 mL) dry red wine

2 cups (500 mL) low-sodium chicken stock

1 tsp Worcestershire sauce

28-oz (796-mL) can whole tomatoes, including juice

1 tsp dried basil

½ tsp dried oregano

½ tsp chili flakes

½ tsp ground black pepper

½ lb (250 g) dried rotini, penne, or other short pasta

4 SERVINGS

PEANUTTY SOBA NOODLES *WITH* KALE

2 tbsp canola oil

1 small onion, chopped

4 garlic cloves, minced

1 tbsp minced fresh ginger

1 block medium-firm tofu

½ lb (250 g) dried soba noodles

½ cup (125 mL) peanut butter (natural peanut butter is best because it's runnier)

¼ cup (60 mL) soy sauce

¼ cup (60 mL) Sriracha sauce

2 tbsp rice vinegar

1 tbsp sesame oil

2 tsp honey (omit or reduce to taste if using peanut butter that contains sugar)

salt and pepper, to taste

½ lb (250 g) chopped fresh kale

1 cup (250 mL) chopped fresh cilantro

½ cup (125 mL) chopped roasted peanuts

This is one of those things that we end up eating a lot of in January, when we're feeling obligated to be virtuous and also when only the kale has survived the first stretch of winter in the garden. Make this dish when it's just too cold to walk to the store—most of it comes from your pantry. If you don't have kale, you can use different fresh greens; a package of frozen spinach also works, but thaw it first and give it a good wring with a clean dish towel. This would also be good topped with fresh bean sprouts.

In a large pan on medium-high, heat oil and add onions, garlic, and ginger. Sauté until fragrant, about 2 minutes.

Pat tofu dry with kitchen towel and chopped into cubes. Add to pan, tossing occasionally.

Meanwhile, bring a large pot of water to a boil on high heat. Add soba noodles, and cook for 3 minutes.

In a small bowl, combine peanut butter, soy sauce, Sriracha, rice vinegar, sesame oil, and honey. Mix well, taste, and adjust seasonings as needed.

After 3 minutes, add kale to pot of boiling noodles. Cook for an additional 3 minutes, then drain. Rinse with cold water and drain again.

Add noodles and kale to onion mixture, and pour peanut sauce over it. Toss with ½ cup (125 mL) fresh cilantro. Divide between four plates, and garnish with another splurch of Sriracha, remaining cilantro, and chopped peanuts.

4 SERVINGS

1 lb (500 g) rapini, chopped

3 tbsp olive oil

1 small onion, chopped

3 garlic cloves, minced

1 lb (500 g) spicy Italian sausage,
   casings removed

1 tsp chili flakes

2 tbsp tomato paste

1 cup (250 mL) dried orecchiette pasta

19-oz (540-mL) can white beans,
   drained and rinsed

½ lemon, zest and juice

½ cup (125 mL) chopped fresh parsley

¼ cup (60 mL) grated Parmesan
   cheese + extra, for garnish

salt and pepper, to taste

RAPINI & SAUSAGE WITH WHITE BEANS & ORECCHIETTE

Rapini can be hard to come by; if you can find it and it's under $2.49 for a bunch, grab some. If not, plain old broccoli will work just fine.

Bring a large pot of lightly salted water to a boil on high heat. Drop chopped rapini in, and boil for 2 to 3 minutes, until wilted and brightened in color. Remove rapini from water, reserving liquid, and plunge into a large bowl of icy water. Set aside.

Return pot to heat and bring water back up to a boil.

Meanwhile, in a large pan on medium-high, heat olive oil. Sauté onions 2 to 3 minutes, until translucent. Add garlic, then crumble sausage into pan. Stir with a wooden spoon, breaking up meat. Stir in chili flakes and tomato paste and continue moving meat around pan.

When water has come to a boil, add pasta and boil until al dente, about 8 minutes.

Drain, but reserve 1 cup (250 mL) cooking liquid. Add rapini to pan, stirring to coat in pan juices. As pasta finishes cooking, add beans and lemon zest and juice, then add pasta. If sauce is too thick, add pasta water as needed, a tablespoon at a time. Add parsley and cheese. Taste and adjust seasonings as needed. Serve with additional cheese if desired.

RIGATONI with TOMATOES & CHICKPEAS

4-6 SERVINGS

A fast, hearty weeknight dish, this pasta is vegan-friendly. The flavors are reminiscent of Italian fennel sausage, but this is gentler on your budget and a great way to go meatless and not really notice. The dish pairs well with off-dry white wine and a simple green salad. Top with grated Parmesan or vegan cheese, if you like.

3 tbsp olive oil

2 tsp chili flakes

1 tsp fennel seeds

1 medium onion, finely chopped

6 garlic cloves, minced

2½–3 lb (1–1.5 g) fresh tomatoes, diced

1 tsp salt

1 tsp ground black pepper

1 lb (500 g) dried rotini

19-oz (540-mL) can chickpeas

½ cup (125 mL) densely packed flat-leaf parsley, chopped

In a large pan on medium-high heat, combine olive oil, chili flakes and fennel seeds and cook until oil begins to sizzle. Add onions, and cook until translucent, 2 to 3 minutes. Stir in garlic and cook for 2 minutes, until garlic is fragrant and just beginning to turn golden. Add tomatoes, salt, and pepper. Reduce heat to medium, and cover. Cook for 10 minutes.

Meanwhile, bring a pot of salted water on high heat to a rolling boil. Add pasta, and cook for 8 or 9 minutes, until just underdone—not quite al dente.

Uncover tomato mixture, and simmer until pasta reaches near-doneness.

Drain and rinse chickpeas.

Drain pasta.

Add chickpeas and pasta to tomatoes and cook until pasta has reached al dente stage and most of the liquid has been absorbed by noodles. Stir in parsley, and serve hot.

4 SERVINGS

SHELLS ~WITH~ BRUSSELS SPROUTS, CHICKPEAS & BACON

4 strips bacon, finely chopped

½ lb (250 g) dried conchiglie (small shell pasta)

3 tbsp butter, divided

3 garlic cloves

½ tsp chili flakes

½ tsp coarse salt

½ tsp pepper

⅛ tsp ground nutmeg

½ lb (250 g) Brussels sprouts, trimmed and halved

14-oz (398-mL) can chickpeas, drained and rinsed

1 lemon, zest and juice

salt and pepper, to taste

chili flakes, for garnish

1 lemon, quartered, for garnish

If all you remember about Brussels sprouts is tiny cabbages boiled to a watery gray death, then it's time to get reacquainted! This is everything I love in one dish of pasta—a little sweet, a little spicy, and buttery. The bacon acts like an herb here, and the meatiness comes from the chickpeas. The sprouts are sweet and tender, having been caramelized. It's not low-cal, but sprouts and chickpeas absolve the dish a little bit. Serve with a crisp white wine and some raw bitter winter greens dressed in olive oil and lemon.

In a large pan on medium-high heat, cook bacon until crispy. Spoon bacon out of pan and onto a plate lined with a paper towel.

Meanwhile, bring a pot of salted water to a boil on high heat. Add pasta, and cook until al dente, 7 to 10 minutes (or follow package instructions).

Return frying pan to stove and reduce heat to medium. Add 2 tbsp butter. Stir in garlic, chili flakes, salt, pepper, nutmeg, and Brussels sprouts. Cook until Brussels sprouts have softened and begun to brown, about 8 minutes. Add chickpeas.

Drain cooked pasta, reserving about ½ cup (125 mL) cooking water.

Pour cooked pasta into pan with sprouts and chickpeas. Add remainder of butter, lemon zest and juice, and stir to coat. If pan seems a little dry, add some pasta water, 2 tbsp at a time, until sauce coats noodles and dish appears glossy and tasty-looking. Taste and adjust seasonings as needed.

Serve with additional chili flakes sprinkled on top and a wedge of lemon to squeeze over pasta.

SIZZLING CHILI NOODLES

4 SERVINGS

There's this fabulous hand-pulled noodle place called Peaceful Restaurant near our old apartment, and it was already crazy busy when Guy Fieri showed up to film a Vancouver-centric episode of *Diners, Drive-Ins and Dives*. They serve fresh noodles fried in chili oil and a ton of garlic, and it's so explosive that if you don't ask for "Western medium," it'll blow your goddamn head off. I miss that place so much, but it's a hard ask to get a feral toddler to wait for a table and food he'll refuse to eat. When Hunter's tame enough to wait in line, we'll go back; for now, I make this reasonable approximation of the dish at home, with store-bought Shanghai noodles and a bottle of sambal oelek. Adjust the spiciness to your taste; serve with a cooling side of sliced, gently salted cucumbers and the kind of beer you'd only drink ice cold.

½ lb (250 g) fresh Shanghai noodles

2 lb (900 g) baby bok choy, trimmed and leaves separated

3 tbsp peanut oil

5 garlic cloves, minced

3 tbsp sambal oelek

2 tbsp soy sauce

4 scallions, finely chopped

Bring a large pot of salted water to a boil on high heat. Add noodles, and boil for 3 minutes. In last minute, add bok choy.

Meanwhile, in a large frying pan on medium-high, heat oil to a shimmer.

Reserving ½ cup (125 mL) noodle liquid, drain noodles and bok choy.

Working quickly, add garlic to pan, stir, then stir in sambal oelek. Add noodles and bok choy, soy sauce, and reserved cooking liquid, and stir to coat noodles in saucy mixture. Cook for an additional 1 to 2 minutes, until noodles are tender but still chewy and well-coated with sauce, which should be slightly absorbed.

Toss with chopped scallions and serve hot from pan.

SHANGHAI NOODLES, OR OTHER FAT, FRESH ASIAN NOODLES, ARE USUALLY SOLD IN THE PRODUCE SECTION, NEAR WHERE YOU'D BUY WONTON WRAPPERS. IF YOU CAN'T FIND THEM IN YOUR USUAL STORE, TRY THE LOCAL ASIAN MARKET; IN A PINCH, YOU CAN SUBSTITUTE FRESH, FROZEN, OR DRIED (AND RECONSTITUTED) UDON NOODLES.

4 SERVINGS

TUNA PENNE

½ lb (250 g) dried penne

3 tbsp olive oil

1 medium onion, diced

4 garlic cloves, roughly chopped

1 tbsp capers (in brine), roughly chopped

½ tsp chili flakes

½ tsp ground black pepper

6-oz (170-g) can tuna in water, 2 tsp water reserved

28-oz (796-mL) can crushed tomatoes

14-oz (398-mL) can cannellini beans

2 tsp Worcestershire sauce

zest and juice of ½ lemon

salt, to taste

3 tbsp chopped fresh parsley

½ cup (125 mL) Parmesan cheese, for garnish

2 tsp chili flakes, for garnish

This is an ideal dish for mid-February, as it uses stuff you'll likely have in your cupboards and refrigerator already. An easy one that comes together in about 20 minutes, it'll fill you up without filling you out—it's reasonably healthy, after all. The thing I like about it is the little bit of Mediterranean flavor that will inject a bit of sunshine into an otherwise dreary day. You can make it anytime, but winter is when this will really shine.

Bring a large pot of salted water to a boil on high heat. Add pasta, stirring occasionally. Cook until just shy of al dente, 9 to 10 minutes, or according to package instructions.

Meanwhile, in a large pan on medium-high. heat olive oil. Add onions, garlic, capers, chili flakes, and pepper, and cook until fragrant and onions are translucent, 2 to 3 minutes.

Reduce heat to medium. Flake tuna into pan with a fork. Add tomatoes, beans, reserved tuna water, Worcestershire sauce, and lemon zest and juice.

Reserve ½ cup (125 mL) pasta cooking water. Drain pasta, then add to pan. Stir, adding pasta water as needed to thin sauce. Taste and adjust seasonings. Just before serving, stir in parsley. Serve with a sprinkle of Parmesan cheese and chili flakes, as desired.

EGGS

Everyone cringed when my grandfather made dinner because his eggs were snotty.

At the time, it was stomach-turning to be served Grandpa's eggs on toast; they were not just slightly undercooked, they were practically mucous, and most people aren't all about eating a sneeze for breakfast. I didn't get it. Why not cook them longer? Why, Grandpa? I wondered if he was just half-assing it, doing a crap job to get out of having to cook again, which is actually a great approach to everything. (I have made a serious and concerted effort at making it look like I have no ability to properly wash a floor, and it's working out pretty great for me.)

But it turns out that snotty is just how he liked them. He'd cook them until the whites were just opaque because it was important that the yolks be completely raw. In my experience, "just opaque" meant "still quite raw," as if a slippery bite of white was an acceptable price to pay for a perfect, runny yolk. When Auntie Lynn would make him his eggs, she'd follow his specific instructions, regardless of how counterintuitive they seemed. He knew what he liked.

Grandpa also preferred to eat his eggs directly from the frying pan. If it was summer and my grandmother had tomatoes turning ripe in pots on the patio, he'd add a couple of slices to the pan. He'd eat his eggs and tomatoes forked onto pieces of toast, sprinkled with a little salt and dried oregano, and he'd leave the last bite for the dog, swiping his hand under the pan to make sure it wasn't too hot for Riley's doggy lips.

At the time, the wet whites seemed very gross, but as an adult I absolutely understand his urge to not overcook the eggs at any cost. An overcooked egg is a tragedy. I will sulk about it. One reason I don't think Nick cooks dinner all that often is that the last time he scrambled a pan of eggs, he was also talking and I watched in horror as he stopped moving the eggs in the pan. It took only a second, but I saw it as soon as my shrieking shocked his stir-hand back into motion: brown. Nick had browned the eggs. It wasn't my finest moment, but I (sputtering with swears and an abject lack of perspective) refused to eat them. There's a pretty good chance I'm just awful to live with, and I suppose I'm willing to change … but I will not budge on the egg issue.

Browned eggs taste like sadness and sulfur and I hate them. A perfect scrambled egg is very soft, still a bit wet, with curds like fluffy yellow clouds. A perfect scrambled egg is whisked with a bit of milk before it's added to the pan, in which a pool of melted butter is waiting. Chef Daniel Boulud, describing the texture of a perfect omelet, once used the word *baveuse*, French for slobber. We're not even 500 words into this intro and already I've gone on at length about snot and slobber, so things are going pretty well, I think? (Food writing: Nailed it!)

I don't need them that smooth, but scrambled eggs a bit underdone and seasoned once they're out of the pan and onto the plate are about the best thing you can make for yourself on a quiet night alone. Some scrambled eggs, a bit of heavily buttered toast, and a cold beer, glass of wine, or a hot cup of tea, paired with a book and a blanket and your favorite armchair—there is no better way to spend an evening, of that I'm sure.

On weekends, those same eggs and a bit of sour cream round out pierogies for breakfast; for lunch, we'll throw them into a folded tortilla with a bit of cheese, maybe half an avocado, and some salsa—homemade or store-bought, it doesn't matter—and have egg quesadillas for lunch. We've just gotten so busy, so scheduled, that eggs are the perfect food—they cook quickly, they cost little, and they'll give you that necessary jolt of protein to get you through the next thing. A scrambled egg is not just sustenance; it's nourishment, and I'm quite certain on some weeknights an egg or two and someone else to fry the bacon has been the thing that's prevented my head from exploding. In two minutes, you have food, and you can sit down. Some days, that's everything.

Right. So. Which eggs should you buy?

The very best eggs you can get are the ones that come from the yards of houses on long, quiet country roads with signs out front that read something like "Eggs, $3 for 12." Bonus points if you can see the chickens just wandering around outside like weird, ugly puppies. Not everyone has country roads, and most of us don't get out of the city anywhere near often enough, so happy-chicken hobby-farm eggs end up being a nice-to-have in a world full of good-enoughs.

Store-bought eggs are likely your main or only option. There is a hierarchy of eggs, with the greatest of these being the SPCA-certified, cage-free organic eggs with yolks as orange as tangerines, a result of the chickens having access to bugs and worms and things to peck and eat outdoors. They are delicious and healthy … and so expensive.

In the middle, there are varying price points for free run, free range, and organic eggs. At the bottom, there are your regular old factory farm eggs, whose yolks range from golden to pale yellow, and they are by far the cheapest; the chickens tend to be fed corn. There are also the omega-3 or vitamin D-fortified "sunshine" eggs, which are pretty much the same as conventional eggs, though the hens who lay them are fed flax or other fortified feed. The eggs cost a dollar or two more, and they often come in Styrofoam cartons. Choosing these eggs is a matter of personal preference; I prefer to save the dollar.

I had been buying the SPCA fancy eggs, but then I got surprise-pregnant and babies cost a lot of money. The place where I buy diapers sends me coupons by email, and eggs are often two dollars per dozen, so I buy the regular ones in the recyclable paper carton. We're all doing the best we can, but I'll admit that in all my trying to do better, I sometimes neglect the chickens.

Truly free range eggs—that is, eggs that come from chickens with access to the bugs and worms that live in the grass outside—are worth the cost if you can afford the splurge. Are they worth it for someone who can't afford six dollars for a dozen? Well, the nutrient content in those fancy eggs is a bit higher—free range eggs are higher in docosahexaenoic acid (DHA, an omega-3 fatty acid), which has been shown to improve brain development and language acquisition in toddlers. According to the US National Institute on Aging, research suggests that DHA may also play a preventative role in the onset of Alzheimer's disease. But eggs in general

Eggs, by type

SPCA-CERTIFIED

SPCA-CERTIFIED EGGS COME FROM PASTURED HENS, AND THEIR ENVIRONMENT INCLUDES NEST BOXES, PERCHES, AND ROOM IN INDOOR AND OUTDOOR SPACES FOR SCRATCHING, FORAGING, AND DUST-BATHING. SPCA-CERTIFIED FARMS HAVE BEEN INSPECTED BY THE SOCIETY FOR THE PREVENTION OF CRUELTY TO ANIMALS AND HAVE BEEN FOUND COMPLIANT WITH THE SPCA'S HIGH STANDARDS FOR FARM ANIMAL WELFARE.

FREE RANGE

HENS THAT LAY FREE RANGE EGGS SPEND MOST OF THEIR TIME IN TEMPERATURE-CONTROLLED OPEN-CONCEPT BARNS. THESE ARE SIMILAR TO FREE RUN EGGS, BUT WHEN WEATHER PERMITS THE HENS CAN ACCESS OUTDOOR SPACES AS WELL.

FREE RUN

HENS THAT LAY FREE RUN EGGS SPEND THEIR TIME IN TEMPERATURE-CONTROLLED OPEN-CONCEPT BARNS. THESE ARE INDOOR ENVIRONMENTS WHERE THE HENS ARE NOT CAGED.

are nutrient-rich and a great source of energy; they are an essential part of low-budget cooking, whether they're two or six dollars per dozen.

I've resolved to do better when I'm better off, which I always assume will come some day. Maybe when Hunter's out of daycare. Maybe after the next new job or promotion or pay raise. Maybe I need to examine whether I'm subconsciously harboring something against chickens. Those farm fresh eggs are the stuff of idyll, and I imagine Nick and I one day living in a place where we can raise our own gross-faced birds and harvest blue- and tan-shelled eggs every morning ourselves. We will wear name-brand rubber boots. I will suddenly be taller.

Eggs are cheap, but are they actually good for you?

Yes! And no! And every shade of yes-kind-of and sort-of-no in between, depending on who you ask and what your underlying health issues include. In general, if you're a healthy person, eggs are fine and you should eat them. If you have high cholesterol or type 2 diabetes, there's research to suggest that more than one or two eggs a day can increase your risk of stroke; the Canadian Diabetes

Association suggests that if you have type 2 diabetes, you limit yourself to two eggs per week. The American Diabetes Association is more generous, allowing three per week.

Though claims that eggs (especially the yolks) contribute to high cholesterol have since been largely debunked (*thank you, science!*), there is evidence to suggest that if your "bad cholesterol" (low-density lipoprotein or LDL) is on the higher side, the small amount that eggs contain can push you into the heart-disease danger zone. Of course, there are a range of factors at play here, and eggs alone are not likely to have you keeling over at brunch, but it is something to keep in mind. I eat eggs fried in butter with reckless abandon, but I also eat cheese and bacon like I'm going to live forever, so I'll let you know how that goes. It may not be the eggs that get me in the end, you know? In the meantime, if you're concerned, it might be a good idea to talk with your doctor.

But if you really, really like eggs and have no current cause for concern, then let's get cracking! (I have waited my whole adult life to make that pun in print.)

ORGANIC

ORGANIC EGGS COME FROM HENS THAT HAVE BEEN FED ORGANIC GRAIN FEED. HENS LAYING ORGANIC EGGS ARE GIVEN ANTIBIOTICS ONLY TO TREAT INFECTIONS OR DISEASE.

CONVENTIONAL

NINETY-FIVE PER CENT OF EGGS IN NORTH AMERICA ARE PRODUCED BY CAGED HENS IN TEMPERATURE-CONTROLLED LAYING BARNS. HENS ARE CONTAINED IN CAGES WITH THREE OR MORE OTHER HENS; IN CANADA, THEY HAVE CURTAINED OFF SPACE WHERE THEY CAN SOMEWHAT PRIVATELY LAY EGGS. CHICKENS ARE SEPARATED FROM THEIR WASTE, AND FOOD AND WATER IS PROVIDED IN THE CAGES.

1 SERVING

BUTTERMILK DUTCH BABY ·WITH· BACON-BAKED APPLE

DUTCH BABY:

1 egg

¼ cup (60 mL) buttermilk

2 tbsp all purpose flour

1 tbsp whole wheat flour

¼ tsp brown sugar

pinch salt

BAKED APPLE:

1 strip bacon

1 small, tart, firm-fleshed apple, such as
   Granny Smith or Braeburn

2 tsp brown sugar

⅛ tsp ground cinnamon

pinch salt

1 tsp butter

This is the kind of thing that's perfect if you've got a morning to yourself; it's equally perfect if you're much too pregnant and it's two o'clock in the morning and you're starving/sleepless/bored. The apples bake while the Dutch baby does, and you can have the whole thing in half an hour if you start right now.

Lightly grease 2 ramekins. Preheat oven to 425°F (220°C). Place 1 ramekin in the oven as it heats.

In a small bowl, whisk together egg, buttermilk, flours, brown sugar, and salt. Set aside.

In a frying pan on medium-high heat, cook bacon until crisp, 2 to 3 minutes. Peel, core, and chop apples to ¼-in (6-mm) dice. Remove bacon to a cutting board, and chop finely. Mix apple, bacon, brown sugar, cinnamon, and salt. Pour into unheated ramekin and top with butter.

Pull heated ramekin out of oven and pour batter into it. Bake both ramekins for 22 to 25 minutes, until Dutch baby is puffed and golden. Don't open the oven too early, or it will fall.

Serve Dutch baby on a plate, with apple mixture on top or on the side.

Butternut Squash Skillet
Strata (page 72)

4-6 SERVINGS **8** AS A SIDE

BUTTERNUT SQUASH SKILLET STRATA

1 tbsp butter

2 tbsp olive oil

1 onion, diced

1 medium butternut squash (about 2 lb [900 g]), ½-in (1-cm) dice

1 head garlic, cloves separated and peeled

1½ tsp salt, divided

5 1-in (2.5-cm) thick slices of day-old French bread, chopped into 1-in cubes

2 cups (500 mL) grated aged cheddar cheese

5 eggs

1½ cups (375 mL) milk

1 tsp dried sage

1 tsp grainy Dijon mustard

1 tsp sambal oelek

½ tsp dried thyme

½ tsp ground black pepper

¼ tsp ground nutmeg

This strata recipe gets pretty good mileage in my kitchen—we use it as a brunch dish, an occasional dinner, and, once the festive season is underway, as a substitute for stuffing once we've had enough turkey dinners that it's time to shake things up. (With most of our family close by, we eat a lot of turkey between October and January.) It's crunchy, creamy, and savory, and stretches 5 eggs a good long way. This works best in a 12-in (30 cm) cast-iron frying pan.

Preheat oven to 375°F (190°C).

In a heavy pan on medium-high heat, melt butter with olive oil. Add onions, squash, garlic, and 1 tsp salt, and sauté until browned, about 8 to 10 minutes.

Meanwhile, in a large bowl, mix bread cubes and cheese.

In a separate bowl, whisk together eggs, milk, sage, mustard, sambal oelek, thyme, pepper, nutmeg, and remaining salt.

Pour squash mixture into bowl with bread and cheese. Toss, mixing well, then return mixture to frying pan.

Pour egg mixture over bread and squash mixture, pressing down on bread so it soaks up eggs and milk.

Place pan in oven and bake for 35 to 40 minutes, until strata has puffed and turned golden. Serve hot.

DEEP-FRIED SRIRACHA EGGS

This is the sort of thing we make when I've boiled too many eggs for the week and there are leftovers. It's great as a simple dinner for two, but I actually quite like just one of these sliced over a quick salad of greens, red onions, and watermelon dressed with a bit of oil and lemon for lunch. It's a nice thing to make when you've got a weekday off; it's also a good, inexpensive first course for brunch if you've got company.

vegetable oil

1 raw egg

1 tbsp Sriracha sauce

1 tbsp milk

½ tsp salt

½ cup (125 mL) all-purpose flour

¾ cup (375 mL) bread crumbs

4 eggs, boiled medium-hard, then cooled and peeled

salt, to taste

In a heavy-bottomed pan on medium-high, heat 2 in (5 cm) oil to 375°F (190°C).

Beat together raw egg, Sriracha, milk, and salt. Set aside.

Measure flour onto a small plate, and bread crumbs into a small bowl.

Roll cooked eggs in flour, then coat with egg mixture, then with bread crumbs.

Drop into oil using a slotted spoon and cook until golden, 60 to 90 seconds, turning as they cook for even browning. Salt and serve immediately, drizzled with additional Sriracha.

EGG & CORN QUESADILLA, FOR ONE OR MANY

1 SERVING

- 1 egg
- 1 tsp milk
- ⅛ tsp salt
- ⅛ tsp ground black pepper
- ⅛ tsp dried oregano
- 12-in (30-cm) flour tortilla
- 1 tbsp salsa (hot or mild, homemade or store-bought)
- 2 tsp canola oil or melted butter
- 2 tbsp frozen or fresh corn kernels
- 1 tbsp finely chopped scallions
- ¼ cup (60 mL) grated cheddar cheese
- 1 tbsp fresh cilantro, chopped

This is a quickie lunch or dinner, and perfect for when you need to eat in 10 minutes or less. It's a great way to use up those last kernels of frozen corn you have kicking around in your freezer; you can also throw in whatever else you've got in the refrigerator. Multiply the recipe by however many you need to feed; if you're making 4 to 8 quesadillas, limit the oil to 2 tbsp, in total. Serve with salsa or sliced avocado and a green salad.

Preheat oven to 450°F (230°C).

Whisk together egg, milk, salt, pepper, and oregano. Set aside.

Place tortilla on a lightly greased baking sheet. Smear top half of one side with salsa.

In a pan on medium-low, heat oil or butter, tipping and rotating pan to coat bottom. Add corn and scallions, and sauté for 1 minute.

Stir in egg mixture, and keep stirring, scraping bottom of pan with a spatula so egg doesn't brown, until it's cooked but still soft, between 30 and 60 seconds. Spoon egg mixture onto half of tortilla that isn't smeared with salsa.

Sprinkle cheese and cilantro over eggs. Fold over tortilla, and bake for 4 minutes. Flip quesadilla and cook for an additional 2 to 3 minutes, until you can hear cheese sizzling and edges of tortilla appear crisp and lightly golden.

Remove finished quesadilla to a cutting board and let it rest for 1 minute before cutting in half. Eat. Enjoy.

EGG & TOMATO CURRY

4
SERVINGS

This is a mild, gentle curry, the kind of thing you might want to eat after a weekend of too much beer and cheese. Serve it with rice and a nice cup of mint tea, and then go to bed early. It's restorative, and won't leave you either uncomfortable or wanting. It is best enjoyed while wearing stretch pants, or no pants at all. Nick and I each like 2 eggs; crack up to 8 eggs to feed 4 people.

2 tbsp butter

1 onion, diced

3 garlic cloves, minced

1 tsp garam masala

½ tsp chili flakes

½ tsp ground cumin

½ tsp salt

¼ tsp ground coriander

¼ tsp ground black pepper

28-oz (796-mL) can whole tomatoes, juices included

14-oz (398-mL) can coconut milk

1 cup (250 mL) frozen peas

4 tbsp chopped cilantro, divided

4–8 eggs

Preheat oven to 425°F (220°C).

In a large pan on medium-high heat, melt butter. Add onions, and cook until translucent, 3 to 5 minutes. Add garlic, garam masala, chili flakes, cumin, salt, coriander, and black pepper. Stir to coat onions in spices, and cook until bottom of pan appears dry.

Add tomatoes, squishing each between your fingers to break it apart as you add it to the pan. Stir in tomato juices.

Add coconut milk and bring up to a simmer. Cook for about 3 minutes, until sauce has reduced slightly and appears to have thickened.

Stir in peas and half of cilantro.

Crack eggs on top of sauce. Put pan in oven, and bake for 10 minutes, until eggs have set but are still soft inside.

Serve hot from the pan, over rice. Sprinkle each serving with remainder of cilantro.

4 SERVINGS

EGGS RABBIT

2 tbsp butter

2 tbsp flour

2 garlic cloves, minced

2 tsp grainy Dijon mustard

1 cup (250 mL) malty beer, such as amber ale

½ tsp chopped fresh thyme

¼ tsp ground nutmeg

½ tsp Worcestershire sauce

1 cup (250 mL) grated aged cheddar cheese

½ cup (125 mL) milk

salt and pepper, to taste

4 English muffins, halved and toasted

8 strips bacon, cooked and drained

8 eggs, poached to desired doneness

chopped parsley, for garnish

This is Eggs Benedict for my friend Corinne, who doesn't like Hollandaise sauce. While I'll never understand that, this is a perfectly lovely alternative—beery, cheesy, and hearty enough for breakfast or breakfast-for-dinner.

In a saucepan on medium-high heat, melt butter and stir in flour, garlic, and mustard to form a paste. Whisk in beer, and reduce to medium heat.

As butter-paste begins to melt into beer and sauce begins to thicken, whisk frequently, adding thyme, nutmeg, and Worcestershire sauce. Once mixture is smooth, stir in cheese and let melt, until mixture is smooth again. Stir in milk. Season with salt and pepper, to taste.

Stack English muffins with bacon and eggs, and pour sauce over. Sprinkle with parsley, and serve hot.

EGGS ~WITH~ CORN & RED BEANS

4 SERVINGS

This is kind of like huevos rancheros and kind of like eggs in purgatory, but it's a whole lot of delicious, especially after a night of eating recklessly. It's got everything you need in it to restore your digestive well-being, and cheese. Serve it with a dollop of yogurt and, if it wasn't just reckless eating you found yourself up to the night before, a couple of Micheladas (equal parts beer and Clamato, plus lime, a squish of Sriracha, and a few shakes of Worcestershire sauce) for good measure.

Preheat oven to 375°F (190°C).

In a large pan on medium-high heat, sauté onions in oil until translucent. Add garlic, corn, bell peppers, and jalapeño, and cook until glistening, about 3 minutes.

Add crushed tomatoes, beans, salt, chili powder, cumin, oregano, and cilantro and simmer for 5 minutes, until reduced and thickened slightly.

Remove from heat, and crack eggs over. Sprinkle with grated cheese, then place pan in oven on middle rack, and bake uncovered for 12 to 15 minutes, until whites are cooked and yolks are done to your liking. Serve over folded tortillas, sprinkled with cilantro.

½ onion, chopped

2 tbsp canola oil

3 garlic cloves, minced

1 cup (250 mL) fresh or frozen corn kernels

1 bell pepper, diced

1 jalapeño pepper, minced

14-oz (398-mL) can crushed tomatoes

14-oz (398-mL) can red beans

1 tsp salt

1 tsp chili powder

1 tsp ground cumin

½ tsp dried oregano

¼ cup (60 mL) chopped fresh cilantro + additional, for garnish

4 eggs

1 cup (250 mL) grated aged cheddar cheese

4 12-in (30-cm) flour tortillas

4-6 SERVINGS

8 eggs

¼ cup (60 mL) all-purpose flour

¼ cup (60 mL) milk

4½-oz (125-g) feta cheese, crumbled

¾ tsp coarse salt

½ tsp ground black pepper

¼ tsp ground nutmeg

½ cup (125 mL) chopped fresh dill

¼ cup (60 mL) chopped fresh parsley

3 tbsp olive oil

1 onion, halved and thinly sliced

4 garlic cloves, minced

1 lb (500 g) spinach, rinsed, dried, and chopped into ribbons

handful chopped fresh dill, for garnish

GREEN EGG BAKE

Ideal for brunch or late-night dinner, this makes efficient use of any greens and herbs you've got wilting in the crisper. I like it best with spinach and dill, because it reminds me of spanakopita. You can substitute a 10-oz (300-g) package of frozen spinach, but thaw it completely and wring it thoroughly in a clean dishtowel before adding it to the pan. Serve with a dollop of Greek yogurt and some quartered tomatoes tossed in olive oil and salt.

Preheat oven to 325°F (165°C).

In a large bowl, whisk eggs, flour, and milk until smooth. Add feta cheese, salt, pepper, nutmeg, dill, and parsley. Stir and set aside.

In a 12-in (30-cm) cast-iron pan on medium-high, heat olive oil. Add onions, and cook until softened, 2 to 3 minutes. Add garlic, stir for another minute, and then add spinach. Cook, stirring frequently, until spinach has wilted and reduced in volume, another 3 to 5 minutes.

Pour egg mixture over, stir quickly to mix in spinach and onions with egg batter, and place in oven. Bake for 30 minutes, until lightly golden and set in the center (shake pan—if eggs slosh around in the middle, give them a bit more time).

Let egg bake rest in pan for 5 minutes before cutting into slices and serving. Serve sprinkled with fresh dill.

PAUL'S TORTILLA ESPAÑOLA

My friend Paul Bell taught me how to make this—he spent time in Spain, and this frittata-like dish was one of his souvenirs. Tortilla Española is great for brunch, as it's impressive but not complicated—you can make it with a hangover. Serve with a dollop of yogurt and store-bought or homemade salsa.

In a 12-in (30-cm) frying pan on medium-high heat, sauté onions in 2 tbsp olive oil until translucent. Add potatoes, tossing to coat in oil and onion mixture, then add ⅓ cup (80 mL) water and cover with a lid. Reduce heat to medium-low, and cook for 20 minutes, shaking pan occasionally to prevent sticking.

Remove potatoes and onions from pan and let cool on a platter for 10 minutes, until there's no more steam rising from mixture.

Preheat broiler and wipe out pan.

Whisk together eggs, salt, and pepper.

On medium-high, heat 1 tbsp olive oil in pan, tipping to coat bottom. Stir cooled potatoes into eggs, then pour into heated pan. Run a spatula along sides every so often as it cooks, 5 to 6 minutes. Place under broiler until center sets and top is golden, 3 to 5 minutes. Check frequently to make sure it doesn't burn.

Turn out onto a dish and let rest for 5 to 10 minutes before slicing and serving.

4 SERVINGS

1 onion, diced

3 tbsp olive oil, divided

2 lb (900 g) yellow-fleshed potatoes, sliced thinly

6 eggs, beaten

½ tsp salt

½ tsp ground black pepper

4 SERVINGS

RED SAUCE EGGS

2 cups (500 mL) Red Sauce (p. 165)
   or store-bought pasta sauce

4 tbsp grated Parmesan cheese,
   divided

4 eggs

1 tsp coarse salt, divided

1 tsp chili flakes, divided

This is my working-from-home "meal for one" scaled up to feed more people. A little leftover pasta sauce, an egg, some toast for dip-scooping—there is no more perfect breakfast or lunch, and I will not debate that fact. If this is lunch, I'll serve it with a chopped piece of fruit or avocado on the side. For breakfast, all you need is a glass of juice (or wine, let's not kid ourselves) and some tea and you're ready for the day.

Preheat oven to 400°F (200°C). Lightly grease four ramekins.

In a saucepan on medium-high, heat sauce until it burbles. Spoon ½ cup (125 mL) sauce into each ramekin.

Sprinkle grated cheese into middle of each ramekin. Using back of a tablespoon, gently make a small indentation in cheese and sauce.

Crack an egg into indentation so that yolk sits in center of ramekin. Sprinkle each egg with salt and chili flakes.

Bake for 8 to 12 minutes, to desired doneness. Eight to 10 minutes will yield a yolk that is runny (more runny with less time); 12 minutes will yield a yolk cooked medium-hard.

BEANS AND LEGUMES

Though we ate a lot of take-out Indian food when I was a kid, I don't recall much in the way of legumes at home. It wasn't until I moved out on my own that I really discovered cooking with them. I moved to a smelly old basement suite near Commercial Drive, a street/neighborhood in Vancouver that's a curious mix of a long-standing Italian community and, well, New Age hippies. It's actually a lot more diverse than that, but at the time it did feel like I was encountering a lot of drum circles.

Vancouver's Commercial Drive has a million little grocery stores with abundant, mountainous displays of fresh produce and tall Lucite cylinders filled with bulk dried goods just waiting to be spilled all over the floor when I fail (again and again) to understand chutes and levers. Because of the area's nutritionally left-leaning population, you can get every kind of bean and lentil that exists in the entire world. Before I moved out on my own, I didn't know there was more than one kind. Truth: there are a lot of kinds.

And in the beginning, I was excited to be able to stock up on super cheap sources of protein that I could cook in large batches and then eat in various incarnations all week long. Of course, I was gassier than I'd ever been, but who doesn't love a fart joke? (Basically, any guy who hits on you in a bar; they do not want to hear your fart jokes. Their loss.) I was also beginning to get bored eating the same thing every day. I desperately want to be the kind of person who can eat the same thing for two of three meals, three days in a row, because it would give me more free time, and maybe I'd use that time wisely for self-improvement or washing the clothes that never leave the bottom of the laundry hamper, but even though it would be cheaper and potentially more convenient over the course of the whole week, I can't do it. We eat dishes containing beans several days a week, but I use canned beans unless I'm making a single meal in the Crock-Pot. When I find canned beans at seventy-seven cents a can, I buy tons.

Dried lentils, canned beans. I'm a busy lady, and if I've already thought ahead to cook rice and pre-chop veggies for the week, then I've used up my allotment for forward-thinking. You can rehydrate small amounts of dried beans, but you've got to have the time to do it. I do not.

What are the drawbacks to canned beans? Well, there is the tiny little issue of bisphenol A, or BPA, which is a toxic chemical that has been shown to mimic estrogen in the body. In 2010, a Statistics Canada report stated that BPA was appearing in measurable—not trace—amounts in the urine of as many as ninety-one percent of Canadians in every age group. BPA appears in some plastics and in the coating inside cans, such as those used for food. It's basically all over the place and in all the things. A 2011 study found that significant prenatal exposure to BPA resulted in symptoms of hyperactivity, anxiety, and depression in girls at three years of age (it didn't find the same severity of these effects in boys). It's the kind of thing you want to be careful with, because research is still looking at the long-term connection between BPA and adverse health events including reproductive cancers, even as other parts of the world have declared it fit for human consumption.

So, am I exposing my family to potentially troubling long-term health outcomes because I'm cranky about eating too many of the same kinds of beans every week? Maybe. But on the other hand, we might not eat any beans at all if it wasn't for the convenience of canned legumes, and beans are extremely valuable as an inexpensive source of fiber and lean protein. Beans and lentils fill you up, they can "stretch" meat meals (reducing the cost and health impacts of eating more meat), and they help regulate your blood sugar. For us, eating fewer beans and lentils would mean replacing the bulk that they provide with starchy foods like pasta, bread, or potatoes. Not a good carb-counting option.

If you're really set on rehydrating dried beans, there are a couple of ways you can do this. First, and possibly most convenient, is in a slow cooker. Soak about 2 lb (900 g) beans overnight in enough water to cover, then drain and rinse. Put beans into a slow cooker, cover with fresh water, add 2 tsp salt, and set to cook on low heat for 6 to 8 hours. I've had mixed success with this—kidney beans and chickpeas have held up well, while others have split and turned to mush. I find that the Crock-Pot most convenient when I can cook something for 10 hours (which covers my work day plus commute). Not all beans will hold up to 10 hours of cooking. If your schedule is more flexible, however, the slow cooker might work out great for you.

Another handy way to rehydrate beans is with a pressure cooker. You can do this in about 20 minutes, I'm told. A pressure cooker will cost between $100 and $200, and it will save you lots of time. I don't own one, but my friends Dan and Dennis have one and swear by its ability to make weeknight cooking a lot less of a hassle. Dennis tells me he makes a fairly rich, very tasty chicken broth in his pressure cooker in 20 minutes.

The easiest and most reliable way to rehydrate beans is on the stovetop. Rinse the beans, but don't bother soaking them first—this will work just fine, and you save yourself a step. Cover 1 to 2 lb (500 to 900 g) beans with about 2 in (5 cm) water, and add 1 to 2 tsp salt. In a heavy pot, such as a Dutch oven, bring beans to a boil on medium-high heat, then reduce heat to medium and simmer for about 90 minutes, give or take a few depending on the size and age of the beans. Beans that have been languishing in the back of your pantry for eons will take longer to cook.

One standard (14-oz [398-mL]) can of beans is equal to about ½ cup (125 mL) uncooked dried beans, which, when rehydrated, will equal about 1½ cups (375 mL). I often buy my beans in 19-ounce (540-mL) cans (the size that always seems to be available in generic brands and on sale), which is about the same as 2 cups (500 mL) of rehydrated dried beans. A pound of dried beans will equal 6 to 7 cups (1.5 to 1.7 L) cooked beans and will cost you very little. If you can buy dried beans in bulk, you'll be even further ahead. If you have the time, it's well worth it to rehydrate a quantity of beans, turn them into meals (as in the recipes that follow), and then package them in serving sizes that work best for your family—meals for four for future dinners, for example, or individual portions for everyone to take to work or school for lunch. Beans freeze well.

As mentioned above, I prefer canned beans for my everyday cooking, and dry lentils, which cook fast enough to not be a problem on weeknights. My experience with canned lentils is that they're a bit soggy, and they fall apart when cooked. Red lentils are an easy way to cram a bit of protein into puréed soups and veggies; they lend starchy bulk, but they're non-confrontational, even for Hunter. They're very mild in both taste and appearance. Green lentils are great for soups and casseroles, and I like the texture of black lentils for tacos because they seem a little more meaty. If you can't find black lentils, green lentils will work just fine. One cup (250 mL) dried lentils equals about 2 cups (500 mL) when cooked.

I think the best thing about lentils is that, if you prepare them in a saucy way, they act like meat and can even pass for it. My sister-in-law Sharon doesn't tell her three boys when they're eating lentils and not hamburger, and everyone's just as happy as they'd be if they were eating ground beef. My father-in-law, an avid carnivore, even admitted after a two-week exercise in clean eating that lentils were an acceptable substitute for meat. Lentils are kind of miraculous that way; they're a great introduction to meatless meals for those who believe that they require meat with every meal. Nick maintains that he prefers meat to lentils, but he prefers lentils to making his own damn dinner, so in the end everyone kind of wins.

A side benefit to lentils? They are highly digestible and contain a small amount of tryptophan, the groggy-making amino acid that makes you sleepy after a big turkey dinner. A lentil-based meal may therefore help you get a good night's sleep. If you're a busy person (and who among us isn't?), lentils are fabulous for many reasons—they make dinner prep uncomplicated, and that counts for so much, especially Monday through Thursday. It makes you wonder what else those New Age hippies were right about. (Please don't let it be drum circles. I can't unselfconsciously sit that close to other people.)

BREAKFAST BEANS

Sometimes Hunter does this adorable thing where he wakes up at, like, 5:45 a.m., which means our mornings are expansive. When that happens, I take the opportunity to whip up these beans, which are more complicated than the smoothies I make while yelling at everyone as we run out the door on regular mornings, but not so complicated that they're not doable, if you have a bit more time than usual. It's not like I'm allowed to just doze on the couch while he watches cartoons anyway. Add additional eggs and a side dish, such as sausage or chopped fruit, and this could stretch to feed 4.

1 tbsp olive oil

1 celery stalk, finely chopped

1 garlic clove, minced

2 tsp fish sauce

1 tsp chopped fresh rosemary

½ tsp grainy Dijon mustard

pinch nutmeg

19-oz (540-mL) can cannellini or navy
  beans

1 tbsp grated Parmesan cheese

½ cup (125 mL) sour cream or thick
  Greek yogurt

salt and pepper, to taste

2 eggs, fried or poached

2 slices of toast

In a pan on medium-high, heat oil. Sauté celery, garlic, fish sauce, rosemary, mustard, and nutmeg for about a minute, until celery is bright green and garlic is fragrant. Stir in beans, then add cheese and sour cream. Sauté another 30 to 60 seconds, until sour cream has melted into beans. Adjust seasonings to taste, and serve hot, topped with eggs on toast.

4 SERVINGS

BUTTERNUT SQUASH & CHICKPEA CURRY

3 tbsp olive oil

1 onion, minced

1 jalapeño pepper, seeded and minced

5 garlic cloves, minced

1 heaping tbsp minced fresh ginger

1 tbsp garam masala

1 tsp chili flakes

1 tsp cumin seeds

1 tsp ground turmeric

½ tsp ground black pepper

2 lb (900 g) butternut squash, diced

19-oz (540-mL) can chickpeas, drained and rinsed

14-oz (398-mL) can coconut milk

14-oz (398-mL) can crushed tomatoes

1 lime, zest and juice

salt and pepper, to taste

3 scallions, chopped

¼ cup (60 mL) chopped fresh cilantro
   + additional, for garnish

While I don't believe in cleanses, this dish is like a reset button when gluttony has left you tired and bloated. It feels good to eat, and all that garlic and ginger will set your stomach right, no matter what it's been through. I like this one with brown basmati rice, partly because it makes me feel virtuous, and partly because the nuttiness of the brown rice pairs well with the chickpeas and squash. Serve with a bit of full-fat yogurt mixed with grated cucumber and minced fresh garlic.

In a large pan on medium-high heat, warm oil and add onions, jalapeño peppers, garlic, and ginger. Sauté until onions are translucent and jalapeño has brightened in color. Add garam masala, chili flakes, cumin seeds, turmeric, and pepper. Stir to coat onion mixture thoroughly, and cook for 2 minutes.

Stir in diced squash and chickpeas. Add coconut milk, tomatoes, and lime zest and juice. Stir to coat squash in curry mixture, then reduce to medium heat, cover, and let cook for 15 to 20 minutes, until squash has softened. Stir occasionally.

Once squash has softened, taste and adjust seasonings as needed. Stir in scallions and cilantro, and serve over rice with an additional sprinkling of cilantro for color.

CHANA MASALA

My first encounter with chana masala was at Kwality Sweets, a tiny place in a tiny strip mall off the highway in Surrey, the town where I grew up. The majority of the place was kitchen, and if you peered in the back, you could see a frenzy of women working quickly. Kwality Sweets sold samosas by the paper bag, three for a dollar, and they were always very, very busy. I think Kwality Sweets provided me with my first taste of chickpeas; at the time they seemed very exotic. Now they're one of my staple foods. When I'm feeling nostalgic, this is the dish that I make. Naan bread is best with this, but any bread will do.

In a large frying pan on medium-high heat, melt butter. Add coriander seeds (if not using ground). Give them about a minute until they begin to pop, then stir in onions, garlic, and ginger. Stir in garam masala, cumin, black pepper, chili flakes, tumeric, cinnamon, and cayenne pepper (and ground coriander, if using).

Reduce heat to medium. Cook for 1 to 2 minutes, until spices are fragrant and onions have softened.

Add tomatoes to pan, juice and all, and scrape up any bits that may have formed on bottom of pan.

Stir in chickpeas, and squish the lime juice over. Reduce heat to medium and simmer to reduce sauce, until juices all but disappear. You want it to be thick and rich, not runny. Taste and adjust seasonings.

Just before serving, stir in about two-thirds of the cilantro, then use the remainder for topping.

1 tbsp butter

1 tsp coriander seeds or ½ tsp ground coriander

1 medium onion, chopped

3 cloves minced garlic

2 tsp finely minced fresh ginger

1 tbsp garam masala

2 tsp ground cumin

1 tsp ground black pepper

½ tsp chili flakes

½ tsp ground turmeric

¼ tsp ground cinnamon

¼ tsp cayenne pepper

14-oz (398-mL) can diced tomatoes or about 1½ cups (375 mL) diced fresh

19-oz (540-mL) can chickpeas

juice of 1 lime

salt, to taste

about ¼ cup (60 mL) cilantro

CHICKPEA SALAD ~WITH~ GARLIC SCAPES

SERVINGS AS A SIDE 4

19-oz (540-mL) can chickpeas, drained
and rinsed

1 pint (454 g) cherry tomatoes, halved

1 lemon, zest and juice

¼ cup (60 mL) olive oil

1 cup (250 mL) chopped garlic scapes

1 tsp chili flakes

1 tbsp chopped basil

salt and pepper, to taste

This is the easiest salad in the world. I like to serve it as a side with something simple like roast chicken, because it's so bright and cheery that it practically steals the show. You can also put it into containers for work—it makes a pretty satisfying lunch with a cup of tea. If you can't find garlic scapes, use chopped scallions or shallots; it just won't be garlicky.

In a bowl, combine chickpeas, tomatoes, and lemon zest and juice.

In a pan on medium-high, heat olive oil until shimmering. Add garlic scapes and chili flakes, and sauté until scapes turn bright green—about 1 minute. Pour scape mixture, oil included, over chickpea mixture, tossing to coat. Chill for 1 hour.

Before serving, stir in basil, salt, and pepper. Adjust seasonings as needed.

LENTIL SALAD

I love this salad so much. So much. It's sweet, it's earthy, there's bacon in it—it's basically everything I need out of life in one simple little salad. It also makes use of what I usually have in my pantry, which makes me love it even more. Also, so much fiber! It's good served warm, so if you're in a hurry, don't feel like you need to cool it off to dig in. It just gets a little better with a rest in the refrigerator. Serve with Pot Roast (p. 166), or Butternut Squash Skillet Strata (p. 72).

Preheat oven to 400°F (200°C).

Place garlic cloves in a ramekin and top with olive oil. Roast, uncovered, for 20 to 30 minutes, until cloves are soft, sweet-smelling, and golden. Drain oil into a bowl and reserve. Set cloves aside.

In a pot on medium-high heat, simmer lentils and bay leaf in 2 cups (500 mL) lightly salted water until tender, 20 to 30 minutes. Drain, then set aside. Discard bay leaf.

In a pan on medium-high heat, fry bacon until crisp, about 5 minutes. Spoon bacon onto a plate lined with a paper towel, and set aside. Save bacon fat for another purpose.

In a large bowl, combine still-warm lentils, roasted garlic, bacon, prunes, celery, and parsley. In a smaller bowl, whisk together still-warm reserved oil, vinegar, mustard, black pepper, and salt. Pour over lentil mixture, toss to coat, and chill for at least an hour, or until cool. Can also be served warm. Give it a quick toss just before serving.

2 heads garlic, cloves peeled and separated

½ cup (125 mL) olive oil

1 cup (250 mL) dried green lentils

1 bay leaf

4 slices bacon, finely chopped

1 cup (250 mL) dried prunes (about 18 prunes), roughly chopped

1 cup (250 mL) diced celery (about 3 stalks)

½ cup (125 mL) packed fresh parsley, roughly chopped

¼ cup (60 mL) red wine vinegar

2 tsp grainy Dijon mustard

1 tsp ground black pepper

½ tsp salt

LENTIL SLOPPY JOES

4 SERVINGS

Sloppy Joes are total kid food. They're also perfect for adults slogging through jobs, parents who just can't cope with all of this right now, and people who have been looking forward all week to spending Friday night on the couch, balancing a plate of comfort food on their thighs while binge-watching Netflix. And these are so healthy, you don't even need to bother with a side salad. Joes go well with chocolate milk and/or weekend-quality red wine. Serve open-faced, on toasted buns.

In a pot on medium heat, simmer lentils and bay leaf in 2 cups (500 mL) lightly salted water until tender, 20 to 30 minutes. Drain, then set aside. Discard bay leaf.

Meanwhile, in a heavy-bottomed pot such as a Dutch oven, on high heat, sauté celery, carrots, and onions in olive oil until glistening, then cover, reduce heat to medium, and cook for 10 minutes.

Remove lid, add garlic, and cook until mixture is caramelized and reduced by two-thirds, 15 to 20 minutes. The longer you cook this, the sweeter it will get.

Add mushrooms and cook until moisture has mostly dissipated and bottom of pan is dry. Add spices, thyme and tomato paste, stir until combined, then add cooked lentils. Stir in 1 cup (250 mL) water with apple cider vinegar and honey. Cook until mix begins to bubble. Taste and adjust seasoning as needed. Serve over toasted hamburger buns.

1 cup (250 mL) dried green, brown, or French lentils

1 bay leaf

2 stalks celery, finely chopped

2 carrots, finely chopped

1 small onion

4 tbsp olive oil

4 garlic cloves, minced

½ lb (250 g) mushrooms, finely minced (or whizzed until almost puréed in a food processor or blender)

1 tsp smoked paprika

1 tsp ancho or other chili powder

½ tsp ground mustard

½ tsp ground cumin

½ tsp ground black pepper

½ tsp dried thyme

5.5-oz (156-mL) can tomato paste

2 tbsp apple cider vinegar

1 tbsp honey

salt, to taste

4-6 SERVINGS

LENTIL TACOS ~with~ AVOCADO CREAM

1 cup (250 mL) dried green lentils

1 bay leaf

2 tsp salt, divided

1 onion, finely chopped

3 tbsp olive oil

2 jalapeño peppers, seeded, membranes removed, minced

3 garlic cloves, minced

1½ tsp ground cumin

1 tsp smoked paprika

1 tsp chili powder

1 tsp dried oregano

½ tsp ground coriander

5.5-oz (156-mL) can tomato paste

2 tsp apple cider vinegar

¼ cup (60 mL) chopped fresh cilantro

20 fresh 6-in (15-cm) corn tortillas

ACCOMPANIMENTS:

½ head shredded lettuce or cabbage

2 cups (500 mL) grated aged cheddar cheese

1 cup (250 mL) salsa (homemade or store-bought)

3 limes (cut into eighths)

Avocado Cream (opposite)

"I don't want you to get the wrong idea, but I actually kind of prefer these to regular hamburger tacos," Nick said once. Lentils in a saucy mixture are a pretty passable ground meat alternative, and in a taco, it's hard to care exactly what protein you're consuming. What's important is that you are eating tacos. Eat more tacos.

In a saucepan on medium-high heat, combine lentils, bay leaf, 1 tsp salt, and 2 cups (500 mL) water. Simmer uncovered for 20 to 30 minutes, until lentils are tender. Drain and set aside.

Meanwhile, in a large pan on medium-high heat, cook onions in olive oil until just translucent, about 3 minutes. Add jalapeño peppers and garlic, and cook for another minute, stirring frequently. Stir in cumin, smoked paprika, chili powder, dried oregano, coriander, and tomato paste. Coat veggies in spices and tomato paste. Cook for another minute, until tomato paste has browned slightly.

Add lentils to pot with ½ cup (125 mL) water, remainder of salt, and apple cider vinegar. Stir in cilantro. Taste and adjust seasonings as needed. If mixture appears dry, add a bit more water, a few tablespoons at a time, until mix is moist and saucy.

To serve, spoon filling into warmed tortillas, and top with accompaniments to taste.

AVOCADO CREAM

In Vancouver, avocados can be a bit pricy—they don't grow here, so we have to bring them in from California. To get the most out of them, I make an avocado-yogurt hybrid that stretches the avocado and plays on another traditional (north of the border) taco accompaniment: sour cream.

1 ripe Haas or other medium-sized avocado (or 2 small avocados)

½ cup (125 mL) Greek or other full-fat plain yogurt

½ tsp salt

½ tsp ground cumin

¼ tsp chili powder

zest and juice of ½ lime

In a large bowl, mash all ingredients together with a fork. Serve with Lentil Tacos (opposite) or with Red Bean Flautas (p. 95).

6 SERVINGS

PUMPKIN & RED LENTIL DAL

¼ cup (60 mL) canola oil

1 medium onion, chopped

5 garlic cloves, minced

1 heaping tbsp minced fresh ginger

2 jalapeño peppers, seeded, membranes removed, and minced

1 tbsp ground cumin

2 tsp chili flakes

1 tsp ground mustard

1 tsp ground turmeric

1 tsp ground coriander

½ tsp ground cinnamon

2 lb (900 g) pumpkin (or other winter squash), peeled and cubed

2 cups (500 mL) dried red lentils, rinsed

14-oz (398-mL) can coconut milk

2 tsp salt, or to taste

2 tsp granulated sugar, or to taste

2 limes, quartered

cilantro, for garnish

This is the stuff of long evenings spent marathoning old episodes of *30 Rock* or *Parks and Recreation*. It's filling but not heavy, warming but not too spicy, and healthy without feeling austere. Serve it with rice and a mug of sweet, milky tea. Best enjoyed on the couch, almost horizontally.

In a large, heavy-bottomed pot, heat oil on medium-high. Add onions, garlic, ginger, and peppers, and sauté until onions are translucent. Stir in cumin, chili flakes, mustard, turmeric, coriander, and cinnamon.

Add pumpkin and lentils, and stir to coat in spices.

Pour in coconut milk, then enough water to just cover pumpkin and lentils (about 3 to 4 cups [750 mL to 1 L]). Add salt and sugar. Bring to a boil, stirring occasionally, then reduce heat to medium-low and cover. Cook for 25 to 30 minutes, until lentils have swelled and broken, and most of liquid has been absorbed. Taste and adjust seasonings as needed.

Let rest, uncovered, 5 minutes before serving.

Garnish with quartered limes for squeezing over and a sprinkling of cilantro.

RED BEAN FLAUTAS

16
FLAUTAS

I didn't learn the word "flautas" until my friend Missy had us over for these; up until then, I'd known them as taquitos, which I'd only had at 7-Eleven under dire, desperate, and probably embarrassing circumstances. These, however, are proper flautas, which are nothing to be ashamed of. Make them when you have a few extra tortillas left over after taco night. Serve flautas hot, with Avocado Cream (p. 93) and your favorite hot sauce.

Preheat oven to 275°F (140°C). Put a wire rack into or over a baking sheet, and leave it in oven while oven heats.

In a large bowl, mix all ingredients but tortillas and oil for frying. Use your hands to ensure ingredients are thoroughly combined.

In a large pan on medium-high, heat ½ in (1 cm) oil until shimmering.

In a microwave oven, heat tortillas 4 at a time: Wrap them in a damp paper towel, then nuke for 30 to 40 seconds, until soft and pliable. If you don't have a microwave, wrap six tortillas in foil and place on a baking sheet in oven while it preheats, for about 15–20 minutes. A standard sheet pan will comfortably hold three of these bundles.

Spoon about 2 tbsp filling into each tortilla, placing it just off-center toward bottom. Gently but firmly roll tortilla away from you. Using tongs, place each roll into pan of hot oil, seam side down. Hold it for a few seconds to seal it shut.

Fry each roll for about 2 minutes per side, until tortilla is crisp and golden. Don't crowd the pan—cook no more than 4 at a time. Place cooked flautas on prepared baking sheet in oven to keep them warm as you cook the remainder. Serve hot.

19-oz (540-mL) can red kidney beans, drained and rinsed

½ lb (250 g) sweet potatoes, peeled, boiled, and roughly mashed

1 cup (250 mL) grated aged cheddar cheese

3 scallions, finely chopped

2 garlic cloves, minced

2 tbsp chopped fresh cilantro

2 tsp Sriracha sauce

1 tsp ground cumin

½ tsp ground coriander

½ tsp salt

½ tsp ground black pepper

¼ tsp dried thyme

16 fresh 6-in (15-cm) corn tortillas

canola or peanut oil, for frying

SWEET POTATO & MIXED-BEAN CHILI

1 medium onion, chopped

1 medium sweet potato, chopped
   (about 2 cups [500 mL])

2 tbsp olive oil

5 garlic cloves, minced

14-oz (398-mL) can diced tomatoes,
   including liquid

19-oz (540-mL) can red kidney beans,
   drained and rinsed

19-oz (540-mL) can black beans,
   drained and rinsed

19-oz (540-mL) can chickpeas, drained
   and rinsed

5.5-oz (156-mL) can tomato paste

½ cup (125 mL) beer, preferably an
   amber ale

4 tsp chili powder

2 tsp ground cumin

1 tsp ground black pepper

¼ tsp ground cinnamon

salt, to taste

It turns out that whether this is chili or not is debatable, and depends entirely on what part of North America you hail from. I was raised on chili with beans, and this is very much like the big pots of chili of my childhood, only with a wider variety of beans crammed in and sweet potato instead of ground beef. It goes rather nicely with the Skillet Cornbread with Blueberries on p. 222. I like mine with a bit of grated cheddar cheese and a dollop of sour cream on top. If you have any left over, this is very good on nachos the next day.

In a large, heavy-bottomed pot on medium-high heat, sauté onions and sweet potatoes in olive oil, about 3 minutes. Stir in garlic and add canned tomatoes. Reduce heat to medium.

Stir in beans, chickpeas, and tomato paste. Stir in beer, ½ cup (125 mL) water, spices, and salt, and simmer, uncovered, for 10 minutes. Taste and adjust seasonings as needed.

Cover and reduce to medium-low heat. Cook for 30 to 40 minutes, until sweet potatoes are soft. Serve hot, in bowls.

SWEET POTATO & RED LENTIL SOUP

My son Hunter, who won't eat any of the items in this soup individually, will gobble this up and ask for more. We call it Toddler Soup around here, because it's pretty much just for him; I make a big batch of it every once in a while, then portion it into little containers and freeze it for his lunches, and I'm certain it's why he's so tall and hardy. With a bit of everything in it, it's just sweet enough that he doesn't notice it's good for him. Serve with slices of lime and (for the grownups) hot sauce.

In a heavy-bottomed pan such as a Dutch oven, on medium-high heat, cook onions in oil until just browned around edges, 4 or 5 minutes. Stir in ginger and garlic, and cook for another minute.

Add celery, carrots, sweet potatoes or yams, and mango, and toss to coat in oil. Add salt, garam masala, turmeric, cumin, and coriander, and cook until veggies have begun to sweat and brighten, about 3 minutes. Add lentils, bay leaf, and stock, and bring to a boil.

Reduce heat to medium, and partially cover. Simmer for 20 to 25 minutes, until veggies and lentils are tender. Fish out bay leaf, then blend using an immersion blender. If you don't have an immersion blender, purée in batches using a stand blender; just be careful—blending hot liquids can be trouble, so work in small batches. Return puréed soup to pot.

Stir in coconut milk and bring back up to heat. Taste and adjust seasonings as needed before serving.

3 tbsp canola oil

1 onion, diced

2 tsp minced fresh ginger

3 garlic cloves, minced

2 celery stalks, trimmed and chopped

2 carrots, peeled, trimmed, and chopped

1 lb (500 g) sweet potatoes or yams, peeled and chopped

1 lb (500 g) mango, peeled, pitted, and chopped

1 tbsp coarse salt

2 tsp garam masala

2 tsp ground turmeric

½ tsp ground cumin

½ tsp ground coriander

1 cup (250 mL) dry red lentils, rinsed

1 bay leaf

8 cups (2 L) low-sodium chicken stock or water

14-oz (398-mL) can coconut milk

CHICKEN

The first roast chicken I ever made was to impress my parents and demonstrate that I really was an adult. I had moved into a real apartment with my boyfriend. We had furniture and nothing leaked or was infested with rats, so I wanted to show my parents that I'd made it. I flipped through all my cookbooks, and there were so many variations on how to roast a bird—start with a very hot oven then reduce the heat, some said; start breast-side down and then flip it, others said. Have you ever tried to flip a half-roasted chicken without the appropriate kitchen tools? Let's just say I've dusted off a few chickens as I blundered toward dinner.

I couldn't decide which recipe was most likely to work, so I panicked and sort of combined them all. An hour after the chicken was supposed to be done, I pulled it from the oven, steaming and golden; its skin was perfect and crisp-looking, and the smell was warm and savory. My mom offered praise for the finished dish until my dad cut into it and discovered it was still raw inside. We ate the side dishes I'd made instead. I apologized ten or twenty times. The relationship with the boyfriend ended a month later. Not because of the chicken, I don't think.

I have eaten many good chickens, and many, many bad ones. Have you ever spent a week looking forward to fried chicken only to find yourself with a carton of greasy, soggy sadness? There is a particular kind of grief that relates to unrequited food cravings, and I can't be the only one who feels it. Chicken is so easy to make, but it's also so easy to ruin. I've eaten overcooked chicken I had to force down my esophagus as if I was trying to swallow a fistful of cotton balls. I've eaten chicken with rubbery, pimply looking skin, just to be polite. I've done some things I regret, and many of them are chicken-related.

The only time I order chicken when I'm out for dinner is when it's fried. When I was a kid, chicken was a regular, everyday thing, but fried chicken was a treat. Picnic food. My dad would take us out to pick my mom up from work, then we'd grab a bucket of chicken from the drive-thru place nearby. We'd find a park with a playground and a picnic table and eat greasy drumsticks and neon-green coleslaw until the evening light turned the whole park yellow and Instagrammy-looking and the air began to cool. Occasionally, my parents would make a breaded version of fried chicken at home, and it was good too, but the real magic was the picnic and the take-out and the feeling that we were doing something special. To this day, when someone says, "Let's have a picnic! We'll get fried chicken!" I get all goofy and excited and shrieky. I have been trying to share my enthusiasm for chicken picnics with Hunter, but he just looks at me like I'm insane (which, I suppose, is exactly how I look with wide eyes and big gestures). I worry that his teenage rebellion is going to be veganism and restraint.

Fried chicken is still special to me, and when I make it at home it's a big treat because it takes a lot of oil and I like to pretend for company that I couldn't possibly eat that way every day. We mostly have roast chicken, because a roast chicken one night means dinner again the next night, and sometimes the night after that. When it was just Nick and me, we'd stretch a single five-pound (2.2 kg) chicken over several days; now that we've got a little person to feed, we roast two at a time so we can have sandwiches, salads, and stews for the rest of the week and little containers of soup to freeze for Hunter's daycare lunches.

Chicken can be difficult: If you're cooking it whole, there's the balance of juicy flesh and crispy skin and cooked-all-the-way-through-ness that must be maintained; if you're frying it in pieces, you have to cook the inside without burning the outside. Chicken cooked poorly is rubbery or chalky or tasteless. Maybe that explains our modern enthusiasm for boneless, skinless chicken breasts—you just chop them into cubes and put them into things and it mostly works out, sort of. It costs more, but a package of boneless skinless chicken is a bland no-brainer for many people come supper time.

(Suppertime no-brainers are no small thing, of course. For many of us, a few simple shortcuts are the difference between a home-cooked meal and just throwing frozen Hungry Man dinners at each individual family member. But you shouldn't have to spend more for less effort.)

Boneless, skinless chicken breasts are the most expensive way to buy chicken, and the least useful. There's just not enough flavor there to make them worthwhile, and without the bones and skin, you risk having to choke down chicken the texture of dry paper towels. If you are going to pay a premium for meat, it should be for fancy meat that makes you feel flush, something you can serve rare and bloody, not something you have to tart up with sauces and spices. When you buy chicken, buy it whole if possible; this is a bit more pricey up front, but the cost of one or two whole chickens is amortized over several meals. If you hit a sale, buy thighs or legs—there's more flavor there than in white meat, and those fattier cuts are more forgiving. Always buy bone-in—even if you're not using the bones, you can save them for stock. If you want lean, inexpensive, easy-cooking boneless protein, pork tenderloin is a good option and infinitely tastier than boneless, skinless chicken breast.

The main challenges with chicken are timing and temperature. When cooked, the internal

Brine that bird!

BRINING IS EASY. AT ITS SIMPLEST, IT'S A MIX OF SALT AND WATER. AND ALTHOUGH THAT'S THE BARE MINIMUM, MOST OF THE TIME IT'S ALL YOU NEED. USE A RATIO OF 1 TBSP KOSHER, COARSE, OR PICKLING SALT PER CUP (250 ML) WATER. IF YOU WANT TO GET FANCY, ADD SOME SLICED LEMONS OR RAW ONIONS, SPICED, BRUISED FRESH HERBS (MUDDLE THEM AS YOU WOULD IF YOU WERE MAKING MOJITOS), OR SRIRACHA.

MIX BRINE IN A LARGE BOWL, AND WHISK TO DISSOLVE SALT. YOU CAN EITHER BRING IT TO A BOIL IN A POT AND THEN COOL IT, OR JUST DO IT COLD. HEATING IT MAKES IT EASIER TO DISSOLVE THE SALT, BUT SOMETIMES THERE'S JUST NO TIME. BRINE BIRD BITS IN A LARGE ZIP-LOCK BAG OR A STORAGE CONTAINER WITH A TIGHT-FITTING LID. IF YOU'RE DOING A BUTTERMILK AND SALT BRINE FOR FRIED CHICKEN, BRINE FOR TWENTY-FOUR HOURS. A WHOLE CHICKEN CAN BE BRINED IN SALT WATER FOR EIGHT TO TWELVE HOURS. CHICKEN IN PIECES CAN BE BRINED FOR UP TO SIX HOURS. KEEP IN MIND THAT YOU WILL NEED TO SEASON CHICKEN LESS IF YOU BRINE IT. (YOU CAN DO THE SAME WITH PORK. YOU CAN BRINE FISH TOO, FOR LESS TIME. DON'T BOTHER BRINING BEEF.)

TO COOK BRINED CHICKEN, SIMPLY REMOVE IT FROM THE BRINE, DAB IT DRY WITH PAPER TOWELS, AND PROCEED AS PER USUAL.

temperature of a piece of chicken should be about 165°F (74°C). At 350°F (180°C), it will take twenty minutes per pound (500 g) to roast. This is a great jumping-off point, but by no means the only way to go. I've had my best luck taking the Ina Garten approach and cooking a four or five pound (1.8 to 2.2 kg) chicken, breast side up, at 425°F (220°C) for ninety minutes. Rotate the pan as you baste the bird, and baste it about four times. If the skin looks like it's getting too dark while there's still a ways to go on the kitchen timer, loosely tent it inside the oven with foil and start to check the internal temperature about fifteen minutes before you expect it to be done. If you have the time, let the chicken rest on the counter for an hour before you roast it—a bird at room temperature will cook more reliably than one still cold from the refrigerator.

If you plan ahead, the easiest way to guarantee a moist and flavorful chicken is to brine it. I'm certain brining has saved my ass on a number of occasions, and on just as many occasions I've wished I'd done it. I once spent twenty-seven dollars on a free-range organic chicken (I am bad at math and didn't realize how much it would be until after the butcher had rung up the bird—at that point I was too embarrassed to slink out of there and, of course, I'd never be able to return). I spiced it and rubbed it the usual way, but it ended up chewy and dry, like jerky, only way more disappointing. Could brining have saved it? It certainly wouldn't have hurt, and then maybe I wouldn't have cried in the shower about a chicken later that evening.

While it's probably not healthy to feel as deeply as I do about a perfectly cooked bird, there is a kind of magic to it, and once you've figured it out, you've got an easy, impressive meal for company or family dinner on a rainy weekend evening. Roast chicken is comforting, like a hug that you eat, only better than a hug because sometimes it comes with gravy. Everyone likes roast chicken, and almost everyone thinks roast chicken is super complicated and time consuming—don't tell them it's not. You'll be a hero.

Relajo (spice mixture). See
Salvadoran Roast Chicken
with Gravy (page 110)

CHICKEN & DUMPLINGS

4–6 chicken thighs, bone-in, skin on

4 cups (1 L) celery, chopped

2 onions, 1 halved, 1 diced

2 bay leaves

1 lemon, halved, zest reserved

3 whole garlic cloves + 3 garlic cloves, minced

2 tsp coarse salt, divided

1 bunch parsley

1 tsp whole coriander seeds

1 tsp whole peppercorns

3 tbsp olive oil

1 lb (500 g) carrots, chopped about ¾-in (2-cm) thick

1 bell pepper, seeded and diced

18 dried apricots, halved

1 tsp ground cumin

1 tsp smoked paprika

½ tsp ground turmeric

½ tsp dried chili flakes

½ tsp ground black pepper

½ tsp chopped fresh thyme

¼ tsp ground coriander

¼ tsp ground cinnamon

¼ cup (60 mL) all-purpose flour

½ cup (125 mL) dry white wine

28-oz (796-mL) can whole tomatoes, including juice

2 tsp honey or brown sugar

1 cup (250 mL) frozen peas

A pot of stew on a cold night is restorative anytime, but a stew flavored with warming spices and a good pop of lemon will not only restore you, it'll transport you as well. We call this "Moroccan-ish stew;" with its Moroccan flavors, it tastes vaguely escapist, even though it feels cozy and familiar. Don't be put off by the long list of ingredients—most of them are spices. I serve this with a simple salad of greens and capers dressed with olive oil and red wine vinegar. A bit of wine or mint tea doesn't hurt either.

In a large pot, place chicken pieces, celery, 1 onion (halved), bay leaves, zested lemon (halved), 3 whole garlic cloves, 1 tsp salt, 6 sprigs parsley, coriander seeds, and peppercorns. Fill pot with water to cover, and bring to a boil on high heat. Once boiling, reduce heat to low, cover, and cook for 40 minutes. Remove chicken from pot, and pass liquid through a strainer. Discard solids, and reserve liquid.

Once chicken is cool enough to handle, remove skin and discard, then pull meat off bones. Roughly chop it, then set aside. Reserve bones for making stock.

Preheat oven to 400°F (200°C).

In a large oven-proof pot on medium-high, heat olive oil. Add diced onions, carrots, bell peppers, and dried apricots. Stir to coat veggies in oil. Cook for 2 to 3 minutes, until veggies have softened slightly and onions are translucent. Reduce heat to medium.

Add minced garlic, remainder of salt, cumin, paprika, turmeric, chili flakes, black pepper, thyme, coriander, and cinnamon. Stir to coat veggies in spices, and cook another minute, until spices are fragrant. Stir in flour and coat veggies.

Stir in wine, and scrape bottom of pan to incorporate well. Add tomatoes and juice, squishing each one through your fingers to break it apart. Stir in honey or sugar. Add 4 cups (1 L) reserved chicken cooking liquid, frozen peas, and about ½ cup (125 mL) chopped parsley.

DUMPLINGS

½ cup (125 mL) all-purpose flour

½ cup (125 mL) whole wheat flour

2 tsp baking powder

½ tsp salt

¼ cup (60 mL) cold butter, diced

¼ cup (60 mL) cold milk

In a medium bowl, whisk together flour, baking powder, and salt. Press butter between your fingers as you add it to the bowl, breaking it apart. Continue gently working butter with your fingers to make a sandy-looking mixture with larger chunks of butter. Stir in milk.

Once chicken mixture has come to a boil, drop ping-pong ball sized pieces of dumpling mixture into pot, distributing evenly around surface of stew.

Bake for 18 to 20 minutes, until dumplings are golden and crisp-looking and stew is bubbling.

Let stew rest for about 10 minutes before diving in.

4 SERVINGS

FRIED CHICKEN & WAFFLES

BRINE

4 cups (1 L) buttermilk

½ cup (125 mL) coarse salt

½ cup (125 mL) Sriracha sauce

1 whole chicken, chopped into 10 pieces

2–4 cups (1 L) peanut oil, for frying

BREADING

3½ cups (825 mL) all-purpose flour

2 tsp coarse salt

2 tsp smoked paprika

1 tsp ground cumin

1 tsp ground mustard

½ tsp ground black pepper

Our friends Greg and Missy are the only people I ever prepare this for, because Missy has prohibited me from making it for anyone else. I could defy her, I suppose, but it's nice to have a thing that you make only for special occasions. Since we've both got young children, we make Chicken & Waffles Night our reason to get together. Serve chicken on waffles, drizzle with maple syrup and Sriracha, and eat with slices of cold watermelon. Drink beer or lemonade. Wear loose pants.

In a deep plastic or glass container with a tight-fitting lid, whisk buttermilk, salt, and Sriracha, then add chicken pieces. Press chicken down to submerge under brine. Refrigerate for up to 10 hours.

In a heavy-bottomed sauté pan or deep cast-iron frying pan, heat 1 in (2.5 cm) peanut oil to between 350° and 375°F (180° and 190°C).

Pour flour, salt, paprika, cumin, mustard, and pepper into a durable plastic bag. Holding bag closed, shake contents to mix thoroughly. In 2 or 3 batches, shake chicken pieces to coat in flour, then gently place into hot oil, skin-side down at first. Fry until golden and crispy, about 8 minutes, then flip and fry other side for another 8 minutes, until internal temperature is 165°F (74°C).

Meanwhile, make waffles.

WAFFLES

1 cup (250 mL) all-purpose flour

½ cup (125 mL) whole wheat flour

3 tsp baking powder

½ tsp coarse salt

1½ cups (375 mL) buttermilk

2 eggs, beaten

¼ cup (60 mL) canola oil

1 tbsp honey

1 cup (250 mL) corn kernels (fresh or frozen)

In a large bowl, whisk together flours, baking powder, and salt. In a separate bowl, whisk together buttermilk, eggs, canola oil, and honey. Pour wet ingredients into dry ingredients, add corn, and stir to combine. Cook according to waffle-maker manufacturer's instructions.

4 SERVINGS

1 whole chicken, chopped into 10 pieces

½ cup (125 mL) yellow (American) mustard

4 tsp salt, divided

2–4 cups (1.5 L) peanut or canola oil

3 cups (750 mL) all-purpose flour

2 tsp ground black pepper

honey, to taste

MUSTARD-FRIED CHICKEN

This fried chicken recipe is just me being cheap and lazy—which, as it turns out, is my recipe for personal success. I wanted fried meat, but had no time for a long brine or any of the usual things for dredging and breading; I had mustard and flour and fat. As luck would have it, that's all you need for some pretty tasty fried chicken. This is great with Grandma Salad (p. 182).

Put chicken pieces, a few at a time, into a sturdy plastic bag. Splurch mustard and sprinkle about 1 tsp salt over chicken. Mush chicken and mustard together in bag, then let sit for at least an hour, or up to 6 hours.

In a heavy-bottomed sauté pan or deep cast-iron frying pan, heat 1 in (2.5 cm) peanut oil to between 350° and 375°F (190°C).

In another plastic bag, combine flour, remainder of salt, and pepper and mix well. Remove chicken from first bag and place in second bag. Hold bag closed and shake chicken like it's 1993 and you're making Shake 'n Bake.

Working in 2 or 3 batches, place chicken in hot oil and cook until crisp and golden on one side (about 8 minutes), then turn and cook for another 4 or 5 minutes, until cooked through (internal temperature should read 165°F [74°C]).

Drain chicken on a wire rack (positioned over a plate for easy clean-up) for 5 minutes. Drizzle lightly with honey, and serve hot.

ROAST PAPRIKA CHICKEN

4 SERVINGS

This sweetly spicy roast chicken is the antidote to the winter blahs. I love it with just a few boiled potatoes and a salad; it's easy, and the prep time is quick—you can do it all ahead of time and stick it in the refrigerator, so long as you let it sit on the counter before roasting—a room temperature chicken roasts more reliably than a cold one. This is perfect for Sunday family dinner.

Let chicken rest at room temperature for an hour. Preheat oven to 425°F (220°C). Place chopped onions, celery, and carrots in a large roasting pan.

In a small bowl, combine oil, garlic, paprika, cayenne pepper, cinnamon, black pepper, and salt. Mash together with a fork until mixture forms a paste.

Using your hands, slather paste all over chicken, sliding your fingers under skin to rub paste into breast, legs, and thighs. Wash your hands, then truss chicken, folding wing tips behind bird. Place chicken in roasting pan with vegetables and pour wine into pan.

Roast chicken for 90 minutes (or 18 to 20 minutes per pound), until internal temperature reaches 165°F (74°C) and juices run clear when poked with a knife between leg and thigh. If chicken browns too quickly, place a piece of foil loosely over it. Baste periodically, adding additional wine or water as needed to moisten bottom of pan. Rotate pan each time you baste to ensure even browning.

Remove from oven and, if you haven't already, tent with foil. Let rest 20 minutes before serving. Serve with roasted veggies from pan.

1 whole roasting chicken, 4–5 lb (1.8–2.2 kg)

1 onion, chopped

3 stalks celery, chopped into 1-in (2.5-cm) pieces

3 carrots, peeled and chopped into 1-in (2.5-cm) pieces

2 tbsp olive oil

3 garlic cloves, minced

1 tbsp smoked paprika

1 tsp cayenne pepper

1 tsp ground cinnamon

1 tsp ground black pepper

1 tsp salt

½ cup (125 mL) dry white wine

6 SERVINGS

SALVADORAN ROAST CHICKEN ·WITH· GRAVY

CHICKEN

1 whole roasting chicken, 6–8 lb (2.7–3.5 kg)

3 tbsp olive oil

1½ tsp kosher salt

1 tsp ground black pepper

1 tsp ground annatto seed (or ground turmeric)

3 lb (1.5 kg) tomatoes, halved

1 onion, chopped

1 head garlic, halved crosswise

1 batch relajo (see below)

1 cup (250 mL) white wine

1 cup (250 mL) chicken stock

2 tsp Worcestershire sauce

salt and pepper, to taste

RELAJO (SPICE MIXTURE)

8 bay leaves

1 tbsp peanuts

1 tbsp pumpkin seeds

1 tsp sesame seeds

1 tsp oregano

1 tsp annatto seeds

½ tsp ground black pepper

There's a town in El Salvador called San Julián, and I spent an afternoon there in September of 2013. At a market in the center of town a woman sold spices and canned goods and little wads of chocolate in plastic sandwich bags. She sold bags of the spice mix for this chicken dish, and I bought a whole bunch without even knowing what to do with it. On the bus back to the town where we stayed, one of the Salvadoran World Vision Canada staff with whom I traveled explained how to use relajo. This is it. Serve chicken with the gravy it makes over rice or buns and curtido-style slaw (p. 180).

Preheat oven to 425°F (220°C).

Let chicken rest at room temperature for an hour. Rub chicken with olive oil, then sprinkle with salt, pepper, and annatto and rub again. Fold wings behind back of chicken and truss legs—tie them together so that they sit close to the body. Set aside.

On medium-low heat, toast all ingredients for relajo until mixture is fragrant and sesame seeds are golden. Remove pan from heat and set spices aside. Place tomatoes, onions, and garlic in pan, sprinkle with relajo, then nestle chicken in middle. Add wine and chicken stock.

Roast for between 90 minutes and 2 hours, until internal temperature reaches 165°F (74°C) and juices run clear when poked with a knife between leg and thigh. Baste every 20 to 30 minutes, rotating pan each time for even browning. If chicken browns too quickly, cover loosely with a piece of foil.

Remove chicken from pan and, if you haven't already, tent it with foil. Let sit for 15 to 20 minutes.

Meanwhile, process roasted veggies and chicken juices through the finest disc on a food mill or press through a fine-mesh strainer back into pan or into a saucepan. Stir in Worcestershire sauce.

Place pan on medium heat and simmer for 10 to 15 minutes. Taste and adjust seasonings as needed.

SRIRACHA BUFFALO WINGS

4 SERVINGS

It's not difficult to make Nick happy—a refrigerator full of cold beer, a pair of pajama pants, and a plate of these wings are all he really needs to experience total bliss. Serve with a plate of crudités and some store-bought ranch dressing. (You could make the dressing if you wanted to, but Nick doesn't care, so I don't either.)

2 cups (500 mL) peanut oil

2 lb (900 g) chicken wings, tips removed

½ cup (125 mL) flour

4 tbsp Sriracha sauce

2 tbsp butter, melted

1 tbsp lime juice

1 tsp salt

1 tsp ground black pepper

chopped scallions, for garnish

In a large pan on medium-high heat, heat oil to about 375°F (190°C).

Preheat oven to 350°F (180°C).

Place chicken wings in a sturdy plastic bag with flour, and shake until wings are covered—you may need to do this in 2 batches. Place half the wings gently into pan, and cook for 8 to 10 minutes, until golden. Flip and cook for 6 minutes on other side. Remove to a plate lined with paper towels, and repeat with second batch of wings.

Meanwhile, in a large bowl, combine Sriracha, butter, lime juice, salt, and pepper. Add fried wings and toss to coat.

Place on a baking sheet fitted with a wire rack. Bake for 25 minutes.

Serve hot and sprinkled with chopped scallions.

4 SERVINGS

1 cup (250 mL) diced mango

1 banana, sliced into rounds

1 large shallot (or small onion), chopped

1 tbsp chopped fresh ginger

3 garlic cloves, smashed

1 lime, zest and juice

1 tbsp fish sauce

2 tsp Sriracha sauce

1 bunch scallions, light green and white parts separated from darker greens

14-oz (398-mL) can coconut milk

2 tsp coarse salt

4–6 chicken thighs, bone in, skin-on

1 tbsp canola oil

2 tsp sesame oil

2 red bell peppers, chopped

1 tsp ground cumin

1 tsp ground turmeric

1 tsp freshly ground black pepper

½ tsp ground coriander

¼ tsp ground cardamom

1 cup (250 mL) frozen peas

½ cup (125 mL) chopped cilantro

SWEET YELLOW CURRY

Need dinner fast? This one's great for when you've got people coming over, or for when you've got ten thousand things to do before bedtime. The curry cooks in about the same amount of time as it takes to steam the pot of rice you'll serve this with.

In a food processor or blender, combine the mango, banana, shallot, ginger, garlic, lime juice and zest, fish sauce, Sriracha, white and light green parts of scallions, and coconut milk. Pulse or blend until smooth. Set aside.

Sprinkle salt over chicken thighs. In a large pan on medium-high heat, sauté chicken in canola and sesame oils, skin-side down first, then flip. Cook for about 6 minutes per side, until skin is crisp and golden. Remove chicken from pan and set aside.

Add bell peppers and cook for 1 to 2 minutes, then stir in cumin, turmeric, pepper, coriander, and cardamom. Coat veggies in spices.

Pour mango-coconut milk mixture into pan, scraping bottom of pan with a wooden spoon to remove any browned bits, and stirring to incorporate spices. The color will be fantastic, possibly alarmingly bright. Stir in peas, then return chicken to pan. Reduce heat to medium and bring to a simmer.

Simmer for 5 minutes, stirring occasionally. Before serving, taste and adjust seasoning as needed, then stir in cilantro and reserved dark green parts of scallions.

TOMATO CHICKEN CURRY

SERVINGS 4

This is not butter chicken, but since it involves similar flavors, it passes when we need it to. It's a bright, easy curry made of stuff you already have in your cupboards and refrigerator. A perfect Tuesday dish, it comes together in about the time it takes to cook a pot of rice. Serve with rice and Chana Masala (p. 87) and a cup of hot black tea.

In a large pot on medium-high heat, melt butter. Sauté onions until translucent. Add chicken, garlic, and ginger. Brown chicken lightly, 5 to 7 minutes.

Add garam masala, chili flakes, cumin, salt, coriander, and pepper. Stir to coat chicken in spices. Add tomato paste, and sauté until bottom of pan appears dry and paste has stuck to chicken.

Add diced tomatoes and coconut milk, scraping bottom of pan for any delicious brown bits. Reduce heat to medium and simmer for 20 minutes, stirring occasionally.

Season to taste. Just before serving, stir in spinach leaves, and cook for an additional minute until spinach has just wilted.

2 tbsp butter

1 medium onion, chopped

4–6 chicken thighs, cubed, skin and
    bones discarded

3 garlic cloves, minced

1 tbsp minced fresh ginger

1 tbsp garam masala

2 tsp chili flakes

2 tsp ground cumin

1½ tsp salt

½ tsp ground coriander

½ tsp ground black pepper

5.5-oz (156-mL) can tomato paste

28-oz (796-mL) can diced tomatoes

14-oz (398-mL) can full-fat coconut
    milk (low-fat's too watery)

salt, to taste

2 cups (500 mL) whole spinach leaves,
    lightly packed

FISH

As a child, many of my finest moments were buffet-related. Early on, I understood the value of seafood in a buffet, and would eschew the filling, less expensive carbs (no pasta, potatoes, or bread) and head straight for the crab legs. I am greedy and competitive, which means I am great at buffets.

My parents didn't have a lot of money then; it was the 1980s-ish and mortgage rates were high, so often we'd pop across the border to Washington state for cheap cheese, milk, and gas. On special occasions, we'd make an evening of it, and if I was very lucky on a Friday night, they'd take me to the King's Table Buffet, a magical place just off the I-5 where I was free to eat as many crab legs as my stomach would hold.

I imagine that watching a scrawny eight-year-old shove pound after pound of crab into her butter-sheened maw was not unlike watching a snake consume an antelope. I have never passed for adorable. Through the years, I have been an insatiable seafood fiend, eating more than my fair share whenever the opportunity presented itself because seafood has always been a treat, whether it's king crab legs at a buffet or a Filet-O-Fish at three a.m. Despite its local ubiquity, I am never certain that I'll get to eat seafood again anytime soon. I think this is how bears must feel in the lead-up to winter.

Fish and seafood have never been everyday food. It was special when Dad barbecued salmon. It was special going to Mo's on the Oregon coast and eating a steamer bucket of clams with a bowl of butter while sweating profusely on a hot, salty summer afternoon. Fish and chips wrapped in newspaper was special, and I'd always try to serve myself first, lest there not be a sufficient excess of tartar sauce for me. It was special picking my own fresh lobster from the tank at the Chinese supermarket on Christmas day during those few years in my early adulthood when it was only my parents and me for dinner. When I went to London with

Auntie Lynn and Uncle George in 2004, I ordered fish and chips every night. They were annoyed at me for never trying anything different, but I didn't know when I'd get back to the UK, so I ate as much battered fish as I could, as if I couldn't get fish and chips everywhere we went.

When I go to a restaurant, I almost always order seafood. And I worry that I'll regret it if I don't.

I get to eat quite a lot of seafood these days— one of the benefits to having Nick around is that he tries to spend as many afternoons as he can throughout the summer and fall drinking beer in boats, so we usually have a freezer full of rainbow trout. Since friends of ours gave us a smoker, we've been smoking four or five fish at a time and eating them whole instead of proper meals. Salmon also runs from the Pacific Ocean up the Fraser River in British Columbia most summers, so we often get a few large sockeye, coho, or pinks. The west coast is a glorious place to live if you love clams and oysters and mussels—they're all here, and they're abundant. You don't have to dig deep to pluck littleneck clams from the sand at low tide; Hunter will spend hours "rescuing" them, digging them up with his fingers and gingerly carrying them one at a time in two hands out to tide pools where I suppose he thinks they can swim away to freedom.

Seafood has been one of my great joys, but like so many of my loves, it's gotten complicated. International demand for fish has never been higher, which has had devastating consequences for the environment, for the fishing industry, and for the communities who rely on fishing as their primary source of income. It is as important to protect the oceans and the species that live within them as it is to protect quality of life for the men, women, and children who work in dangerous conditions catching and processing seafood for commercial sale. Unchecked demand for fish and seafood products leads to corruption in the fishing industry, particularly in countries that are already straining to meet the needs of their populations, especially those in poverty.

If that sounds dire, take heart—it's not all bad, and there are steps you can take to make sure you're eating fish you can feel good about. I spend most of my time in a breathless panic about how everything's terrible and we're all going to die, but even I'm reassured by some of the measures folks smarter than me are taking to protect the world around us. Choosing sustainable seafood doesn't mean giving up the stuff you love altogether. Farmed shellfish is gentler on the environment than wild-caught shellfish. Local crustaceans are often okay, and so are some wild-caught ocean and lake fish. Some farmed fish—tilapia, Atlantic salmon—are not bad, and clever people in some places have even figured out how to farm shrimp in tanks on land.

Whenever possible, however, choose wild, line-caught fish from local fisheries, or fish farmed in an environmentally friendly manner. This is an easy solution when you live on a coast, but what if you don't? In that case, choose sustainably sourced fish, either fresh, frozen, or canned—in North America, look for the Ocean Wise logo or the Seafood Watch seal; in the UK, look for certification from the Marine Stewardship Council or Marine Conservation; in Australia, choose seafood certified by the Australian Conservation Foundation. (For further information on these resources, see pp. 245–247.)

And remember that thing I told you about buffets? No potatoes, no pasta, no bread. Now, you go get your money's worth.

4
SERVINGS

FISH SAUCE SALMON

½ cup (125 mL) fish sauce

¼ cup (60 mL) honey

2 tsp Sriracha sauce

2 garlic cloves, smashed

2 1-lb (500 g) salmon or trout fillets, about ¾ in (2 cm) thick

1 tsp toasted sesame seeds

2 scallions, finely chopped

Every year, Nick catches too many small fish whose fillets are thin and cook quickly, often lake trout or pink salmon, fish that are certainly not above the help of rich sauces and bold flavors. This dish was inspired by the fish sauce wings at Pok Pok in Portland and has since become our go-to preparation for cheap and otherwise mild-tasting fish. It also works well with cod or tilapia. Serve with Savory Fruit Salad (p. 196) or a bit of steamed rice and lightly dressed greens.

Preheat oven to 375°F (190°C). In a small saucepan, whisk together fish sauce, honey, and Sriracha. Add garlic cloves.

Arrange fillets on a baking sheet lined with parchment paper or greased aluminum foil. Dip a brush into fish sauce mixture and brush some over fillets.

Bake for 8 to 10 minutes, until just cooked through. Fish should flake when separated with tines of a fork.

Meanwhile, heat remainder of fish sauce mixture on medium-high heat, whisking frequently until reduced by half to two-thirds, about 5 to 7 minutes. Mixture should resemble a thin caramel sauce. Watch it carefully, as this can burn if left unsupervised. (You may find the task of eliminating the burned fish sauce smell from your home … daunting.)

Brush sauce over cooked fillets until no sauce remains, letting them rest for a minute between brushings so sauce can firm up a bit and get sticky. Sprinkle with sesame seeds and scallions.

SALMON BALL CASSEROLE

My mom made this dish with Campbell's Cream of Mushroom soup, and it was delicious and I loved it. Those condensed cream-soup-based dinners of our youth were really wonderful, weren't they? This is very similar, with that same richness, but with less sodium and a fresher taste. It's a nice make-ahead meal, because you can form the fish balls a day ahead and save yourself some time. Serve with rice sprinkled with fresh parsley.

Preheat oven to 350°F (180°C).

In a large bowl, combine salmon, rice, carrots, celery, onions, parsley, lemon zest and juice, eggs, olive oil, salt, and pepper. Mash together with your hands until thoroughly combined. Form into 16 balls of equal size, about 1½ in (4 cm), and set aside.

In a large pan on medium-high heat, add oil and onions and sauté until onions are translucent, 3 to 5 minutes. Add garlic, mushrooms, savory, Worcestershire sauce, pepper, and cayenne, and cook until mushrooms have sweat and no liquid remains at bottom of pan, about 5 minutes. Stir in flour, then add milk and sour cream. Cook until liquid comes to a gentle boil. Taste and adjust seasonings as needed.

Ladle a small amount of cream sauce into a 1.5–2 qt/L casserole dish. Place a layer of salmon balls on sauce, then ladle half of sauce over them. Place remainder of salmon balls on top, then finish with remainder of sauce.

If you're using a shallow casserole dish, place a cookie sheet beneath it before putting in oven, as sauce will bubble up around sides. Cover and bake for 1 hour. Garnish with parsley.

1 lb (500 g) cooked salmon, chilled, bones removed, or 2 8-oz (250-g) cans of salmon

½ cup (125 mL) uncooked long-grain white rice

1 carrot, finely grated

1 celery stalk, diced

½ onion, diced (use other half in sauce)

¼ cup (60 mL) chopped fresh parsley

1 lemon, zest and juice

2 eggs

1 tbsp olive oil

½ tsp salt

½ tsp ground black pepper

MUSHROOM CREAM SAUCE

2 tbsp olive oil

½ onion, diced

3 garlic cloves, minced

1 lb (500 g) mushrooms, chopped

1 tsp dried savory

1 tsp Worcestershire sauce

½ tsp ground black pepper

⅛ tsp cayenne pepper

2 tbsp all-purpose flour

1½ cups (375 mL) milk

1 cup (250 mL) sour cream

salt, to taste

chopped fresh parsley, for garnish

SERVINGS AS LUNCH **4** **6** AS A SIDE

SARDINE PANZANELLA

½ loaf whole wheat day-old French bread, chopped into 1-in (2.5-cm) cubes, about 6 cups (1.5 L)

½ English cucumber, quartered lengthwise and chopped into 1-in (2.5-cm) pieces, about 2 cups (500 mL)

4 tomatoes, diced to 1 in (2.5 cm), about 4 cups (1 L)

5.5-oz (160-g) tins water-packed sardines, drained and torn into chunks, bones removed (if preferred)

1 cup (250 mL) whole basil leaves

1 shallot or small red onion, thinly sliced

1 tbsp capers, roughly chopped

¼ cup (60 mL) red wine vinegar

⅓ cup (80 mL) olive oil

1 tbsp fish sauce

2 garlic cloves, minced

½ tsp coarse salt

½ tsp ground black pepper

½ tsp dried oregano

½ tsp chili flakes

This is the kind of thing that's nice to pack into containers and take to the beach on a sunny afternoon in late August when it doesn't matter how bad your breath is afterward. It's bright-flavored, fresh, and filling. Make a meal of it by pairing it with Roasted Tomato & Garlic Soup (p. 195) and a glass or two of Vinho Verde.

Preheat broiler.

Place bread cubes on a baking sheet. Toast for 2 to 3 minutes, checking frequently to make sure they haven't burned.

In a large bowl, combine cucumbers, tomatoes, sardines, basil leaves, shallots, and capers. Add bread cubes, and toss gently, using your hands.

In a separate bowl, whisk together red wine vinegar, olive oil, fish sauce, garlic, salt, pepper, oregano, and chili flakes. Taste, and adjust seasonings as needed. Pour half of dressing over salad mixture, toss with your hands, then add remainder of dressing.

Let panzanella rest for at least 15 minutes. Toss again before serving.

Roasted Tomato & Garlic Soup
(page 195)

6
APPETIZER-SIZED

SARDINOÏADE

½ cup (125 mL) whole almonds (skins on), toasted

2 garlic cloves

5.5-oz (160-g) tin smoked sardines packed in oil

2 tbsp chopped fresh parsley

1 tsp lemon zest

1 tbsp lemon juice

1 tsp grainy Dijon mustard

½ tsp salt

1 tsp pepper

¼ cup (60 mL) olive oil + extra, for drizzling

Although we're sometimes very tired and messy, we entertain a lot. Often inadvertently, as people tend to just stop by. A few chopped veggies, some toasted bread, and a bit of dip can be nice to serve unexpected guests. This sardine-based dip uses simple ingredients and comes together in the time it takes to receive the call that someone's coming over. It will resemble pâté and will work as either a spread or dip. Best served with pickles, slices of hard-boiled eggs, and a baguette.

You can do this two ways.

The faster way is to grind almonds and garlic in a food processor, then add remainder of ingredients (including oil from sardines) and pulse until mixture achieves texture you prefer. I like making it this way for parties.

The other way, which is also easy but has more steps, is to chop almonds as finely as possible and mince garlic. In a bowl, combine almonds and garlic, then add tin of sardines, oil included, and mash until it's a texture you like. Stir in remainder of ingredients until well combined. This works better as a spread. It's less attractive than the above, but just as tasty.

Scoop either variation into a ramekin, and drizzle top with olive oil.

If you have any left over the next day, thin it out with a bit more olive oil and toss with pasta, a few capers, and hardboiled eggs. Top with fresh herbs and a handful of grated hard cheese.

SMOKED FISH CAKES

When I was a kid we'd eat fish cakes at least once a week, probably because they were fast, and because Mom was at work and Dad knew I'd eat them without complaints. Ours were very simple, a mix of canned salmon and mashed potatoes fried in butter until golden brown, with edges that were lacy and crisp. This version uses even cheaper canned herring or leftover smoked fish.

In a bowl, combine potatoes, scallions, and garlic.

In a separate bowl, whisk together eggs, mustard, sambal, and dash each of salt and pepper.

Crumble fish into bowl with potatoes, stir to quickly combine, then pour egg mixture over and mix thoroughly.

Form into 6 cakes, about 3 in (8 cm) in diameter and 1 in (2.5 cm) thick.

In a pan on medium-high, heat oil until it shimmers and moves easily about the pan. Fry fish cakes in small batches (do not crowd the pan); they should sizzle when they hit the pan. Cook for about 2 minutes per side, until they form a nice crust.

Serve with ketchup, more hot sauce, or fancy mustard.

4 cups (1 L) mashed potatoes*
  (2 large or 3 medium Russets)

2 scallions, finely chopped

1 garlic clove, minced

2 eggs, beaten

2 tsp grainy Dijon mustard

1 tsp sambal oelek or other hot sauce

salt and pepper, to taste

6.5–6.7-oz (180–190-g) tin smoked
  herring or mackerel (drained), or
  about 1 cup (250 mL) chunked
  smoked fish

2 tbsp canola oil, for frying + more as
  needed

* You can use leftover mashed
  potatoes to make this even easier.
  Or, if you're making them fresh, let
  them cool until you can handle them
  comfortably with your bare hands.

6-8 SERVINGS

TUNA & DILL PICKLE CASSEROLE

7-oz (190-g) broad egg noodles

3 tbsp butter

1 lb (500 g) leeks, white and light
    green parts only, thinly sliced

2 garlic cloves, minced

¼ cup (60 mL) all-purpose flour

1 cup (250 mL) chopped dill pickles

¼ cup (60 mL) pickle brine

2½ cups (625 mL) milk

2 6-oz (170-g) cans tuna in water,
    drained

1 tsp coarse salt

1 tsp ground black pepper

19-oz (540-mL) can cannellini beans,
    drained and rinsed

3 tbsp chopped fresh dill, divided

2 oz (60 g) plain potato chips

I love tuna casserole. Love it. I also love pickles and potato chips. To reduce the indulgent quality of this homey casserole, I've cut the amount of pasta in half and added a can of white beans; this makes it a little bit more filling and lowers the glycemic load. What you end up with is a curiously nostalgic-feeling dish that hits every feel-good note in your tuna casserole-loving heart … while not clogging the arteries (too much). Serve with a simple salad and a big glass of milk.

Preheat oven to 400°F (200°C). Grease a 9x13-in (3.5-L) casserole dish.

Bring a pot of salted water to a boil on high heat. Add noodles and cook until they're just shy of al dente—about 4 minutes, but refer to package instructions to be sure.

Meanwhile, in a large pan on medium-high heat, melt butter. Add leeks and cook until wilted, about 2 minutes. Add garlic, cook 1 more minute, then stir in flour and coat the leeks and garlic thoroughly.

Add pickles and pickle brine, and stir until liquid is mostly absorbed. Add milk, stirring and scraping bottom of the pan to lift any browned bits. Add tuna, salt, and pepper, and cook until thickened, about 3 minutes.

Drain pasta, then add pasta and beans to mixture. Stir in 2 tbsp dill. Taste and adjust seasonings as needed.

Pour mixture into prepared casserole dish. Gently crush potato chips inside bag, then sprinkle crushed chips over casserole.

Bake for 20 minutes, rotating halfway through, until sauce is bubbly and topping is golden brown.

Sprinkle with remaining dill.

TUNA CHOWDER

This has a slightly Thai flavor, thanks to the coconut milk and lemongrass. It's a nice deviation from a traditional fish chowder, and it's a bit healthier—there's no flour or white potatoes, so it's a good option for when you need to keep your blood sugar in check. We eat this as a main course, but it can also be served for lunch, with a salad or sandwich. (*Note:* This recipe works just as well with salmon.)

In a large, heavy-bottomed pot on medium-high, heat oil. Add onions, ginger, garlic, and lemongrass and sauté quickly, until golden. Add sweet potatoes and 1 cup (250 mL) corn. Add stock. Scrape bottom of pot with a wooden spoon to scrape off any browned bits. Stir in tuna. Add fish sauce, lime zest and juice, and Sriracha.

Bring to a gentle boil, then reduce heat to medium. Simmer for 10 to 15 minutes, until sweet potatoes are fork-tender.

Add bell peppers, coconut milk, and remainder of corn. Simmer for 5 minutes. Season to taste. Stir in most of the basil. Sprinkle remainder of basil over chowder for garnish.

4 SERVINGS

2 tbsp canola oil

½ onion, finely chopped

2 tbsp minced fresh ginger

4 garlic cloves, minced

1 lemongrass stalk, trimmed and minced

1 lb (500 g) sweet potatoes, diced

3 cups fresh or frozen corn, divided

4 cups chicken stock

2 6-oz (170-g) cans tuna in water, drained

1 tbsp fish sauce

1 lime, zest and juice

1 tbsp Sriracha sauce, or to taste

1 large red bell pepper, diced

14-oz (398-mL) can coconut milk

3 tbsp chopped fresh basil

salt and pepper, to taste

TUNA SALAD with CELERY & BLACK-EYED PEAS

4 SERVINGS

This is my cheap work lunch. I make a big bowl early in the week, spoon it into lunch-sized containers, and take it with me to the office. It's bright and flavorful and has the right balance of fiber and protein and good fat to keep you from ravenously rattling the vending machines for free chips around three p.m. The ingredients are sturdy and don't wilt, so this salad can live in the refrigerator for a few days and keep you going for most of the week.

In a large bowl, combine diced celery, scallions, black-eyed peas, and tuna.

In a smaller bowl, whisk together lemon juice, olive oil, capers, mustard, celery salt, black pepper, coarse salt, and Worcestershire sauce.

Pour dressing over tuna mixture, and toss to coat. Serve immediately, or refrigerate for up to 3 days. Stir or shake it up before serving to redistribute dressing.

4 celery stalks, diced (leaves included)

4 scallions, white and light green parts only, chopped

19-oz (540-mL) can black-eyed peas, drained and rinsed

6-oz (170-g) can tuna, packed in water, drained

¼ cup (60 mL) lemon juice

¼ cup (60 mL) extra-virgin olive oil

1 tbsp capers, roughly chopped

1 tsp grainy Dijon mustard

1 tsp celery salt

½ tsp ground black pepper

½ tsp coarse salt

½ tsp Worcestershire sauce

2-4 SERVINGS

TUNA TARTARE

¼ lb (125 g) frozen albacore tuna

1 avocado, diced

2 tbsp chopped scallions, light and
    dark green parts only

1 tbsp minced radishes

1 lime, zest and juice

1½ tsp rice vinegar

1 tsp sesame oil

1 tsp ketjap manis

1 egg yolk

Sriracha sauce, for garnish

1 chopped scallion, for garnish

This is an appetizer for four, or a really lovely dinner for two. It's very mild, and it feels fancy when it's really just a hunk of frozen tuna, dressed up all saucy. Raw tuna and egg yolks aren't for everyone. If they are for you, then serve simply—with some lightly dressed greens, and a bit of buttered toast, quartered.

Line 2 small ramekins (I use Pyrex custard cups) with plastic wrap.

Tuna should be frozen but workable. Mince it. Mince the hell out of it. In a bowl, combine tuna with avocado, scallions, and radishes.

In a small bowl, mix remaining ingredients except Sriracha and scallions. Pour over fish mixture, toss to coat, and press into ramekins.

Turn mixture out onto serving plates, pulling ramekins away and peeling off plastic. Serve with Sriracha and additional chopped scallions.

PORK

In the spring of 2011, my friend Grace and I went to France to celebrate her thirty-fifth birthday—and to eat as many things as we could. I put a big damper on the trip by accidentally getting pregnant, but made up for all the wine I couldn't enjoy by eating twice as much.

I met Grace at a job interview in 2007; she hired me as an intern at the publishing company where she was an editor. By the end of our summer working together, we were friends on our way to a well-established karaoke routine and picnic habit. We're eaters. And pretty good pop singers, if you've had a few drinks. We decided to go to France together one evening after I don't know how many whiskey sours and bottles of rosé; since then, that is how I've made all my important decisions and large purchases.

Our second dinner in France was a garden party at Jim Haynes' atelier, a Sunday supper club that Allen Ginsberg once attended; there were British expats and local Frenchmen and boxed wine and crusty bread and a man named Claude. We ate a hearty stew and mingled with all kinds of people from everywhere. I think I was the youngest person there, and felt terribly awkward as I was the only one without wine, but Claude made conversation, and that's when I realized I don't actually speak French—that C+ on my French 12 final must have really boosted my confidence in my language skills. Soon Grace joined us, English was spoken, and at the end of the night Claude walked us to the Metro, then rode with us, then walked us to our rental apartment in the Marais. He lived nearby, he explained. There's no stranger danger in Paris.

Grace is meticulous—she is a brilliant editor and a careful trip planner (our personalities clash occasionally in that regard, as I am chaotic and irrational and frequently a stumbling block), and she plotted our course so that we'd hit as many affordable French restaurants as possible from a list of places mentioned and adored by the likes of David Lebovitz, Dorie Greenspan, and Anthony Bourdain. And while we wanted to do and see different things during our travels, we always came together over a meal.

The French do comestibles well. That's common knowledge, but I didn't anticipate how many delicious things they do with swine. We ate paper-thin sheets of pork jowl curled up on crostini, and ribbon-thin strips of marbled, salty cured ham, and regular ham piled atop buckwheat crepes, and chops of acorn-fed pork from the south of France, from pigs our server described in heavily accented English as "cute, with bushy black hairs over their eyes." We ate head cheese and croque-mon-sieurs, and terrines, rillettes, and pâtés. It was salty, porky heaven. The greatest dish of all was at Bistroy…Les Papilles, a little bistro in the Latin Quarter whose walls were lined with shelves of organic and biodynamic French wines in a range of prices. There was no menu because you simply ate what was being served that day. (Side note: This is the best way to eat—no menus, just delicious surprises from the kitchen.)

Claude joined us there for dinner. We met at his apartment, which really was a short walk from where we were staying. When you are in Paris, the kind of thing you might interpret as a red flag at home only registers as vaguely concerning, but a worthwhile risk. When you are in Paris, sometimes the city compels you to cram your ham-bloated body into an elevator the size of a phone booth with a simi-larly ham-bloated friend to meet an eighty-year-old man in his apartment, where you don't have any

way of knowing if he'll greet you at the door with a butcher's knife. We were lucky as Claude was kind. Also because Claude was from a family of vintners in Sauternes, and he had a fifty-year-old bottle of his family's wine on hand, just waiting for a special occasion.

There are few occasions more special than sitting in the dusty library of an octogenarian scientist's beautiful, aged apartment, sipping well-aged Sauternes while looking out over the rooftops of the Marais as the sun fades on the horizon. Pregnant or not, this was not likely to ever happen again, so I had a small glass; it was sweet and bright and concentrated. You would think that after half a century it'd be no good, but there was nothing off about it—it had just reduced somewhat in the bottle over time, so when you swished the liquid around, it drizzled back down to the bottom of the glass like syrup. It tasted like peaches in mid-August at the exact moment when they are at their ripest, and dried apricots plumped with a little bit of apple brandy.

The bistro was busy, but Grace had made reservations (*en français*!), and although we had added a third member to our party en route, we were seated fairly quickly. So good was the main that I have no recollection what the first course was. The entrée came to our table sizzling, fat sparkling, in a metal serving dish piled with gently roasted garlic and fresh spring vegetables, peas and carrots and radishes and fresh thyme. The meat was pork belly, braised and then sliced into thick strips and cooked once more until crisp. It cut like room-temperature

butter, oozing its juices into the beans on the plate. I sopped the mess up with crusty bread while sipping another small glass of cold wine. I briefly considered proposing to Claude then and there in an attempt to remain in the country.

I can't think of much I wouldn't do for a life of international wine and swine.

Pork is the greatest meat, mainly because of bacon, but also because it is both sweetly delicious and endlessly versatile. It tends to be a bit cheaper than other meats—though other people have noticed this as well and things aren't as affordable as they used to be. If you're looking for something lean that's not boneless, skinless chicken breast, try pork tenderloin. Need to feed a dinner party of eight people on a tight budget? Order bone-in pork shoulder from your butcher—eight to ten pounds (3.5 to 4.5 kg) will leave you with enough left over for subsequent meals at a price significantly lower than you'd expect. Like bacon? Then you'll like pork belly too.

When purchasing budget-friendly meat, think French and look to inexpensive cuts (and ground)— you'll save a lot of money over more conventional or popular cuts, like ribs, loins, and some chops. The secret to inexpensive cuts of meat is time—they are very flavorful, but you've got to melt the fat and connective tissue and coax out texture and tenderness slowly, under low heat. Good cuts for this include pork butt, shoulder, and belly, but you're going to need a few hours. For this reason, I advise either investing in a Crock-Pot (see p. 14), or saving your low-and-slow meat adventures for the weekends.

CANDIED PORK BELLY

I almost feel bad telling you about this, because it's not like you can just have a single piece. It's meat candy, pure and simple, the kind of thing you should eat with waffles or maybe fruit salad. The only person I make this for is my friend Aimee—her enthusiasm for it is so compelling, I hardly notice that it's just the two of us who have polished off most of a pan all on our own. *Note:* This one's going to require a bit of planning; let it marinate for up to 24 hours, plus an additional 3 to 8 hours to cook, chill, and finish.

1 cup (250 mL) brown sugar, divided

½ cup (125 mL) soy sauce

2 lb (900 g) pork belly, skin removed

1 cup (250 mL) apple cider or unsweetened apple juice

½ tsp smoked paprika

½ tsp ground cinnamon

½ tsp salt

¼ tsp cayenne pepper

Whisk together 4 cups (1 L) water with ½ cup (125 mL) brown sugar and soy sauce until sugar has dissolved. Place pork in a large, sturdy zip-lock bag or container with a lid, and pour brine over. Seal and let marinate in refrigerator for 24 hours.

Remove pork belly from brine and place fat side up in a 9x13-in (3.5-L) baking dish. Preheat oven to 300°F (150°C). Pour apple cider or juice over pork belly, cover with aluminum foil, and bake for 2½ hours.

Remove from oven, let cool completely, and refrigerate—still in pan— for at least 3 hours, preferably overnight.

Cut chilled pork belly in half widthwise (with grain of meat) and then into lengthwise slices (across grain) about ¼-in (6-mm) thick.

Preheat broiler.

Line a rimmed baking sheet with parchment, and lay slices of pork belly evenly across sheet. Mix remainder of brown sugar with smoked paprika, cinnamon, salt, and cayenne pepper. Sprinkle half of spice mixture over pork belly slices.

Place baking sheet on highest rack of oven. This part is going to require constant vigilance—it will take just a second to burn, so you need to pay attention. Watch surface of pork belly; watch for sugar to melt and bubble. Immediately remove sheet from oven, flip slices, and sprinkle remainder of sugar mixture over them. Return sheet to under broiler and wait for sugar to sizzle. Immediately remove from oven. Serve hot.

6 SERVINGS

FRENCH BISTRO PORK & BEANS

DAY 1

3 lb (1.5 kg) skinless pork belly

1 tbsp coarse salt

1 tsp whole black peppercorns

1 tsp coriander seeds

2 bay leaves

2 thyme sprigs

1 lemon, sliced

1 head garlic, halved crosswise

1 onion, trimmed and quartered

This is my take on a beautiful Paris bistro meal with our eighty-something gentleman-friend, Claude. A two-day effort, be sure to have ingredients ready the day before you want to eat it. It's perfect for a lazy weekend in late September, when the weather has begun to cool and the farm markets are abundant with the best fresh produce of the year. This is worth your time, ideal for entertaining, and it's pretty. Serve with crusty bread and cold pink wine.

Preheat oven to 275°F (140°C). Place pork belly in a 9x13-in (3.5-L) pan. Sprinkle both sides of the pork with salt, rubbing to ensure it sticks. Add peppercorns, coriander seeds, bay leaves, thyme, lemon slices, garlic, and onion quarters to the pan, surrounding pork belly. Fill pan with water so it is level with top of pork. Bake, uncovered, for 2½ hours.

Remove pork from the oven, and allow to cool. Wrap pork in plastic wrap and refrigerate for at least 4 hours, until firm; discard pan juices and solids.

Preheat oven to 400°F (200°C).

CONTINUED ON PAGE 140

CONTINUED FROM PAGE 138

DAY 2

3 tbsp olive oil, divided

1 onion, diced

1 head garlic, cloves separated and peeled

2 carrots, peeled and sliced on the diagonal

2 stalks celery, trimmed and sliced on the diagonal

4 plum or Roma tomatoes, quartered lengthwise

½ lb (250 g) fresh snap peas, trimmed

1 tsp salt, divided

5 sprigs + 1 tsp chopped fresh thyme

1 tsp smoked paprika

1 tsp ground mustard

½ tsp chili flakes

½ tsp ground black pepper

2 19-oz (540-mL) cans white beans, such as cannellini or navy, drained and rinsed

½ cup (125 mL) dry white wine

28-oz (796-mL) can whole tomatoes, including juices

1 lemon, zest and juice

Slice pork belly into six pieces lengthwise, so that pieces resemble very thick slices of bacon. In a large pan on medium-high heat, sear pork belly slices until crisp and golden brown on each side. Remove pork from pan, and set aside.

Add 1 tbsp oil to pan, then add onions and garlic. Sauté until onions have softened and garlic has begun to brown, about 3 minutes.

Meanwhile, in a bowl, toss carrots, celery, fresh tomatoes, and peas with remainder of olive oil, ½ tsp salt, and 1 tsp chopped thyme. Set aside.

Add paprika, mustard, chili flakes, pepper and remainder of salt to pan. Stir in beans. Add wine, scraping browned bits off bottom of pan. Squish canned tomatoes between your fingers into pan, then add can juices. Stir in lemon zest and juice. Bring to a boil.

Nestle pork belly slices in tomato and bean mixture. Carefully spoon vegetable mixture into pan over pork slices. Add sprigs of thyme, strewing over veggies.

Bake for 20 to 25 minutes, until veggies have cooked and charred slightly and pan sauces have reduced somewhat. Let rest for 5 minutes before serving.

NICK'S SWEET SOY PORK TENDERLOIN

3-4 SERVINGS

We started to buy pork tenderloin once I got my first real grown-up, out-of-school job because it was Costco's best value, pork-wise. And then we discovered how delicious it is. This is Nick's favorite way to eat pork tenderloin. The salty, savory, slightly spicy marinade works brilliantly with the pork, and a benefit of the soy sauce is that it further tenderizes this already tender cut of meat. Great in summer—you can make it ahead, then chill it in the refrigerator, slice it cold, and put it into sandwiches.

1 lb (500 g) pork tenderloin

3 tbsp ketjap manis

3 tbsp Sriracha sauce

1 tbsp sesame oil

4 garlic cloves, minced

1 tsp minced fresh ginger

½ tsp coarse salt

1 lime, zest and juice

2 tbsp canola oil

Trim any silver skin—the tight, sort of shiny membrane along the side of tenderloin—then set pork aside.

In a small bowl, whisk together remainder of ingredients except canola oil. Reserve 2 tbsp marinade in a separate bowl.

Place pork in a heavy-duty zip-lock plastic bag, then pour in marinade. Seal bag, squeezing air out. Squish pork around in bag to coat in marinade. Marinate at room temperature for at least 30 minutes, or up to 2 hours.

Preheat oven to 425°F (220°C).

In an oven-proof frying pan on medium-high, heat canola oil. Sear pork for 2 minutes per side.

Bake for 12 to 15 minutes, until pork reaches an internal temperature of about 145°F (63°C). Pull it out of the pan and let rest for 3 to 5 minutes. Paint with remaining marinade before slicing into thin rounds.

6
SERVINGS

PORK & BEAN COTTAGE PIE

1 onion, halved

3 garlic cloves

1 tbsp chili powder

1 tbsp apple cider vinegar

1 tsp ground cumin

½ tsp ground coriander

½ tsp dried oregano

¼ tsp ground cinnamon

¼ tsp cayenne pepper

3 tsp coarse salt, divided

1 lb (500 g) ground pork

1 tbsp olive oil

2 bell peppers, diced

19-oz (540-mL) can black beans,
   drained and rinsed

14-oz (398-mL) can diced tomatoes

6-oz (156-mL) can tomato paste

½ cup (125 mL) chopped fresh cilantro

4 lb (1.8 kg) yams or sweet potatoes,
   peeled and cubed

4 tbsp cold butter

When Nick was diagnosed with type 1 diabetes, the dietitian at the endocrinology clinic gave us a package of handouts, one of which was a handy reference sheet about common foods and their place on the glycemic index. Sweet potatoes and legumes? Both on the low end. The sweet potatoes lend a bit of an indulgent flair to this dish, and the beans will fill you right up. This is spicy and loaded with complex carbohydrates—great for weeknight dinners and subsequent workday lunches. Serve with lightly dressed greens.

Preheat oven to 400°F (200°C).

Chop half of onion and place in a food processor or blender with garlic, chili powder, vinegar, cumin, coriander, oregano, cinnamon, cayenne pepper, and 2 tsp salt. Blend until smooth.

Place pork in a bowl and pour blended pepper mixture over. Mix with your hands until well-combined. Let marinate for 15 to 30 minutes.

Mince other half of onion. In a large pan on medium-high, heat olive oil. Add onions and peppers, and sauté until they've begun to sweat, about 3 minutes. Add pork, breaking it apart with a wooden spoon, and then add black beans, tomatoes, and tomato paste. Simmer until liquid has reduced, about 10 minutes. Stir mixture regularly while it simmers. Add cilantro, and remove from heat.

Meanwhile, in a large pot on high heat, bring yams or sweet potatoes in salted water to a boil. Reduce heat to medium and simmer until tender, about 20 minutes. Drain and mash with butter and remaining salt.

Pour pork mixture into a 9 x 13-in (3.5-L) baking dish. Pour yam or sweet potato purée over and spread to cover.

Bake for 35 to 40 minutes, or until golden on top and bubbling around the sides. Let rest 5 to 10 minutes before serving, so that filling can set.

SAUSAGE & "GRITS"

Grits are an American thing and harder to come by in Canada than I'd like. You can use coarse polenta, but that too may be hard to find. This recipe uses fine-ground cornmeal. On the one hand, you don't get the chewier, more interesting texture of coarse grits; on the other hand, it takes only 10 minutes to make. Although the recipe calls for just ½ cup (125 mL) cheese, Nick wanted you to know you can add as much as you like. Of course, he doesn't manage the grocery budget around here.

In a large frying pan on medium-high heat, brown crumbled sausages in olive oil.

Add onions, celery, bell and jalapeño peppers, garlic, and lemon zest. Sauté until veggies begin to sweat, then add tomatoes, salt, paprika, chili powder, cumin, and oregano.

Meanwhile, bring chicken stock and 2 cups (250 mL) water to a boil. Reduce heat to medium, then slowly whisk in cornmeal. Cook until thick, about 5 minutes, stirring regularly to prevent grits from sticking to bottom of pot.

As grits thicken, add beer and lemon juice to sausage mixture. Simmer until liquid has reduced slightly and thickened. Add parsley.

Stir in yogurt, corn kernels, butter, and cheese to grits until smooth. Serve sausage mixture over "grits."

1 lb (500 g) spicy pork sausage, casings removed

1 tbsp olive oil

1 onion, chopped

2 celery stalks, quartered lengthwise and chopped

1 bell pepper, chopped

1 jalapeño pepper

3 garlic cloves, minced

1 lemon, zest and juice

2 cups (500 mL) diced tomatoes (about 4 Roma or plum tomatoes)

1 tsp salt

1 tsp smoked paprika

1 tsp chili powder

½ tsp cumin

½ tsp dried oregano

½ cup beer, such as lager or pilsner

handful fresh parsley, chopped

GRITS

2 cups (500 mL) chicken stock

1 cup (250 mL) cornmeal

¼ cup (60 mL) yogurt

1 cup (250 mL) fresh or frozen corn kernels

1 tbsp butter

½ cup (125 mL) grated aged cheddar cheese

MAKES ABOUT 20

SLOW-COOKER CABBAGE ROLLS

1 head green cabbage

1 large onion

2 carrots

2 celery stalks

4 garlic cloves

½ packed cup (125 mL) fresh parsley

2 lb (900 g) ground pork

1 cup (250 mL) uncooked long-grain white rice

2 eggs

2 tbsp olive oil

1 tbsp Worcestershire sauce

1 tbsp grainy Dijon mustard

2½ tsp kosher salt

2 tsp smoked paprika

1 tsp dried savory

1 tsp ground black pepper

28-oz (796-mL) can crushed tomatoes

2 cups (500 mL) chicken stock

salt and pepper, to taste

I hardly ever made cabbage rolls until I discovered this one weird old trick to simplify the process and make it less likely that I'd burn my clumsy hands. The secret? Freeze the cabbage leaves. Freezing breaks down the cellular structure of the leaves so that once they've defrosted they become malleable and much easier to work with. Save time! Don't burn yourself! Everybody wins. Thanks for the tip, Mrs Booy. Make a full batch of these and freeze half. Serve with pickles and well-buttered crusty bread.

The night before, put entire cabbage in freezer. The next morning, remove it and put in a colander in the sink to defrost. Your mileage here may vary—my apartment tends to be on the warm side, so the cabbage defrosts in 8 hours at room temperature, meaning I can make the cabbage rolls the same day I take the cabbage out of the freezer. If you are unsure, start to defrost cabbage in refrigerator a day or two before making recipe.

Finely chop onions, carrots, celery, garlic, and parsley. Divide mixture evenly between two bowls. Set aside.

Add pork, rice, eggs, oil, Worcestershire sauce, mustard, salt, paprika, savory, and pepper to one bowl of vegetables and mix to combine thoroughly. (You can do this a day ahead as well; just cover and refrigerate until ready to use.)

In other bowl, add crushed tomatoes and chicken stock. Season with additional salt and pepper to taste. (Again, feel free to make this ahead of time and set it aside.)

When you're ready to roll, pour about 1 cup (250 mL) sauce into a slow cooker. Cut core from cabbage and discard. Peel off leaves, and cut out thick part of center rib. Place 3 tbsp meat mixture on top part of leaf, then roll up, folding in sides. Place each roll into slow cooker, ladling tomato sauce over each layer.

Pour remainder of sauce over, cover with lid, then either refrigerate until you're ready to make these, or cook them right away. Set slow cooker to low, and cook for 10 hours.

SLOW-COOKER GOCHUJANG PULLED PORK

6-8 SERVINGS

I love pulled pork, but not most barbecue-esque slow-cooker versions, which can be too cloyingly sweet. I do love the texture the slow cooker gives pork, however, and this version provides all the ease and convenience of traditional slow-cooker pulled pork, but it tastes different—better, spicier. It also freezes well. Make a full batch and freeze half, and you've got dinner for another evening. You can serve this on buns, but I like it folded into a piece of soft butter lettuce with a spoonful of rice and cold, spicy kimchi. *Note*: You'll need to start this recipe the day before you plan to serve it.

The night before you want to eat this, make a paste of the gochujang, minced garlic, sugar, and salt. Then rub it all over your butt. The pork. Rub it all over your pork butt.

If you have the kind of slow cooker from which the crock is removable, place onions in slow cooker. Add soy sauce and beer, then nestle pork butt in center of crock. Cover and refrigerate overnight. If you do not have that kind of slow cooker, prepare all the pieces, then assemble in slow cooker in the morning.

Set slow cooker to low, and cook for 10 hours.

When the pork is cooked, scoop out 1 cup (250 mL) cooking liquid and strain into a small saucepan on medium-high. Add sugar, rice vinegar, gochujang, sesame oil, and garlic. Bring mixture to a boil, then reduce heat to medium and cook until mixture has reduced by half, 5 to 7 minutes. Taste and adjust seasonings as needed. Pour mixture into a large bowl, and set aside.

Using 2 forks, shred pork into bowl containing sauce. Using tongs, toss pork so that it's thoroughly coated in sauce. If mixture looks dry, add additional pan juices to moisten pork.

Sprinkle with toasted sesame seeds, and serve with accompaniments.

PORK

3 tbsp gochujang (Korean hot pepper paste)

3 garlic cloves, minced

1 tbsp granulated sugar

1 tbsp coarse salt

4 lb (1.8 kg) pork butt

2 onions, halved and sliced

½ cup (125 mL) soy sauce

½ cup (125 mL) beer, such as amber ale

SAUCE

1 cup (250 mL) cooking liquid, strained

½ cup (125 mL) granulated sugar

6 tbsp rice vinegar

3 tbsp gochujang

1 tbsp sesame oil

3 garlic cloves, minced

salt, to taste

toasted sesame seeds, for garnish

ACCOMPANIMENTS

6 cups (1.5 L) cooked white rice

1 head butter lettuce

2 cups (500 mL) kimchi

1 diced long English cucumber

¼ cup (60 mL) sesame oil

SPICY PORK & TOFU STEW

This is a good autumn dish, the kind of thing you might eat after a long afternoon of hayrides and corn mazes and picking just the right pumpkin. It's hearty and satisfying, but lighter than you might expect from a pork stew. A nice mix of textures, the butternut squash is what takes this into the realm of comfort food. Serve over rice with an off-dry white wine to dull the burn.

Place pork, soy sauce, Sriracha, and 1 tbsp starch in a sturdy plastic bag. Seal, pressing out all of the air, and squish pork around, coating in marinade. Let marinate at room temperature for 30 minutes.

In a heavy-bottomed pot such as a Dutch oven, on medium-high, heat oils. Add pork cubes, reserving marinade. Brown pork, about 3 to 4 minutes a side, then scoop out of pot and set aside.

Add onions and sauté until translucent. Stir in celery and squash. Stir in garlic and ginger, and cook for 1 to 2 minutes, until veggies have softened and garlic and ginger have begun to turn golden.

Stir in beer, scraping bottom of pot to collect any browned bits. Add stock and reserved marinade.

Mix remainder of starch with about 1 tbsp water to form a slurry. Stir into mixture in pot.

Return pork to pot, and add tofu. Reduce heat to medium-low, and cover pot partially with lid so some steam escapes. Cook for 45 minutes, occasionally lifting lid to stir pot. When pork is tender, sprinkle with scallions and sesame seeds and serve.

1–1½ lb (500–750 g) cubed pork shoulder or pork shoulder steak

½ cup (125 mL) soy sauce

¼ cup (60 mL) Sriracha sauce

2 tbsp corn or tapioca starch, divided

1 tbsp canola oil

1 tbsp sesame oil

1 onion, halved and thinly sliced

4 celery stalks, chopped into 1-in (2.5-cm) pieces

1–1½-lb (500–750 g) butternut squash, peeled, seeded, and cubed

4 garlic cloves, minced

1 tbsp minced fresh ginger

½ cup (125 mL) beer, such as pilsner or lager

2 cups (500 mL) low-sodium or homemade chicken stock

⅔ lb (350 g) block medium-firm tofu, cubed

4 scallions, chopped

2 tsp toasted sesame seeds

4 SERVINGS

1 cup (250 mL) all-purpose flour

1 cup (250 mL) milk or buttermilk, at
    room temperature

4 eggs, at room temperature

1 tsp grainy Dijon mustard

pinch, salt and pepper

2 strips bacon, chopped

2 tsp butter

1 medium onion, sliced

1 lb (500 g) pork sausages, such as
    English bangers or bratwurst

TOAD IN THE HOLE

I grew up eating this dish, usually for dinner. It's the kind of thing you have on, like, a Thursday night when the week has been too long and nobody's up for a lot of standing upright. Of course, it's also a hearty brunch. For best results, start with eggs and milk at room temperature, so take them out of the refrigerator 20 minutes or so before you start cooking. My dad would serve this with a small, simple salad and a glob of HP Sauce for dipping. Go ahead and do the same.

Preheat oven to 425°F (220°C).

In a large bowl, whisk together flour, milk, eggs, mustard, and salt and pepper until smooth. Set aside.

In a cast-iron pan on medium-high heat, fry bacon. When cooked, remove from pan and drain on plate lined with a paper towel.

Add butter to pan and let melt. Add onions and sauté until translucent with brown bits around their edges, about 3 minutes.

Add sausages, and brown them too—it doesn't matter if they are cooked through, but brown on all sides. Remove from pan and slice into bite-sized pieces.

Return bacon and sausages to pan. Pour batter over, and bake for 25 minutes, until batter has puffed and turned golden. Slice and serve immediately.

BEEF

As a kid, my experience with beef was limited to what was affordable, so we ate a lot of ground beef, a lot of pot roast, and the occasional really overcooked steak. Nick and I joke about the beef of our childhood, which was so often gray and board-like, a weathered shingle of beef. Nick recalls, fondly of course, a dish his mother made regularly called Hamburger Mush, a mix of ground beef and Campbell's Cream of Mushroom Soup that was grayer than dinner ought to be. It was the 1980s and early '90s, and everyone was busy, and everyone had kids and mortgages, and yet dinner kept happening every single day, and we were lucky to get food at all. I get it. Hamburger Mush for everyone!

Ground beef was a staple in my parents' kitchen; they'd buy it cello-wrapped and heaped in big styrofoam trays from Costco, and my dad would portion it out into 1 lb (500 g) balls and wrap them in plastic to store in the freezer. There were always wads of frozen ground beef around, and they went into everything—stuffed bell peppers, meatballs, pasta sauces, soups, and the occasional casserole. Some things were great, like the stuffed peppers, which were basically cabbage rolls in a different wrapper (Dad doesn't like cabbage); other things were just gross, like Dad burgers. I was excited when I learned that Nick had eaten Dad burgers too, as apparently the burgers of his youth were much like mine—a ball of ground beef that started out as a patty but shrank, charred on the outside and dry in the middle. The result was a burger whose ratios were all off—it was mostly bun and condiments, except where it was just a dense rock of indigestible meat. An informal poll of friends who grew up in the same era revealed that we all ate Dad burgers. A rite of passage?

Nick and I were just married and fresh out of university when our student loan repayments began to kick in and we moved into our first grown-up apartment. We were finally both working full time and could afford to live without roommates, but that's about all we could afford. I was in the middle of my "I'm an adult and I do what I want and I do not want to eat red meat" phase, which excluded cold cuts and fast food burgers, and we were broke anyway so there just wasn't much meat in those early days. There was a little produce market with a small meat counter and a lot of Asian ingredients nearby, and

for most of that first year our diet was mainly plant-based; you could buy big bags of baby bok choy at the market for about a dollar, so we'd eat stir fries and curries and heaping piles of steamed greens most nights of the week. I don't blame Nick at all for rebelling.

"Damn it, I just want a goddamn steak," he declared one night, probably on a Friday after a long week of being responsible adults with jobs. There were two big grocery stores nearby; at one, he'd be able to get a bunch of steaks on a styrofoam tray covered in plastic for probably eight dollars. The other was Whole Foods. I don't know if it's because he was feeling fancy, or if he'd just never bought meat at an actual meat counter before, but somehow he managed to spend thirty-five dollars on two steaks; he didn't realize how much they'd be until they were wrapped up and handed over the counter. When he got home he apologized: "They were, like, seventeen dollars apiece," he said. "You're cooking them, then," I told him, backing away from the kitchen.

It was more than I'd spend on a week's worth of groceries at the time, and it wouldn't even leave us with leftovers for lunches the next day. I don't know if it was because we would never buy meat like that again, or because it was just so much better than any steak I'd encountered in my life, but that extravagant piece of meat was the best steak I've ever had, simply salted, peppered, rubbed with garlic, and grilled perfectly rare. I honestly never knew beef could be like that.

I have the advantage of a partner who hunts, so for most of the year, our freezer is full of wild deer or moose; when the woods come up short, we share a large beef order with a friend and get a quarter or half of a grass-fed cow. Of course, this is a reasonably big investment—you've got to come up with around $250 all at once, and then you have to store all that meat. Check Craigslist or local classifieds for a used deep freezer—someone's always selling one cheaply, or if you're lucky, giving it away. We don't have much room to store ours, but our decor is fairly crappy and primarily second-hand, so our dinged, paint-smeared deep freezer fits right in. We like to think of our home as rustic.

If you don't have room for a deep freezer, talk to a butcher about freezer packs of grass-fed meat. Many butchers will provide freezer packs to accommodate apartment kitchens or refrigerator freezers. Buying more meat at a time can cost more, but it's cheaper in the long run.

Can someone on a budget expect to be able to enjoy grass-fed beef? Yes, but nothing cheap comes easy, of course, so what you will sacrifice in convenience (especially from steaks and other prime cuts that tend to be lean and don't require long cooking), you make up for in the depth of flavor. Cuts such as bone-in front and hind shank, oxtail, neck, chuck, cross rib, and cheeks are all reasonably priced and delicious, though you'll need to coax out the flavor and texture of these cuts with braising or stewing. If you work full time (or more), these meats may be better suited to weekend or Crock-Pot cooking.

Quick-cooking cuts such as ground meat and sausage are cheap, easy to find options; skirt steak (sometimes called bavette) and heart are

IF YOU'RE PRESSED FOR TIME, A SLOW COOKER IS YOUR VERY BEST FRIEND. ANY RECIPE THAT WOULD GENERALLY TAKE 2 TO 3 HOURS OF BRAISING OR STEWING IN THE OVEN WILL COOK FOR 10 TO 12 HOURS ON LOW IN A SLOW COOKER. FOR ME, 10 HOURS IS PERFECT, AS I CAN SEAR THE MEAT AND TURN ON THE CROCK-POT BEFORE I LEAVE FOR WORK, AND BY THE TIME EVERYONE'S HOME, DINNER IS READY. FOR RECIPES THAT AREN'T SOUPS OR STEWS, AND DEPENDING ON THE SIZE OF THE SLOW COOKER, REDUCE THE AMOUNT OF LIQUID IN THE RECIPE BY ABOUT HALF. IF THE RECIPE CALLS FOR PASTA OR RICE OR FRESH HERBS (SUCH AS ROSEMARY OR THYME), ADD THESE IN THE FINAL 40 MINUTES OF COOKING. FOR SOFTER HERBS, SUCH AS PARSLEY OR BASIL, AND FOR GREENS SUCH AS SPINACH OR CHARD, ADD IN THE FINAL 10 MINUTES IF YOU GET HOME AND FIND YOU'VE ADDED TOO MUCH LIQUID (I ERR ON THE SIDE OF ADDING MORE LIQUID TO AVOID SCORCHING INGREDIENTS), FINISH THE DISH IN A PAN ON THE STOVE TO EVAPORATE ANY EXCESS AND TO THICKEN THE SAUCE.

A SLOW COOKER WILL COST YOU ANYWHERE FROM $20 TO $100 DEPENDING ON THE SIZE AND FEATURES; I RECOMMEND SOMETHING IN THE 5 TO 6 QT/L RANGE, AND PROGRAMMABLE IF YOU CAN SWING IT—THAT'LL RUN YOU BETWEEN $45 AND $60, BUT IT SHOULD LAST FOR YEARS AND YOU'LL USE IT OFTEN.

inexpensive and will also cook quickly, but may require a trip to the butcher. Ground is my go-to weeknight meat, as it's cheap and fast, and if you forget to take it out in the morning before work, it defrosts well in the microwave. And you can do so much with it—there are so many different kinds of meatballs!

There are plenty of ethical concerns around eating meat, and the environmental impact of industrial beef production is staggering, but grass-fed, free-range meat is something I feel pretty okay about eating. On the one hand, livestock production accounts for as much as twenty percent of global greenhouse gas emissions; on the other hand, supporting small-scale farmers of grass-fed beef means voting for the environment, because though it runs counter to my hippy-dippy idealism, the only thing that's going to change the world is where we spend our money. Of course, I am in a relatively privileged position in that I am able to work out my finances to buy in bulk, when it is considerably cheaper; I recognize that this is not easy or possible for many people. Buy better, and eat less.

Okay, but is red meat even healthy to eat anymore? Again, yes. One of the great myths of modern nutrition is that red meat is linked with high cholesterol and heart disease. A Swedish study recently found that "high total red meat consumption was associated with progressively shorter survival." That the culprit wasn't the meat itself, but rather the volume being consumed and the fact that it had been processed into things like fast-food burgers. The fifteen-year study concluded that "consumption of non-processed red meat alone was not associated with shorter survival." As with all things, it's not what you consume but how much of it—and how it's made—that's the problem. I wish we could move past this strange idea that there are foods we can't and foods we must eat in order to be healthy. Eating a nutritious diet is simple, but there's no formula. It's not a matter of Kale + Chickpeas - Bread - Beef = I'M GOING TO LIVE FOREVER. So we might all be happier and better off to just eat a damn steak once in a while. (Just please don't overcook it.)

6 SERVINGS

3 tbsp olive oil, divided

4 lb (1.8 kg) bone-in beef shank

1 tbsp coarse salt

2 celery stalks, trimmed and chopped
  into 2-in (5-cm) pieces

2 carrots, trimmed and chopped into
  2-in (5-cm) pieces

1 onion, trimmed and quartered

4 garlic cloves, crushed

1 bay leaf

4 sprigs fresh parsley

4 sprigs fresh thyme

½ lb (250 g) leeks, green tops trimmed
  and reserved

1 tbsp whole black peppercorns

1 cup (250 mL) pearl barley

12-oz (355-mL) bottle dark beer, such
  as stout or dark lager

1 tsp Worcestershire sauce

1 cup (250 mL) frozen peas

1 tsp chopped fresh thyme

BEEF STEW with BARLEY

This one's a little time consuming, but it's worth it, because while you cook the beef, you also make the broth that will form the basis for this homey, hearty stew. Beef shank is cheap and requires a long time to become tender. It mostly rains all winter in Vancouver, and this is the kind of thing that makes staying inside so wonderful. Let it rain, I don't care—I've got beef stew and slipper socks and *Star Trek*, and nowhere I'd rather be. Serve with dark beer and toasted rye bread.

In a large, heavy pot such as a Dutch oven, heat 2 tbsp oil on medium-high heat. Sprinkle both sides of beef shanks with coarse salt. Sear beef shanks on each side about 4 minutes, until brown.

Add celery, carrots, onions, and garlic. Tie bay leaf, parsley, and thyme to form a bouquet garni; add to pot. Add green tops of leeks and peppercorns. Fill pot with warm water to cover.

Reduce heat to medium. Simmer, partly covered, for 2½ hours, until beef is tender enough to fall apart when pulled apart with a fork, broth has reduced and turned deep brown, and veggies are a shadow of their former selves. If it boils, reduce heat to medium-low to keep at a simmer.

Remove beef and bouquet garni, and strain mixture into another large pot, pressing out as much moisture as possible. Discard solids.

Trim beef from bones. If any marrow remains, scoop this out, chop it roughly, and add to pot with broth. Remove any rubbery bits and discard. Chop beef into bite-size pieces and set aside.

Cut white part of leeks lengthwise down middle, then thinly slice.

Return pot to medium heat. Add remainder of olive oil and leeks, and sauté until softened, about 3 minutes. Stir in barley. Add chopped beef to pot. Add beer, scraping any browned bits off bottom of pot. Add reserved broth and Worcestershire sauce. Taste and adjust seasonings as needed. Simmer, partially covered, for another 20 to 30 minutes, until barley is cooked through.

Just before serving, add peas and remaining fresh thyme. Cook for another minute, until peas are warmed through.

Adapt this to the slow cooker!
IN A LARGE FRYING PAN ON MEDIUM-HIGH HEAT, SEAR BEEF, THEN PLACE IN A SLOW COOKER WITH CARROTS, CELERY, ONIONS, GARLIC, BOUQUET GARNI, GREEN TOPS OF LEEKS, AND PEPPERCORNS. ADD TAP WATER TO COVER, AND COOK ON LOW HEAT FOR 10 HOURS. THEN STRAIN STOCK, REMOVE BEEF, AND DISCARD VEGETABLE SOLIDS; CONTINUE AS PER REST OF INSTRUCTIONS. YOU'LL SAVE YOURSELF A FEW HOURS OF WAITING AROUND AND WILL HAVE DINNER READY IN ABOUT 40 MINUTES.

COTTAGE PIE

8 SERVINGS

If you're having friends over on a weeknight, make this—hell, make it for them on a weekend, especially a rainy one. This is pure comfort; don't be put off by the weight of the pan as you put it in the oven; it's meant to be hearty. You can make the filling and boil the veggies for the topping ahead of time, which is a bonus. It also freezes fairly well, so it's a great dish for work lunches or to deliver to a friend who's just had a baby. It's also easy to halve. Serve with salad, red wine, and country bread.

Preheat oven to 375°F (190°C). Lightly grease a 9x13-inch (3.5 L) baking dish.

In a large pot of salted water on high heat, bring cubed potatoes and rutabaga to a boil. Reduce heat to medium-high and continue to cook for about 25 minutes.

Meanwhile, begin to make filling: In a large pan on medium-high, heat olive oil. Add onions, celery, and carrots, and sauté for 2 to 3 minutes, until veggies have brightened. Add garlic and cook for another minute Add ground beef, breaking into pieces with hands as you drop into pan. Stir, cooking until meat has browned. Stir in rosemary, Worcestershire sauce, mustard, and pepper. Stir in flour until absorbed. Add wine, scraping bottom of pan with spoon, and cook another minute or 2.

Add stock and simmer until sauce has thickened and reduced just slightly. Taste and adjust seasonings as needed. Stir in peas and parsley. Remove from heat. Pour meat mixture into prepared baking dish.

Drain potatoes and turnips once cooked—they should pierce easily with a knife. Return to pot and mash, or process in a food mill. Add butter, stir to combine, then add eggs. Stir quickly. Taste and adjust seasonings to taste.

Dollop potato mixture over meat. Spread to coat evenly, ensuring potato mix reaches edges as much as possible. Drag fork tines over topping.

Bake for about 25 minutes, until topping is golden and meat bubbles around sides. Let rest for 10 to 15 minutes before serving.

TOPPING

4 lb (1.8 kg) starchy potatoes such as Russets, peeled and diced

2 lb (900 g) rutabaga, peeled and diced

½ cup (125 mL) butter

2 eggs, beaten

salt, to taste

FILLING

¼ cup (60 mL) olive oil

1 onion, diced

2 celery stalks, diced

2 carrots, diced

3 garlic cloves, minced

2 lb (900 g) lean ground beef

1 tbsp chopped fresh rosemary

1 tbsp Worcestershire sauce

2 tsp grainy Dijon mustard

1 tsp ground black pepper

½ cup (125 mL) all-purpose flour

1½ cups (375 mL) dry red wine

2½ cups (625 mL) beef stock

salt, to taste

2 cups (500 mL) frozen peas

½ cup (125 mL) chopped fresh parsley

4 SERVINGS

CURRY BRAISED BEEF

2 tbsp canola oil

3–4 lb (1.5–1.8 kg) chuck roast, cubed

1 tsp salt

1 onion, diced

2 tbsp minced ginger

2 tbsp minced fresh lemongrass

2 tbsp minced fresh cilantro stems
(leaves reserved)

6 garlic cloves, minced

2 jalapeño peppers, seeded and
minced

2 tsp ground turmeric

2 tsp ground cumin

1½ tsp ground coriander

1 tsp ground black pepper

½ tsp ground cardamom

¼ tsp ground cinnamon

3 tbsp fish sauce

3 tbsp brown sugar

2 14-oz (398-mL) cans coconut milk

1 lime, zest and juice

3–4 kaffir lime leaves (optional)

2 red Thai bird chilies (optional)

1 lb (500 g) cubed sweet potatoes

1 medium red bell pepper, chopped

I'm lucky in that for the past six years I've worked at academic institutions that shut down over the holidays, so I get the week between Christmas and New Year's off. This is one of the things I like to make then, as it takes a while but still feels celebratory; it isn't another freaking turkey, and it's gluten-free, so it's good for visiting relatives for whom gluten is a concern. This will make your home smell wonderful. Serve over rice with a sprinkling of fresh cilantro leaves.

Preheat oven to 325°F (165°C).

In an oven-proof pot on medium-high, heat oil. Add beef and season with salt. Brown beef deeply on all sides, about 3 minutes, but don't let it burn. Remove to a plate and set aside.

To same pot, add onions, ginger, lemongrass, cilantro stems, garlic, and jalapeño peppers. Sauté until fragrant, 2 to 3 minutes. Add turmeric, cumin, coriander, black pepper, cardamom, and cinnamon, and cook another 2 to 3 minutes, until bottom of pan looks dry.

Add fish sauce, sugar, coconut milk, and lime zest and juice. Add kaffir lime leaves and Thai chilies, if using. I leave my chilies whole. Return beef to pot with meat juices. Cover and put on middle rack of oven. Braise for 2 to 2½ hours, stirring occasionally.

In last 45 minutes, add sweet potatoes and cover pot.

Remove pot from oven, uncover, and return it to stove on medium heat. Add bell peppers and cook an additional 10 minutes until peppers are tender and sauce has reduced slightly.

DUTCH MEATBALLS

This is another of Nick's favorites. I make a full batch, as they're even better the next day, sliced and served cold in sandwiches with mayonnaise, grainy Dijon mustard, and dill pickles. The Dutch (and Nick's mom) use a spice mix called Gehakt (which sounds slightly Klingon, doesn't it?) that's a blend of salt, coriander, ginger, mace, nutmeg, cardamom, and chili. Adding a bit of nutmeg and ketjap manis to 2 to 3 tsp garam masala is a pretty close approximation. Serve these over boiled potatoes with pan juices.

2 lb (900 g) lean ground beef

1 cup (250 mL) bread crumbs

2 eggs

1 onion, finely chopped

4 garlic cloves, minced

2 tbsp ketjap manis (or 1 tbsp each soy sauce and brown sugar)

2 tsp garam masala

½ tsp ground nutmeg

½ tsp salt

½ tsp ground black pepper

½ cup (125 mL) all-purpose flour

½ cup (125 mL) butter

2 cups (500 mL) beef stock or water

Mix beef, bread crumbs, eggs, onions, garlic, ketjap manis, garam masala, nutmeg, salt, and pepper. Form into 10 large meatballs.

Measure flour out onto a plate or clean surface, then roll each meatball in flour to coat.

In a large pan, melt butter on medium-high heat. Add meatballs and sprinkle any remaining flour over. Brown meatballs all over.

Add stock or water, reduce heat to medium, and simmer for 30 minutes. If liquid evaporates too quickly, reduce heat and cover pan with a lid.

4-6 SERVINGS

ED'S POTATO MOUSSAKA

6 tbsp olive oil, divided

2 onions, halved and sliced

4 garlic cloves, minced

1 lb (900 g) lean ground beef

3 tsp coarse salt, divided

½ tsp chopped fresh thyme

½ tsp ground black pepper

1 cup (250 mL) Greek or Balkan-style yogurt

4 eggs, beaten

¼ tsp ground nutmeg

4 lb (1.8 kg) Russet potatoes (5 or 6 medium), peeled and thinly sliced

I once worked with a rather intense Bulgarian web programmer named Ed. One day I brought in a container of leftover moussaka for lunch, which I'd made with eggplant, zucchini, and feta cheese. The dish offended him; according to Ed, this was not moussaka but some other thing—it was wrong. "A *real* moussaka," he explained, "is just potatoes, meat, and yogurt." So I made it again, and this version passed Ed's rigorous inspection. Serve with salad and a bold, opinionated red wine.

Preheat oven to 400°F (200°C). Grease a 9x13-inch (3.5-L) baking dish.

In a frying pan on medium-high, heat 3 tbsp olive oil. Add onions and sauté until translucent and edges have begun to brown, about 5 minutes. Add garlic, and sauté for an additional minute, until garlic is fragrant but not yet brown. Add beef, using a wooden spoon to break apart. Add 1 tsp salt, thyme, and pepper, and cook until meat has browned, 5 or 6 minutes.

Meanwhile, in a bowl, combine yogurt, eggs, nutmeg, 1 tsp salt, and remainder of olive oil. Thin mixture with 2 cups (500 mL) water. Set aside.

Layer half of potatoes in baking dish. Spoon meat mixture on top. Layer remainder of potatoes on top of meat.

Pour yogurt mixture over, sprinkle with remainder of salt, and cover with aluminum foil. Bake for 60 minutes. Remove foil cover, turn on broiler, and broil until top is golden and crispy, 8 to 10 minutes, turning halfway for even browning. Let rest for about 15 minutes before serving.

HAMBURGER STEW

Hamburger stew is as fancy as it sounds, but fancy is hardly the point. This stew is about quick, easy, and hearty, the kind of thing you'd eat under a tarp at a rainy campsite or after soaking yourself to the bone on some grass field somewhere. The first time I made this, it was late November and I'd been playing field hockey on a dark evening with the rain coming in sideways. This stew simmered while I showered, and when I got out, warm and clean, this was the perfect bowl to unwind with. Serve with a slice of good buttered bread.

In a large pot on medium-high, heat oil. Add beef, salt, chili flakes, and pepper. Cook beef until mostly browned.

Add onions, carrots, celery, and garlic, and cook until veggies are glistening and bright, 2 to 3 minutes. Add tomato paste, stirring to coat veggies and disperse paste. Add rice and lentils.

Add 6 cups (1.5 L) water, and reduce heat to medium. Add bay leaves, oregano, and basil, and simmer for 20 to 30 minutes, until rice is cooked and lentils are tender. Stir occasionally.

Add lemon zest and juice. Taste and adjust seasonings as needed. Stir in parsley, and serve in bowls.

2 tbsp olive oil

1 lb (500 g) lean ground beef

1 tbsp coarse salt

½ tsp chili flakes

½ tsp ground black pepper

1 onion, diced

4 carrots, peeled and chopped

4 celery stalks, trimmed and chopped

6 garlic cloves, roughly chopped

6-oz (175-g) can tomato paste

½ cup (125 mL) long-grain white rice

½ cup green lentils

2 bay leaves

1 tsp dried oregano

½ tsp dried basil

½ lemon, zest and juice

3 tbsp chopped fresh parsley

24 MEATBALLS

MEATBALLS ⟶ WITH ⟵ RED SAUCE

1 lb (500 g) lean ground beef

1 lb (500 g) ground pork

1 medium onion, finely chopped

3 garlic cloves, minced

2 eggs

2 tbsp butter, bacon fat, or olive oil

1 rounded tbsp tomato paste

1 tsp Worcestershire sauce

1 cup (250 mL) dry bread crumbs

½ cup (125 mL) grated Parmesan cheese

1 tsp salt

1 tsp dried oregano

½ tsp ground black pepper

I thought this was everyone's meatball recipe—it's not unlike my mom's and it's apparently very much like my friend Tracy's Nonna's recipe. These meatballs are so good that they converted a vegetarian, which is, I'm sorry to admit, a source of great pride for me. You can easily halve the meatball recipe if you want to feed a family of four; I like to make the full batch and freeze half for later. Serve with spaghetti and Red Sauce (recipe following). Garnish with fresh basil, and choice of cheese. As my friend Grace would say, "serve family style."

Preheat oven to 375°F (190°C).

In a large bowl, combine all ingredients. Squish together with your hands to ensure that crumbs and eggs are thoroughly combined with meat, but don't worry if meat isn't completely combined—it's better to have meat sort of separate, so that you can taste pork and beef distinctly. And you must use your hands. There is no other way.

Line a baking sheet with aluminum foil. Roll meat mixture into balls roughly 1½ in (4 cm) in diameter. There should be about 2 dozen—if you have many more, your balls are too small. (Snicker.) And the reverse is true too.

Place balls on lined baking sheet. Bake for 25 to 30 minutes.

To serve, drop them into pot of Red Sauce as it cooks, then spoon mixture over a big plate of cooked spaghetti.

3 tbsp butter

1 tbsp olive oil

1 onion, diced

4 garlic cloves, minced

1 tsp chili flakes

1 tsp salt

½ tsp ground black pepper

½ cup (125 mL) dry red wine

2 28-oz (796-mL) cans whole
   tomatoes, juices included

RED SAUCE

In a heavy-bottomed pot such as a Dutch oven, melt butter and olive oil on medium-high heat. Add onions and sauté until translucent, about 3 minutes. Add garlic, chili flakes, salt, and pepper, and cook for another minute or 2, until garlic is fragrant but not yet browned. Add wine, scraping browned bits off bottom of pot.

Add tomatoes, one by one, squishing each between your fingers as it goes into pot. Stir in remaining can juices. Reduce heat to medium-low, then partially cover pot with a lid. Allow mixture to simmer for about 45 minutes, until tomatoes have broken down. If you like a smooth sauce, purée with an immersion blender before adding meatballs.

This recipe is scalable; the full amount makes enough for a big plate of pasta (about 8 servings), or 12 servings of Red Sauce Eggs (p. 80).

4-6 SERVINGS

4–5 lb (1.8–2.2 kg) beef chuck roast

2 tsp coarse salt

½ tsp ground black pepper

3 sprigs parsley + 2 tbsp chopped
   parsley, for garnish

1 sprig thyme

2 bay leaves

3 tbsp bacon fat or olive oil

2 large onions, quartered

1 head garlic, cloves separated, peeled,
   and chopped

12-oz (355-mL) can cola

1 tbsp Worcestershire sauce

2 tbsp instant coffee granules

1 lb (500 g) carrots, peeled and
   chopped into 2-in (5-cm) chunks

2–4 cups (500–1 L) beef or chicken
   stock

POT ROAST

My grandmother made a kick-ass pot roast, and though she was notoriously secretive about her recipes, she let me watch her make this once. I have no idea why, but I'm happy that she did. I've adapted it a bit to suit my own tastes (by which I mean I added an unseemly amount of garlic, as I do), but it's flavorful, and even better the next day piled onto soft white buns with a bit of cheddar cheese and mustard. Serve with buttered noodles or mashed potatoes.

Preheat oven to 275°F (135°C).

Generously season beef with salt and pepper. Set aside.

In a piece of cheesecloth, bundle parsley and thyme sprigs and bay leaves. Roll tightly, then tie with string to secure. Set aside.

In large pot on medium-high, heat bacon fat or oil. Add onions and sauté about 8 minutes, until browned, then remove to a plate.

Add beef to pot, and sear each side until deep brown. Remove meat to a plate and set aside.

Add garlic to pot and cook for about 1 minute, stirring frequently. Add cola to deglaze, scraping browned bits off bottom of pot using a wooden spoon. Stir in Worcestershire sauce and coffee granules.

Return onions to pot, spreading so that they cover entire bottom. Return roast to pot, placing on top of onions. Add herbs and carrots. Cover with enough stock to come halfway up sides of meat. Give it a quick taste—is it delicious? Yay! Not salty enough? Add more salt.

Cover and cook for 4 hours. Remove herbs, then sprinkle with fresh parsley for a bit of color.

4-6 SERVINGS

PATTIES

1 lb (500 g) lean ground beef

¾ cup bread crumbs

2 eggs

1 medium onion, finely chopped

3 garlic cloves, minced

1 tsp Worcestershire sauce

1 tsp grainy Dijon mustard

1 tsp coarse salt

½ tsp ground black pepper

1 tbsp canola or olive oil

GRAVY

2 tbsp butter

1 medium onion, sliced

½ lb (250 g) mushrooms, roughly
   chopped

2 garlic cloves, minced

1 tsp chopped fresh thyme (or ½ tsp
   dried thyme)

2 tbsp all-purpose flour

½ tsp ground black pepper

½ tsp salt or to taste

3 cups (750 mL) beef stock

SALISBURY STEAK

This is not a beautiful dish—it's all shades of brown, like the 1980s on a plate, so you should definitely serve it with a vegetable, preferably one that goes well with gravy. (They all do.) This is one of those meals my Dad made on weeknights when I was a kid—it's economical and not quite good for you (quintessential dad food, really), and it's best served over white rice, buttered pasta, or a heap of mashed potatoes, with maybe a salad, and a cold, dark beer.

In a large bowl, combine beef, bread crumbs, eggs, onions, garlic, Worcestershire sauce, mustard, salt, and pepper. Mush together with your hands until thoroughly combined. Form into six patties of equal size and thickness—about ¾-in (2-cm) thick. Set aside.

In a large cast-iron pan (or Dutch oven) on medium-high heat, add oil and swirl to coat bottom of pan. Add patties, and cook for 2 to 3 minutes per side, until both sides are seared and brown. Remove from pan, and set aside.

Add butter to pan, and once melted, add onions. Cook until onions have softened and become translucent, 3 to 4 minutes. Add mushrooms and cook until they're soft and most of liquid has evaporated, another 3 minutes. Stir in garlic and thyme. Reduce heat to medium-low, then stir in flour and pepper and salt. Add stock, scrape bottom of pan to loosen browned bits, and then nestle beef patties in pan.

Simmer, uncovered, for 25 to 30 minutes, flipping halfway, until sauce has thickened and patties are cooked through—they should register an internal temperature of around 160°F (71°C). Serve, being generous with the gravy.

FRUITS AND VEGETABLES

The thing I enjoy seeing most when I travel is local supermarkets and farmer's markets. In San Salvador, I spent an hour of our highly-scheduled trip just pacing the aisles of Super Selectos, a local chain of grocery stores, looking at stuff. I bought little packages of every spice I didn't think I could get at home and marveled at the eggs, not refrigerated but stacked neatly and nearly four feet (1.2 m) high on paper flats at the end of an aisle. Apparently, egg refrigeration isn't a universal thing, and much of Europe doesn't refrigerate them either. Who knew?

In Paris and Lyon, I'd duck into every market I passed, admiring the little crocks of individual yogurts and pretty jars of chestnut paste and every kind of mustard. In London, I enjoyed Waitrose and Marks & Spencer, especially their wide array of potato chip flavors and the abundance of single-serve meal choices designed for people with limited kitchen space. Even when I cross the border into the US, I love the grocery stores with their long aisles of food we just don't have in Canada—different brands, different flavors, bigger blocks of less expensive cheese. Supermarkets are the museums of right now, and a brilliant way to peer into and learn about the modern lifestyles of whoever's culture you're visiting.

Open air markets are the best way to find new types of fruits and vegetables. I love fruit the way other people love chocolate, and so for me there is no greater gustatory pleasure than discovering a new variety of something sweet and juicy. In El Salvador, my favorite "new" fruit was jocote, a small, musky tropical fruit about the size of a fresh date, with skin that ranged from green to red. In Lyon, I bought and ate an unreasonable quantity of *fraises du bois*, little wild strawberries that taste like those squishy red strawberry marshmallows you get in five-cent candy bins in 7-Elevens everywhere. In San Francisco, I bought Chardonnay grapes and then wouldn't stop talking about them, and that wasn't annoying for my travel companions at all. "You guys, you should taste these! These are wine grapes! They taste like wine!" My enthusiasm is not infectious, but it is extremely repetitive.

A little closer to home, there's a wonderful

market down the hill from where my parents live, and though it's forty-five minutes away from us, we still go there most Sundays. The market is seasonal and open only from May to the end of October. So when we go, we get a little ridiculous, partly because the cost of produce is much lower than in the city, and partly because it's all so good. The family who runs the market also operates the farm around it, and they grow the most wonderful greens, new potatoes, giant zucchini, squash, and purple and orange cauliflower, among other things. They even grow broccoflower, a broccoli-cauliflower hybrid that is the best of both brassicas. They also bring in most of what they don't grow from other local farms, and what is imported is clearly marked. Their produce isn't certified organic, but it couldn't be fresher—much of it is picked the same morning or the day before it's sold. They don't take credit cards, just cash or debit, and they'll pack your produce in either bags or big cardboard boxes. We always end up with the cardboard boxes filled to the brim for about twenty-five dollars.

We mostly don't buy organic produce. For a while I bought the organic version of everything on the Environmental Working Group's "Dirty Dozen" list (see p. 172), but to keep our costs down we've always eaten mostly seasonally, so we just don't eat many of the items on that list for most of the year. I don't buy organic nectarines, for example, because we only get nectarines in the summertime, and they come from farms just six hours away. The organic nectarines in the grocery store near my apartment are from California. They're smaller and harder than the ripe, juicy ones at the farm market. I don't know

how old they are or when they were picked or who picked them. So we don't eat nectarines unless it's nectarine season in British Columbia's Okanagan Valley. I live all year for my first taste of fresh stone fruit, and when I can finally get my hands on it, there is no one shriekier or more filled with delight. Food is cheaper and tastes better when it's in season. We get by with cold-stored apples and pears and whatever fruit we've frozen for most of the year, so by the time those first spring fruits and veggies hit the market in March or April, we're fully ravenous for them.

Depending on where you live, organic produce can be quite costly; it can also come from anywhere. Organic means that the fruit was grown using organic soils, fertilizers, and pesticides, but doesn't include any criteria for the kind of labor used to harvest the fruit. While on the one hand, produce from an organic farm is gentler on the environment, it may have been picked by people who are not being paid a living wage or who are employed under slave-like conditions. This makes it difficult to feel like you're making the "right" choice by buying organic. And it's not like we can all just stop eating fruits and veggies.

I am privileged to live in a place with a lot of very good seasonal produce and to have the time to put a lot of it up for the winter, either by canning or freezing. There's a farmer's market two blocks from home every Sunday during the summer and a winter farmer's market at the local baseball stadium, also not far from home, which means we can talk to local farmers and ask questions about their products. It's more expensive, but when we're able to afford

The Dirty Dozen
(and the Clean Fifteen)

EVERY YEAR, THE ENVIRONMENTAL WORKING GROUP (*EWG.ORG*) COMES OUT WITH A LIST, THE DIRTY DOZEN, OF PRODUCE THAT YOU SHOULD BUY ORGANIC, IF POSSIBLE, DUE TO HIGH LEVELS OF PESTICIDE RESIDUES IN CONVENTIONAL PRODUCTS. IT ALSO PRODUCES A LIST OF CONVENTIONALLY GROWN FRUITS AND VEGGIES THAT HAVE LESS PESTICIDE RESIDUES—THESE ARE THE CLEAN FIFTEEN. ORGANIC PRODUCE IS NOT PESTICIDE FREE, HOWEVER, SO NO MATTER WHAT KIND OF PRODUCE YOU BUY, BE SURE TO WASH IT THOROUGHLY BEFORE YOU COOK WITH OR EAT IT. USE A BRUSH TO SCRUB PRODUCE WITH THICK SKINS, SUCH AS POTATOES AND APPLES, AND RINSE ANYTHING YOU'RE NOT GOING TO PEEL, ESPECIALLY CELERY AND LEAFY GREENS. IF YOU WANT TO BE EXTRA SUPER CAREFUL, FILL A SPRAY BOTTLE WITH A SOLUTION THAT'S ROUGHLY THREE PARTS VINEGAR TO ONE PART WATER, AND SPRAY PRODUCE BEFORE RINSING IT UNDER RUNNING TAP WATER FOR UP TO THIRTY SECONDS.

it we do make the effort to buy what we can. I like to know where my food comes from, how often it's sprayed with pesticides, when in its life cycle it's been sprayed, and that the people involved in the harvest are paid fairly for their work. For me, it's easy to eat locally and seasonally first. This is not the case for everyone. Especially for people who live in places that get serious winter.

So what do you do when you want to eat more fruits and veggies but there isn't a thrilling variety of fresh, local produce available to you at the moment? Frozen and canned fruits and vegetables are often healthier than off-season fresh produce because they are usually picked at the peak of ripeness, making them more nutrient-rich than produce that's picked early, sprayed with chemicals, and shipped across the continent or overseas. Frozen and canned produce are also a lot cheaper. For example, as I write, a bundle of fresh spinach at my local supermarket is $1.99. A roughly half-pound (270 g) plastic bag of baby spinach leaves is $2.79. But a brick of frozen spinach? Ninety-nine cents. And it's not been sitting around deteriorating and being handled by hordes of people who may have just sneezed into their hands. So there's that to feel good about. Spinach is currently two bunches for a dollar at my little farm market, so I'm going to buy a ton and freeze it. To freeze spinach, just blanch it quickly, squeeze out all the water, and place it in tightly packed containers. You can also just freeze it as-is in pillowcases overnight (the pillowcases keep the delicate leaves from becoming freezer-burned), then package according to your preference.

Buy canned vegetables packed in water or their

own juices, and if you're concerned about sodium, just drain the veggies in a colander and rinse them before using them in a recipe. A standard 14- to 15-ounce (398- to 450-mL) can of corn or peas will work out to about 2 cups (250 mL) of its fresh or frozen counterpart; a 28-ounce (796-mL) can of diced tomatoes is equivalent to about 2 lb (900 g) tomatoes. Use canned whole tomatoes for most recipes where you don't need the tomatoes to keep their shape; if you need identifiable pieces of tomato, choose diced tomatoes, which have been treated with calcium chloride to prevent them from disintegrating. (Calcium chloride is a kind of salt and common food additive used as both a preservative and a thickening agent. Though associated health risks are minor, it can cause irritation to mucous membranes, including eyes, nose, and stomach.)

If you are concerned about where your canned and frozen produce has come from and who has picked it, call, write, or email the company who produced it. If you like buying a specific product but are concerned about labor practices or packaging or anything else, let the manufacturer know. Pressure the people who make products you like to do better. The positive changes that we have seen in improved access to organic produce, in a greater variety of fair-trade products on store shelves, in better labeling—all of that has been a result of consumer pressure. Nagging works, both at home and in business. Which reminds me, the refrigerator is starting to smell again … Nick?

We're all doing the best that we can, and I think that's sometimes hard to remember when looking

I REALLY CAN'T GET ENOUGH FRUIT, AND THERE ARE SO MANY WAYS TO ENJOY IT. I LOVE DESSERT, BUT I DON'T LOVE TO FOLLOW A MEAL WITH ANYTHING TOO RICH OR TOO HEAVY; FRUIT-BASED DESSERTS ARE MY GO-TOS FOR ENTERTAINING, BUT FOR FAMILY DINNERS OR EVEN WHEN I'M EATING ALONE, I LIKE TO END A MEAL WITH FRESH SUMMER FRUIT WITH A TINY BIT OF CREAM AND JUST A DUSTING OF WHITE SUGAR OR A DRIZZLE OF HONEY. IN WINTER, PEAR OR APPLE SLICES SAUTÉED IN BUTTER AND SUGAR OR A COMPOTE MADE OF FROZEN FRUIT IS LOVELY WITH A BIT OF ICE CREAM. DRIED FRUIT SIMMERED AND PLUMPED IN A SYRUP OF WINE OR BRANDY AND SUGAR CAN BE LOVELY WITH A PIECE OF SIMPLE POUND CAKE. AND ANY TIME OF YEAR, YOU CAN'T GO WRONG WITH A FEW PIECES OF FRUIT AND A CHUNK OF CHEESE. FRUIT: AN OPPORTUNITY TO EAT MORE CHEESE. SEIZE IT.

at all the things there are in the world we can do better. The best advice I've heard on this was from Cheryl Hotchkiss, Senior Manager for Public Engagement and Brand Development at World Vision Canada. You can burn yourself out trying to save the world with every single purchase—that in itself is not sustainable, and if you're broke it's pretty easy to find yourself making compromises and feeling bad about them. She suggested choosing the cause that matters most to you, and making a difference there. So, for example, if you buy a lot of canned veggies, find a brand whose values you share and support them. If supporting your local farmer is important to you, go out and meet him or her and ask questions about the products they sell. If eating the very best nectarines is important to you, wait until August and buy them from a farm or pick them yourself and eat them still warm from the sun and let them blow your mind each and every year. And then acquire too many and freeze them, so you can enjoy them in February (which is the worst month, as everyone knows).

Fruit and vegetables are two of the most important elements contributing to our nutrition and well-being. A diverse diet rich in a variety of plant-based foods will go a long way toward strengthening your immunity and protecting your health—anything you can do to eat more of them is a good thing. Even if that means blending them frozen with a bunch of rum and lime juice. Which, honestly, is my second-favorite thing about traveling.

BORSCHT WITH BEETS & RED CABBAGE

Most of the year, we eat our beets raw and shredded over salads, roasted (again, on salads), or pickled. But for the 3 or 4 months it's just non-stop cold and rainy on the west coast, we take our beets brothy and warm, with a dollop of thick, full-fat yogurt and a smattering of caraway seeds and fresh dill. Nutritionally rich and calorically sparse, it's a nice thing to eat on weeknights in December when it feels like every weekend is a two-day butter binge. I like to make this on Sunday, as it's a bit time-consuming, and serve it for dinner the next day.

In a stock pot or other large pot, heat peppercorns and caraway seeds on medium-high heat for 2 to 3 minutes, or until spices are fragrant and caraway seeds start to pop. Add 4 qt/L water, beets, bay leaves, parsley, garlic, and salt, and cook, partially covered, for 90 minutes.

Remove beets to a bowl of icy water, and strain liquid from pot through a fine-mesh strainer into a container you can pour easily from. Discard solids. Peel, trim, then dice beets. Set aside.

In a large pot on medium-high, heat oil and add carrots, celery, onions, and garlic. Sauté until glistening, then add beets, cabbage, and reserved stock. Reduce heat to medium, add ¼ cup (60 mL) lemon juice, and simmer for 20 to 25 minutes, until cabbage is soft.

Taste, adding sugar and additional lemon juice as desired. Adjust seasonings, and serve with a dollop of yogurt or sour cream and a sprinkling of caraway seeds or fresh dill.

STOCK

2 tsp whole black peppercorns

1 tsp caraway seeds

1 lb (500 g) beets, scrubbed clean but not trimmed or peeled (3 to 4, about the size of baseballs)

2 bay leaves

½ bunch fresh parsley

1 head garlic, halved crosswise

1 tbsp kosher salt

SOUP

2 tbsp olive oil

2 carrots, quartered lengthwise and chopped

2 celery stalks, quartered lengthwise and chopped

1 onion, finely chopped

3 garlic cloves, minced

2 cups (500 mL) shredded red cabbage

¼–½ cup (60–125 mL) fresh lemon juice (start with ¼ cup, and adjust to taste)

2 tbsp brown sugar

salt and pepper, to taste

¾ cup (175 mL) yogurt or sour cream, for garnish

3 tsp caraway seeds and/or 6 tbsp chopped fresh dill, for garnish

BROCCOLI *WITH* TOFU & PEANUTS

For us, this dinner is the ultimate in cheap eats. It's rich in fiber and protein, colorful, fast, and so jam-packed with sweet, salty, spicy flavors that it manages to feel a little indulgent. Tip: If your peanut butter contains added sugar, scale back on the sugar in this recipe a bit and then adjust the sweetness to your taste. Serve over rice.

In a dry frying pan on medium heat, toast peanuts, and watch them diligently. In 3 to 4 minutes, when they start to smell like roasted peanuts, turn golden, and sweat, remove from heat and set aside. Divide into two piles and chop one pile.

Blanch broccoli by plunging it into a pot of boiling water. Boil for 2 minutes, then remove immediately and immerse in ice water for 1 minute. Reserve ½ cup (125 mL) blanching water and set aside.

In a large frying pan, heat peanut oil on medium-high heat. Add shallots, garlic, and ginger, and sauté until just golden, about 2 minutes. In a bowl, combine peanut butter, soy sauce, sesame oil, Sriracha, sugar, and lime juice. Taste. If it needs more sugar, add more. Add pepper and taste again. If it needs to be spicier, add more Sriracha.

Add bell peppers and tofu to pan. Stir ⅓ peanut sauce into pan. Add ¼ cup (60 mL) blanching water; if it is still too thick, add more water, 1 tbsp at a time, to thin. Cook until peppers have softened, about 2 minutes. Add broccoli and remainder of peanut sauce. Stir to coat, then toss in whole peanuts. Sprinkle with chopped peanuts before serving.

1 cup (250 mL) unsalted peanuts

1½ lb (750 g) broccoli, chopped into bite-sized pieces

2 tbsp peanut or vegetable oil

1 shallot, minced

3 cloves garlic, minced

1 tbsp minced fresh ginger

½ cup (125 mL) peanut butter

½ cup (125 mL) soy sauce

1 tbsp sesame oil

1 tbsp Sriracha or favorite hot sauce, to taste

1 to 2 tbsp dark brown sugar

1 tbsp fresh lime juice

½ tsp fresh ground pepper

1 red bell pepper, diced

12-oz (350-g) pkg firm tofu, cubed

4-6
SERVINGS

CORN & ASPARAGUS SALAD

This is summer in a bowl! It's a great mix of textures and the colors are fabulous. Make it a couple of hours before serving, as it's best when cold. It's easy, fast, and a nice accompaniment to summer potlucks and beach picnics. Fresh and tasty, too.

1 lb (500 g) asparagus, trimmed, chopped into bite-size pieces

2 large cobs corn, about 1½ cups (125mL) kernels, fresh or frozen

2 cups (500 mL) diced fresh tomatoes

2 diced roasted piquillo or red bell peppers

1 large shallot, minced

½ cup (125 mL) garlic scapes or scallions, finely chopped

½ cup (125 mL) grated Parmesan cheese

1 lemon, zest and juice

¼ cup (60 mL) extra-virgin olive oil

2 tbsp minced fresh basil

1 tsp chili flakes

1 tsp kosher salt

½ tsp ground black pepper

In a large pot of boiling water, blanch asparagus for about 1 minute. Cool in an ice-water bath until cold.

Scrape corn from cobs into a large bowl or thaw frozen corn. Stir in tomatoes, peppers, shallots, garlic scapes, cheese, lemon zest, and asparagus.

In a small bowl, whisk lemon juice, olive oil, basil, chili flakes, salt, and pepper. Taste and adjust balance of flavors as needed. Pour over vegetables and toss to coat. Serve immediately.

CUCUMBER SALAD

My mom always made this when we were going to eat salmon. Her version used dill and sour cream, but the effect was the same—a creamy, cool side dish to go with something rich, a way to balance the flavors on the plate. Depending on what herbs you use, this is lovely with fish (dill or parsley), spicy foods such as curry (mint and cilantro), or fried chicken (parsley and cilantro).

In a large bowl, combine cucumber and onion slices and sprinkle with salt. Toss to coat. Cover, and place in refrigerator for 2 hours.

Drain liquid from veggies. Add herbs, yogurt, lime juice and zest, cumin seeds, and pepper, and toss to coat. Cover and place in refrigerator until serving time. Serve chilled, garnished with more chopped herbs.

1 English cucumber, sliced into very thin rounds

1 small onion, sliced paper-thin

1 tsp salt

½ cup (125 mL) chopped herbs (parsley, mint, dill, or cilantro)

½ cup (125 mL) Greek-style yogurt

1 lime, zest and juice

½ tsp cumin seeds

ground black pepper, to taste

6
CUPS (1.5 ML)

1 lb (500 g) napa cabbage, thinly
  sliced

1 lb (500 g) carrots, peeled and grated

1 onion, halved and thinly sliced

6 tbsp apple cider vinegar

2 tsp brown sugar

1 tsp salt

1 tsp ground black pepper

1 tsp dried oregano

CURTIDO

Curtido is somewhere between coleslaw and kimchi—it's a Salvadoran fermented cabbage condiment, usually served with pupusas, thick corn tortillas stuffed with cheese, beans, or meat. This is a short-cut, a recipe you can make when you want the idea of curtido, but don't have time to let the cabbage succumb to science. At my local pupusa spot, this is served as a slaw. In El Salvador, restaurants often kept it on the tables in big plastic jars with spoons inside so diners could help themselves.

In a large bowl, toss cabbage, carrots, and onions to combine well.

In a small bowl, whisk vinegar and 2 tbsp water, brown sugar, salt, pepper, and oregano until sugar has dissolved.

Pour dressing over veggies and mix, using your hands. Squeeze veggies as you mix so that cabbage really takes on flavor of dressing.

Refrigerate for at least 1 hour—ideally for 24 hours—before serving.

DELICATA TACOS ~WITH~ CORN

4
SERVINGS

Delicata squash, sometimes sold as "potato squash" or "sweet potato squash" is perfect for weeknight cooking—you don't need to peel it, and it cooks pretty quickly. Its flesh is sweet and a bit dryer than butternut squash, which makes it perfect for tacos—it soaks up the flavors around it while maintaining great taste and texture. Have friends over and make a batch of these and a batch of Lentil Tacos (p. 92); you'll never feel more virtuous and healthy after Taco Night.

In a large pan on medium-high, heat oil. Add onions, and sauté until just translucent, about 4 minutes. Add garlic, jalapeño peppers, and cumin seeds. Sauté until peppers have softened, about 5 minutes.

Add squash, chili powder, salt, and pepper. Stir to coat veggies with spices. Stir in beer, lemon juice, and corn. Reduce heat to medium. Cook until squash has softened, about 10 minutes. Stir occasionally to prevent squash from browning too much.

Add scallions in last 2 minutes of cooking. To serve, spoon filling into warmed tortillas (see below), and top with accompaniments to taste.

Microwave: warm tortillas 4 at a time, wrapping them in a damp paper towel, then cook on high for 30 to 40 seconds, until soft and pliable.

Oven: Wrap six tortillas in foil and place on a baking sheet in 350°F (180°C) oven for 15 to 20 minutes. A standard sheet pan will comfortably hold about three of these bundles.

3 tbsp canola oil

1 onion, diced

4 garlic cloves, minced

2 jalapeño peppers, seeded and minced

2 tsp cumin seeds

1 lb (500 g) delicata squash, trimmed, seeded, and diced

1 tsp chili powder

½ tsp salt

½ tsp ground black pepper

½ cup (125 mL) beer, such as lager

juice of ½ lemon

2 cups (500 mL) fresh or frozen corn kernels

4 scallions, chopped

20 fresh 6-in (15-cm) corn tortillas

ACCOMPANIMENTS

½ head shredded lettuce or cabbage

2 cups (500 mL) grated aged cheddar cheese

1 cup (250 mL) salsa (homemade or store-bought)

4 limes (cut into eighths)

Avocado Cream (p. 93)

Pico de Gallo (p. 188)

6
SERVINGS

GRANDMA SALAD

2 tbsp Greek yogurt

1 tbsp mayonnaise

1 tbsp white vinegar

1 tsp grainy Dijon mustard

½ tsp smoked paprika

½ tsp honey

½ tsp coarse salt

1 head iceberg lettuce, torn into rough
   pieces

4 scallions, finely chopped

2 medium avocados, diced

Nick's grandmother makes something his family calls "Beppe Slaw"; my grandmother made something similar. Basically, it's iceberg lettuce and onions in a creamy dressing, and it goes well with most things. Our version is lighter on the mayonnaise and uses avocado for extra creaminess. This one doesn't keep, so insist that everyone has salad and lots of it. You know, like your grandma would have.

In a large bowl, whisk together yogurt, mayonnaise, vinegar, mustard, paprika, honey and salt. Taste and adjust seasonings as needed.

Add lettuce, scallions, and avocados to bowl. Toss to coat lettuce in dressing, and serve immediately.

HONEY MUSTARD BEETS

4 SERVINGS

Given how vibrantly colored and dense they are, it's no wonder beets are good for you. They're high in fiber! They're rich in nutrients! That have antioxidant properties and are kind to your liver! Eat more beets. If you think you don't like them, try them again—this sweet and sour dressing brings out the best in them.

1 lb (500 g) beets

2 tbsp apple cider vinegar

1 tbsp honey

1 tsp olive oil

1 tsp grainy Dijon mustard

½ tsp salt

¼ tsp ground black pepper

In a medium pot covered with a tight-fitting lid on high heat, bring beets in salted water to a boil. Boil beets until tender, about 30 to 40 minutes. (If beets are quite large, this can take up to 1 hour.)

Drain beets. Place in a bowl of cold water, and shuck off skins once beets are cool enough to handle. Slice beets thinly.

In a small bowl, whisk apple cider vinegar, honey, olive oil, mustard, salt, and pepper. Pour over still-warm beets, mixing well to coat each slice. Refrigerate until completely cooled. Serve cold, first giving beets another quick stir to coat in dressing.

KIMCHI &
SOFT TOFU STEW

2 tbsp canola oil

2 tsp sesame oil

1 onion, diced

4 garlic cloves, roughly chopped

2 cups (500 mL) cabbage kimchi,
   roughly chopped

3 tbsp gochujang sauce

2 tbsp fish sauce

2 tbsp corn or tapioca starch

1 tsp coarse salt

1 lb (500 g) soft or silken tofu

juice of ½ lemon

4 scallions, chopped

With a toddler in daycare, we get just about every virus that goes around from October through March. These are congested times. This stew is magic because it'll clear your sinuses, warm your bones, and get itself onto your table and into your mouth in under 20 minutes. It pairs nicely with slippers and sweatpants.

In a large pan on medium-high heat, heat canola and sesame oils. Add onions and sauté until edges are just browned, about 4 minutes. Stir in garlic, kimchi, and gochujang. Cook for 2 to 3 minutes, until bottom of pan begins to look dry.

Add fish sauce, 4 cups (1 L) water, and a slurry made of starch and additional 2 tbsp water. Add salt, and bring mixture to a simmer. Add tofu by heaping tablespoonful, then reduce heat to medium. Simmer for 10 minutes.

Add lemon juice, stirring gently. Taste and adjust seasonings as needed. Sprinkle scallions over and serve hot in bowls.

KIMCHI PANCAKES

There's a Korean market two blocks from my apartment that makes their own kimchi and tofu, among other things, and it's really, really good. This recipe takes under 10 minutes to make, if you've got kimchi, and it hits several satisfying notes—it's fried, which is always good; it's spicy and tangy, with few ingredients; and it uses kimchi, which is one of those fabulously probiotic things that contributes to a healthy microbiome and overall sense of well-being. It pairs nicely with That Korean Restaurant Soup (p. 199) and is also good with cold soju (a Korean spirit) or a handful of vodka sodas with lime. (*Note*: these may diminish benefits to microbiome; I'm a lush, not a scientist.) Serve with Sauce for Kimchi Pancakes, below.

2 cups (500 mL) cabbage kimchi, chopped

2 eggs

1 cup (250 mL) all-purpose flour

1 tsp sesame oil

½ tsp salt

½ cup (125 mL) club soda

3 tbsp vegetable oil

SAUCE FOR KIMCHI PANCAKES

2 tbsp ketjap manis

2 tbsp rice vinegar

2 tsp minced ginger

2 garlic cloves, minced

In a large bowl, combine kimchi, eggs, flour, sesame oil, and salt. Stir together until thoroughly combined. Add soda, and gently fold in. You want to keep as many bubbles as you can, because bubbles make this light.

In a large frying pan on medium-high, heat oil. Divide batter into 4 pancakes of roughly equal size. Cook for about 3 minutes per side, until golden and crispy, especially around edges. Cut pancakes into quarters to serve.

In a small bowl, whisk together all ingredients for sauce. Serve in ramekins or little bowls wide enough to dip a slice of pancake. Double recipe if serving 4 people.

4-6 SERVINGS

MUSHROOM COTTAGE PIE

2 lb (900 g) Yukon Gold or other yellow-fleshed potatoes, diced

½ cup (125 mL) grated Parmesan cheese

4 tbsp extra-virgin olive oil, divided

¼ cup (60 mL) + 1 tbsp milk, divided

2 eggs

1 tbsp butter

1 shallot, minced (about 2 tbsp)

3 garlic cloves, minced

1 cup (250 mL) finely chopped leeks (white and light-green parts only, about 2 medium leeks)

2½ lb (1 kg) mushrooms, assorted varieties if possible, roughly chopped

2 tsp chopped fresh thyme

1 tbsp all-purpose flour

½ cup (125 mL) dry red wine

2 tbsp soy sauce

1 tbsp grainy Dijon mustard

1 tsp Worcestershire sauce

1 tsp ground black pepper

¼ tsp ground nutmeg

1 tbsp chopped fresh parsley

salt, to taste

If you grew up eating Shepherd's Pie and haven't gone back to it for complicated Shepherd's Pie-hating reasons, this one might just bring you back. It's savory and rich, and goes very well with red wine. We serve this with Grandma Salad (p. 182).

In a large pot of water on high heat, boil potatoes until tender, 15 to 20 minutes. Drain and mash or process through a potato ricer or food mill until smooth. Whip in cheese, 2 tbsp olive oil, ¼ cup (60 mL) milk, and eggs. Taste and adjust seasonings as needed. Set aside.

Preheat oven to 400°F (200°C).

In a large frying pan on medium-high, heat remainder of oil and butter until butter begins to bubble and foam. Stir in shallots and garlic, and sauté for 2 minutes, until translucent. Add leeks and sauté until shallots have melted down, about 3 minutes.

Add mushrooms and thyme to pan, stirring to coat. Allow mushrooms to sweat, about 5 minutes, stirring occasionally. Sprinkle flour over mushrooms and mix until flour is absorbed. Stir in wine, soy sauce, mustard, Worcestershire sauce, pepper, and nutmeg. Reduce heat to medium and allow to thicken slightly, 2 to 3 minutes. Stir in parsley and remainder of milk. Taste and adjust seasonings as needed.

Remove mushrooms from heat and pour into a 1½- to 2-qt/L casserole dish. Top with mashed potato mixture, spreading to cover completely.

Bake for 20 to 25 minutes, until potatoes are golden on top and mushroom sauce is bubbling out from around sides.

PEAS & CARROTS

4 SERVINGS

Peas and carrots are the simplest thing, but so easy to half-ass. It doesn't take any longer to make peas and carrots with a little bit of care, and the payoff is that you get a simple, colorful, and flavorful side dish out of stuff you just have in the refrigerator and freezer anyway. This dish is more than the sum of its parts, with all the benefits of nostalgia and visual appeal. It's also fairly universal—serve it with grilled meat, Thanksgiving dinner, or as a side to any casserole.

1 tbsp butter

1 tbsp olive oil

2 cups (500 mL) chopped carrots, ¼-in (6-mm) thick

2 cups (500 mL) frozen peas

½ cup (125 mL) chopped fresh parsley

2 tbsp chopped fresh mint

salt and pepper, to taste

In a medium frying pan on medium-high, heat butter and oil until butter melts and begins to bubble. Add carrots, and cook until just soft, stirring frequently, 6 to 8 minutes. Add peas and cook for an additional 5 minutes. Peas should be soft but still bright.

Stir in parsley, mint, salt, and pepper. Taste, and adjust seasonings as needed.

3 CUPS (700 ML)

PICO DE GALLO

4 plum or Roma tomatoes, chopped,
about 2 cups (500 mL)

1 small red onion, finely chopped

1 garlic clove, minced

1 jalapeño pepper, seeded and minced

1 lime, zest and juice

1 tbsp olive oil

½ tsp salt

½ tsp ground black pepper

Pico de gallo is best made in September or October, when tomatoes are bursting their skins, they're so ripe and ruddy. If you have a food processor, use it; this does not require uniform chopping. It's supposed to be juicy, a little messy, and a lot flavorful.

In a large bowl, combine all ingredients. Refrigerate for 1 hour before serving. Taste and adjust seasonings as needed.

POTATO & KALE QUESADILLAS

8 SERVINGS

Every culture has some twist on potatoes and cabbage; for the Dutch, it's *boerenkool*—a mix of potatoes and kale, which often comes in cans. Nick ate this throughout his childhood, usually with sausage and as much butter as possible. My mother-in-law still keeps cans of it in her pantry, mostly for my nephews. Here, fresh potatoes and kale fill tortillas for a vegetarian-friendly take on quesadillas. To make it really Dutch, serve with a side of chilled applesauce.

In a frying pan on medium-high heat, place 2 tbsp olive oil. Add onions and sauté for 3 to 4 minutes, until onions begins to soften and become fragrant. Reduce heat to medium-low and cook for 25 to 30 minutes more, or until onions have caramelized and are deeply browned.

Meanwhile, bring a large pot of water to a boil on medium-high heat. Add diced potatoes and cook for 10 to 20 minutes, until tender when pierced with a fork.

Stir chopped kale into pot and cook for 3 minutes more, or until kale begins to become tender. Drain.

Mash potatoes with remainder of olive oil, garlic, and yogurt. Season with nutmeg, cayenne pepper, and salt.

In a nonstick frying pan on medium-high heat, place a tortilla. Place ⅛ of potato mixture on one side of tortilla, then ⅛ of cheese. Top with ⅛ of caramelized onions. Cook for 2 to 4 minutes, fold tortilla over to close, flip to other side, and cook another 2 to 4 minutes, until cheese has melted. Repeat with remainder of tortillas and fillings until used up.

3 tbsp olive oil, divided

1 large onion, diced

4 medium Russet potatoes, peeled and diced

4 packed cups (1 L) finely chopped kale

2 garlic cloves, minced

½ cup (125 mL) plain yogurt

¼ tsp ground nutmeg

¼ tsp cayenne pepper

salt, to taste

8 12-in (30-cm) whole wheat flour tortillas

2 cups (500 mL) shredded Gouda cheese

4 SERVINGS

RICE NOODLE SALAD WITH ALL THE VEGGIES

DRESSING

Makes about ¾ cup (375 mL)

3 tbsp fish sauce

3 tbsp rice vinegar

2 tbsp honey

1 tbsp sambal oelek

1 tbsp sesame oil

1 lime, zest and juice

1 garlic clove, minced

SALAD

10-oz (300-g) rice vermicelli

4 lettuce leaves, sliced into thin ribbons

1 bell pepper, quartered and thinly sliced on the diagonal

1 tomato, quartered and diced

1 celery stalk, thinly sliced

½ English cucumber, quartered and diced

1 beet, peeled, trimmed, and grated

1 carrot, peeled, trimmed, and grated

1 large or 2 small avocados, halved and thinly sliced

4 scallions, finely chopped

½ cup (125 mL) chopped fresh cilantro

4 tsp chopped fresh mint

½ cup (125 mL) peanuts, roasted and roughly chopped

This is my summer super lunch—it's cool, it's healthy, and it uses a little bit of everything, so you can make it with whatever's popping up in your garden. You can sub any of this out for other things—I like to switch the tomato for a mango when the price is right. It's surprisingly filling, but it won't weigh you down; keep your energy up by pairing with a tall glass of iced green tea.

In a jar with a lid, combine dressing ingredients with 2 tbsp water, and shake. Taste and adjust seasonings as needed. Set aside.

In a large bowl, place rice vermicelli. Fill up kettle and let it come to a boil. Pour boiled water over noodles and let sit until softened, 2 or 3 minutes. Drain noodles, them add to bowl of very cold water until cool enough to touch, but not ice cold, 15 to 20 seconds. Drain again, and return noodles to large bowl.

Shake up dressing again, then spoon 2 tbsp over noodles, tossing to coat. Divide noodles between 4 serving bowls.

Place shredded lettuce over noodles. Arrange remainder of veggies around bowl. Sprinkle with scallions, then herbs. Finish with peanuts. Pour remainder of dressing evenly over four bowls.

IN THE DEAD OF WINTER, THIS DRESSING FINDS NEW LIFE AS A SAUCE FOR ROASTED OR STEAMED BROCCOLI, CAULIFLOWER, OR KALE. SIMPLY TOSS COOKED BRASSICAS IN A FEW TABLESPOONS OF DRESSING, AND SERVE SPRINKLED WITH TOASTED SESAME SEEDS. IT WILL LIVEN UP YOUR PLATE AND YOUR MOOD!

ROASTED ALOO GOBI

2 lb (900 g) cauliflower, trimmed and
  chopped into florets

1 lb (500 g) Russet potatoes, diced

2 plum or Roma tomatoes, diced, about
  1 cup (250 mL)

½ cup (125 mL) plain Greek or other
  full-fat yogurt

1 tbsp olive oil

4 garlic cloves, minced

2 tsp sambal oelek

1½ tsp salt

1 tsp minced fresh ginger

1 tsp cumin seeds

1 tsp garam masala

1 tsp ground turmeric

½ tsp ground black pepper

½ tsp yellow mustard seeds

4 scallions, chopped

To be honest, this one requires the potatoes only if you feel like it—you could make it with just cauliflower and it would still be fabulous. But the potatoes make it a bit more filling, and I suppose one cannot live on cauliflower alone. (Says Nick, though he doesn't love cauliflower like I do.) Serve this with rice or Chana Masala (p. 87), a dollop of yogurt, and a squish of fresh lime.

Preheat oven to 400°F (200°C). Grease a 9x13-inch (3.5-L) baking dish.

In a large bowl, combine cauliflower florets, diced potatoes, and tomatoes.

In a small bowl, whisk together yogurt, oil, garlic, sambal oelek, salt, ginger, cumin seeds, garam masala, turmeric, pepper, and mustard seeds. Pour mixture over potatoes and cauliflower, and mix well.

Pour veggie mixture into baking dish and roast for 40 to 50 minutes, until veggies are fork-tender and golden. Stir after about 20 minutes, for even cooking. Sprinkle with chopped scallions just before serving.

Clockwise from left: Roasted Aloo
Gobi, Chana Masala (page 87),
Cucumber Salad (page 179)

4 SERVINGS

ROASTED RADISHES & GARLIC

2 bunches radishes, greens removed

2 tbsp olive oil

1 head garlic, cloves peeled and
    separated

2 tsp chopped fresh parsley

2 tsp fresh lemon juice

pinch of salt

Radishes are the first things out of the garden each year, and I plant an unreasonable number of them. If there's a theme to my life in the garden, it's a lack of expectation: I never assume anything will turn up, so whenever anything does, holy crap. While radishes are lovely raw on sandwiches and in salads, I love them roasted and served with a fat, juicy steak. They're sweet and surprising and, even if you don't grow them yourself, wickedly cheap as a side.

Preheat oven to 425°F (220°C).

Trim each radish, top and bottom, removing roots and tops. Slice in half lengthwise, if radishes are of average radish size, or in quarters if very large.

In an oven-proof frying pan on medium-high heat, sear radishes quickly in olive oil, no more than 1 minute a side. Add whole garlic cloves.

Bake for 15 to 18 minutes, turning radishes and garlic halfway through cooking time, until both sides are deep golden brown.

Toss radishes and garlic with parsley, lemon juice, and salt, and serve immediately.

WHAT SHOULD YOU DO WITH THOSE RADISH GREENS? EAT THEM! RADISH GREENS ARE A GREAT SOURCE OF IRON, VITAMIN C, AND FOLIC ACID. YOU CAN TREAT THEM MUCH THE SAME WAY THAT YOU'D TREAT FRESH SPINACH—WASH THEM, PAT THEM DRY, AND THEN EITHER STEAM (2 MINUTES WITH A BIT OF WINE, STOCK, OR WATER IN A COVERED POT) OR SAUTÉ IN BUTTER WITH GARLIC UNTIL WILTED AND SERVE WITH ROASTED RADISHES. TO STRETCH THIS SIDE DISH, TOSS A BUNCH OF SPINACH, SWISS CHARD, OR KALE INTO THE MIX.

ROASTED TOMATO & GARLIC SOUP

Garlic is the best flavor in the world. And I have no idea how to just eat a little bit of it. Fortunately, I married someone who feels the same way—we could never make out with other people, which is probably for the best. This soup is nice as part of a stinky lunch—pair it with Sardine Panzanella on p. 122 and prepare to enjoy an afternoon alone.

5 medium field tomatoes

3 heads garlic + 3 cloves, peeled

¼ cup (60 mL) olive oil + 2 tbsp

1 tsp coarse salt, or to taste

1 medium onion, diced

2 tsp ground black pepper

1 tsp chili flakes, or to taste

½ tsp dried oregano

4 cups (1 L) vegetable or chicken stock

½ packed cup (125 mL) fresh basil leaves

½ cup packed (125 mL) fresh parsley leaves

olive oil, for garnish

Lightly grease a 9x13-in (3.5-L) pan. Preheat oven to 300°F (150°C).

Quarter tomatoes, and line up in pan. Scatter peeled garlic cloves from 3 heads over pan. Drizzle ¼ cup olive oil over tomatoes and garlic, and sprinkle 1 tsp coarse salt over. Roast for 90 minutes to 2 hours, until tomatoes have withered and garlic is deeply golden. (You can do this in advance; I like to roast a lot of tomatoes and garlic in the fall and stick them in freezer bags for easy weeknight dinners during the winter.)

In a large, heavy-bottomed pot on medium-high, heat 2 tbsp olive oil. Add 3 remaining garlic cloves and onions. Sauté for about 4 minutes until translucent, then add pepper, chili flakes, and oregano, stirring to coat. Add tomatoes and garlic, scraping up any solids to incorporate.

Stir in stock and reduce heat to medium. Simmer for 10 to 15 minutes, until fresh garlic cloves have softened. With an immersion blender or in a stand blender, purée mixture. Be careful when blending hot liquids. Taste and adjust seasonings as needed, then add basil and parsley and purée again. Add water to thin to desired consistency, if needed. Serve drizzled with additional olive oil.

4 SERVINGS

SAVORY FRUIT SALAD

This is the stuff of pregnancy cravings. I ate it every other day while gestating Hunter. It hits every single note—it's sweet, spicy, salty, and just tart enough, and goes perfectly with fried everything (might I recommend Mustard-Fried Chicken? p. 108). If you have a pregnant person in your life, this may just be the thing to win her over for that time you did that thing wrong. (You did. And you may never know what it was.)

DRESSING

1 tbsp soy sauce

1 tbsp rice vinegar

1 tbsp sesame oil

1 tbsp Sriracha sauce

2 tsp honey

1 lime, zest and juice

SALAD

4 cups (1 L) diced seedless
   watermelon

1 English cucumber, diced

2 avocados, diced

1 mango, diced

4 scallions, finely chopped

2 tbsp chopped fresh cilantro

toasted sesame seeds, for garnish

In a small bowl, whisk together all dressing ingredients. Taste and adjust seasonings as needed.

In a large bowl, combine watermelon, cucumber, avocado, mango, scallions, and cilantro. Toss with dressing, and sprinkle with sesame seeds. Serve cold.

SIMPLE GREEN SALAD

I like big, complicated salads, but most of the time at my table, a salad is a thing that goes with other things. Here's my basic recipe for "lightly dressed greens," my simple most-of-the-time side dish. A traditional vinaigrette follows a ratio of 3 parts oil to 1 part acid, but I like the oil scaled back a bit so I can really taste the acidity, especially because this is so plain. Add things, subtract other things—make it to your liking.

In a large bowl, whisk together olive oil, lemon juice or vinegar, mustard, honey, salt, and pepper. Taste it. Does it need anything? Add the thing it needs.

Wash and dry lettuce and chop into ribbons. In bowl with dressing, toss lettuce with herbs. Leave until just before serving, then toss again to coat lettuce and herbs with dressing.

2 tbsp extra-virgin olive oil

1 tbsp lemon juice or red wine vinegar

2 tsp grainy Dijon mustard

½ tsp honey

½ tsp coarse salt

½ tsp ground black pepper

1 head green or red leaf lettuce

½ cup (125 mL) roughly chopped fresh
   soft herbs, such as parsley, dill, mint,
   or basil

STRAWBERRY SALSA

2 cups (500 mL) diced strawberries

1 large avocado, diced

1 large or 2 medium jalapeño peppers, seeded and minced

3 scallions, finely chopped

¼ cup (60 mL) packed fresh cilantro, roughly chopped

1 lime, zest and juice

2 tbsp extra-virgin olive oil

1 tsp freshly ground black pepper

½ tsp sea salt

This goes well with chips. That alone is probably enough for most people, but for the unconvinced, strawberries have that tart, sort of musky quality that tomatoes take on somewhere between August and late September; this makes them a natural substitution where salsa is concerned. If you don't love cilantro, basil is also fabulous here. Serve over chicken, fish, grilled halloumi, or in a bowl on its own with all the chips you can eat.

Place all ingredients in a large bowl. Toss to combine, and let sit for 30 minutes in refrigerator before serving.

THAT KOREAN RESTAURANT SOUP

4-6 SERVINGS

There's a Korean restaurant in Vancouver's West End that serves pork belly and banchan, little dishes of sides and condiments that go with the meat and rice. To start, you get a bowl of soup that's very much like the one below, and while it's good with dinner, it's perfect if you're at home in footie pajamas, fighting a cold. If you can't find gochujang, use Sriracha sauce instead.

In a large, heavy-bottomed pot on medium-high heat, sauté onions in oils until translucent, about 6 minutes. Add garlic and sauté until golden. Add zucchini, tomato paste, and stock or water. (*Note*: If using stock, you may want to lessen amount of soy and fish sauce, especially if stock is very salty. Definitely start with less and add more to taste.)

Add soy sauce, fish sauce, gochujang, and lemon juice. Bring to a gentle boil, then reduce to a simmer. Add tomatoes, tofu, scallions, and seaweed (if using), and simmer for 5 to 10 minutes. Taste and adjust seasonings as needed.

1 medium onion, chopped

1 tbsp canola oil

1 tbsp sesame oil

4 garlic cloves, sliced

2 cups (500 mL) diced zucchini

5.5-oz (156-mL) can tomato paste

6 cups (1.5L) chicken or vegetable
    stock or water

2 tbsp soy sauce

2 tbsp fish sauce

1 to 2 tbsp gochujang sauce

juice of 1 lemon

2 cups (500 mL) diced tomatoes

1 lb (500 g) firm tofu, diced

½ cup (125 mL) chopped scallions

½ cup (125 mL) chopped dried
    seaweed (optional)

salt and pepper, to taste

4-6 SERVINGS

1 medium onion, diced

1 cup (250 mL) diced carrot

1 cup (250 mL) diced celery

1 cup (250 mL) diced sweet potato

5 garlic cloves, minced

2 tbsp olive oil

1 jalapeño pepper, minced

2 tsp ground cumin

1½ tsp chili powder

½ tsp dried oregano

½ tsp ground black pepper

4 cups (1 L) vegetable stock

5.5-oz (156-mL) can tomato paste

28-oz (796-mL) can hominy, rinsed

14-oz (398-mL) can diced tomatoes,
   including juice

14-oz (398-mL) can black beans,
   rinsed

1 cup (250 mL) diced red bell peppers

1 lime, zest and juice

salt, to taste

½ cup (125 mL) chopped cilantro

VEGETARIAN POSOLE

Posole is a Mexican soup traditionally made with pork and hominy, a lye-cured corn used in the cuisines of Mexico and the southern United States. It is delicious and hearty and satisfying. This vegetarian version comes together quickly, for a weekend lunch or the first course of a Latin-inspired dinner party. Follow with Lentil Tacos (p. 92).

In a large pot on medium-high heat, sauté onions, carrots, celery, sweet potatoes, and garlic in olive oil until colors have brightened, 2 to 3 minutes. Add jalapeño, cumin, chili powder, oregano, and pepper, and stir to coat.

Stir in vegetable stock and tomato paste, and bring to a gentle boil. Reduce heat to medium. Simmer for 10 to 15 minutes, until sweet potatoes have softened.

Add hominy, diced tomatoes, black beans, and bell peppers. Stir in lime zest and juice. Taste and adjust seasonings as needed. Just before serving, stir in a handful of cilantro. Sprinkle with additional cilantro for garnish.

VEGGIE STEW WITH DUMPLINGS

6 SERVINGS

This is late summer in a pot, and it's endlessly adaptable to what you have on hand. Keep quantities the same, but feel free to make substitutions for what's in season or in the freezer. If you need to, I suggest subbing the green beans for frozen edamame (ones without shells) or lima beans, and the zucchini for red-skinned potatoes or delicata squash. Serve with a simple green salad dressed with oil and lemon.

In a large, heavy-bottomed pot on medium-high heat, melt butter. When it starts to bubble and foam, add onions, celery, bell and jalapeño peppers, and sauté until colors have brightened, 2 to 3 minutes. Add garlic, paprika, cumin, savory, black pepper, and salt, and cook for another 2 minutes.

Add zucchini, green beans, and corn. Stir to coat in butter and spices. Stir in flour to coat veggies. Add stock. Bring mixture to a boil, then reduce heat to medium.

Meanwhile, prepare dumpling batter. In a medium bowl, combine flour, cornmeal, baking powder, salt, and cheddar cheese. Mix to combine well.

In a separate bowl, whisk together soured milk, oil, and honey. Let both mixtures rest separately until stew has come to a boil.

When heat is reduced to medium, whisk together dry and wet dumpling ingredients. Drop batter by heaping tablespoons directly into stew. Place dumplings so they have room to spread as they cook.

Cover pot with a lid, and cook for 18 to 20 minutes, until dumplings have puffed and spread out over stew, and stew has bubbled up around them. Serve stew and dumplings topped with chopped scallions.

4 tbsp butter

1 onion, diced

2 cups (500 mL) chopped celery (about 4 stalks)

1 red bell pepper, diced

2 jalapeño peppers, seeded and chopped (remove membranes for a milder dish)

3 garlic cloves, minced

2 tsp smoked paprika

2 tsp ground cumin

1 tsp dried savory

1 tsp ground black pepper

1 tsp salt

4 cups (1 L) diced zucchini

2 cups (500 mL) chopped green beans

1 cup (250 mL) fresh or frozen corn kernels

4 tbsp all-purpose flour

4 cups (1 L) vegetable or chicken stock

4 scallions, chopped, for garnish

DUMPLINGS

1 cup (250 mL) all-purpose flour

¾ cup (175 mL) cornmeal

1½ tsp baking powder

½ tsp salt

½ cup (125 mL) grated aged cheddar cheese

1 cup (250 mL) milk + 1 tsp apple cider vinegar

2 tbsp canola oil

1 tsp honey

ZUCCHINI PARMIGIANA SANDWICHES

6-8 SERVINGS

I don't know about you, but every year I end up with a dozen enormous zucchinis. I don't even plant them—people just give them to me—my mom, my mother-in-law, friends who have grown more than they ever imagined would in their tiny community garden plots. Nobody ever plants zucchini and ends up with just a couple. It's not a bad problem to have—it fries up deliciously for sandwiches. These are great with cold beer and are best enjoyed on a patio.

8 buns, such as Kaiser or Calabrese

3 large eggs, beaten

1 tbsp Sriracha or other hot sauce

1 cup (250 mL) bread crumbs

zest of 1 lemon

1 lb (500 g) zucchini, sliced into ½-in (1-cm) rounds (about 24 pieces)

4 tbsp olive oil, for frying

salt, to taste

3 tbsp butter, at room temperature

3 tbsp olive oil

2 garlic cloves, finely minced

1 tsp chili flakes

salt and pepper, to taste

1 cup (250 mL) marinara or Red Sauce (p. 165)

1 cup (250 mL) grated Provolone cheese

2 tomatoes, thinly sliced

16 basil leaves

Slice buns in half horizontally and set aside.

In a large bowl, whisk together eggs and Sriracha.

In a small bowl, combine bread crumbs with lemon zest, and stir to combine.

Dredge zucchini slices first in egg, then in bread crumbs.

In a large pan on medium-high, heat olive oil. Fry breaded zucchini slices until golden, 90 seconds to 2 minutes per side. Place on a plate lined with a paper towel and sprinkle with salt while still hot.

Set oven to broil.

Meanwhile, in a small bowl, combine butter, olive oil, garlic, chili flakes, and salt and pepper. Taste and adjust seasonings as desired. Divide equally between 8 buns, spreading on top half only. Place buns on a large baking sheet.

Place 2 to 3 zucchini slices on other half of each bun. Top with 2 tbsp each marinara sauce and Provolone, and place on same baking sheet as top halves.

Broil 2 to 3 minutes, until cheese has melted and buttered half has turned golden.

Finish each sandwich with fresh tomato slices and basil leaves.

Fruits & Vegetables

FLOUR

My friend Grace made serious notes and plans and prepared a thorough brief for me before our trip to Paris. We had once gone on a weekend trip with friends to British Columbia's Sunshine Coast, and Grace prepared individual duotangs for five people with everything we'd need to know about ferry rides, clam digging, and red tide, so naturally her preparation for a ten-day trip abroad was considerable.

Among her notes on places to go and things to eat were instructions on etiquette, and I recall specifically one point, which I disregarded almost immediately: The French don't eat while walking (or driving, or on the Metro). It would be an embarrassing and obviously touristy move for me to not wait until I was seated somewhere appropriate before cramming food into my face in public. It would be very gauche, and I didn't want the French to think I was gauche. The first day, the day I spent finding my bearings with Grace, I didn't eat and walk; but on the second day, as soon as I stepped out of a boulangerie alone with a bag of still-warm croissants, I broke the rule. I never went back. I have no regrets. I am a tacky tourist with crumbs on my face, and I can't change.

Bread is my thing. It's a vehicle for cheese and meat, my other things, which is why it's so essential to my personal happiness. And it doesn't have to be sliced from a loaf; tortillas, crêpes, dosas, waffles—all of it, I want it, and I don't care that I'd be thinner without it. I'd rather be roly-poly with cinnamon buns than have a thigh gap and no cinnamon buns. Life is short. Mine might be shorter, but it will have been a delicious ride.

I remember my parents saving Folger's coffee tins when I was a kid, and my dad using them to bake cylindrical loaves of homemade bread that we'd spread—still warm—with gobs of butter and my mom's homemade raspberry jam. My parents were busy and it didn't happen often, but when it did I remember wiggling with excitement, the kid version of intoxicated, over the smell of baking bread. The bread, made without the benefit of preservatives, would go stale pretty quickly so we'd have to eat as much of it as we could right away. This was never a problem.

If it's bread, it's going into my face. Anytime my mom bought croutons, especially the flavored ones, I ate them. When I discovered fried bannock and corn syrup at Mr and Mrs White's house when I was about seven years old, life changed irreparably—I learned you could deep-fry dough. There would be no going back to the way things were before. Fried bread and syrup. Forever. Anytime I was at a friend's house and they ordered Crazy Bread with an order of Little Caesar's Pizza (ham and pineapple, if I was lucky!), I ate most of it. When focaccia bread with oil and vinegar was a big thing in restaurants in the late 1990s, I consumed liters of olive oil and balsamic vinegar, spoiling my dinner on the bread basket every single time.

Bread is one of those things that we're all so persnickety about now—think of the gluten, the carbohydrates, the candida! Do we think bread is going to kill us? But what is a bowl of soup without the heel of a crusty loaf to sop up the last dregs of broth too low in the bowl to scrape up with a spoon? Breakfast would be nothing without a piece of buttered toast to dip into a runny, salted egg yolk or two. And a grilled cheese sandwich simply would not exist without two pieces of bread to hold it all together. While bread certainly will add a few pounds to your middle if you eat too much of it (what won't?), it is one of those things that I am not prepared to live without, because it is essential to the ritual of eating. Bread is about culture as much as it is about sustenance, and the joy of eating a

piece of warm wheat bread smeared with melting butter or dragged through olive oil is as important to our health as any nutrient.

Health is bigger than just the sum of calories and vitamins and minerals, and life is about more than the endless pursuit of physical fitness. Like almost everything else, if you ask: Is it good for me? the answer is yes—and also no; it's up to you to find the balance. And if you're on a budget, a bit of bread with dinner can be the difference between wanting more and having enough. The heartier the bread, the better.

If you're really keen and really frugal, you can make your own bread pretty easily. Books and the Internet abound with endless recipes and tips and tricks to make soft sandwich bread, crusty artisan-style bread, sourdough from homemade starter, and everything else you could possibly ever want or need to know about bread making. I make bread *and* I buy it, depending on what I'm doing and how much free time I have. I don't use a bread machine because I don't like spending money on appliances that have a single purpose, and I have so little room to store stuff that baking bread is perhaps less convenient than it could be for me. Lately I've been fermenting a milk kefir-based sourdough bread starter on my kitchen counter, and my apartment smells a bit like a not-very-good brewery; this is inconvenient, but I enjoy it.

Speaking of ferments and sourdough, there is evidence to suggest that sourdough bread is more digestible than regular bread, and that it may not raise blood glucose to the same levels as unfermented wheat breads. Sourdough is the result of a mix of good bacteria and wild yeast; over time, the process of fermentation converts the sugars that occur naturally in flour into lactic acid—that's where the sour part of the sourdough comes from. It's gentler on your gut and definitely tastier in your mouth. Apparently also a source of probiotics, research suggests that sourdough can help you cultivate a healthy microbiome (with regular consumption). Gouda is also probiotic, and you should put the two together. With some butter. In a pan.

But dough need not be sour for bread to be delicious. I like making focaccia, because I never got over the joy of dipping bread in oil, and I like making quick breads and biscuit breads and bannock, which is as good with strawberry jam as it is with corn syrup. One trick I learned somewhere along the way was to substitute a bit of the water in a yeasted bread recipe for a bit of Nick's open beer (he drinks a lot of pilsners and lagers); I'd never use my own, of course, and Nick doesn't always notice that he's been bilked. The beer makes the bread taste breadier, but it doesn't take much—a quarter cup is plenty.

BREAD SOUP

6-8 SERVINGS

I don't break out the good olive oil often, but when I do it's for something simple, like this dish, where the taste of the oil really comes through. This is nice for when it's cold and you just want to be anywhere warm. It's also suitable for a weekend lunch with friends; pair with a loaf of crusty bread and a bit of Lentil Salad (p. 89).

In a large pot on medium-high, heat olive oil. When hot, add garlic and sauté until fragrant and lightly golden, about 2 minutes.

Meanwhile, whizz bread cubes in a food processor or blender until they resemble coarse crumbs. Don't grind bread too finely, or you'll end up with a boring texture—and no one wants that.

Add bread crumbs to oil, and stir to coat. Immediately begin squishing tomatoes into mix, adding juice quickly and scraping bottom of pot to ensure nothing burns. Stir in wine and stock. Reduce heat to medium and simmer, uncovered, for 30 minutes.

Add beans, cheese, parsley, lemon zest, and pepper. Taste and adjust seasonings as needed. Simmer an additional 5 minutes, until parsley has wilted and soup smells magnificent. Serve drizzled with a little bit more olive oil.

¼ cup (60 mL) extra-virgin olive oil

5 garlic cloves, roughly chopped

½ lb (500 g) stale bread, cubed and toasted (about 4 thick slices)

2 28-oz (796-mL) cans whole tomatoes, juice reserved

½ cup (125 mL) red wine

4 cups (1 L) chicken stock

19-oz (540-mL) can cannellini beans

½ cup (125 mL) grated Parmesan cheese

½ cup (125 mL) chopped fresh parsley

1 tbsp lemon zest

1 tsp ground black pepper

salt, to taste

FERGAZZA BREAD ~WITH~ GARLIC SCAPES

1 LOAF

1 cup (250 mL) lukewarm water

1 tbsp granulated sugar

1 tsp yeast

3 cups (750 mL) all-purpose flour + additional for kneading

¼ cup (60 mL) beer

4 tbsp extra-virgin olive oil, divided

1½ tsp coarse salt

1 tsp dried oregano

½ tsp ground black pepper

1 tbsp sambal oelek, Sriracha sauce, or other chili paste or hot sauce

1 garlic clove, minced

½ cup (125 mL) garlic scapes, chopped

½ lb (250 g) cubed aged cheddar cheese

additional coarse salt, to sprinkle over loaf

This bread is the best. It's pretty, it's cheesy, it's garlicky—there is nothing that's not completely delightful about it. And as far as I can tell, it's a regional specialty—I've never seen it anywhere but here on the west coast of Canada. It's not fougasse; it's unique. I have eaten it my whole life, usually greedily. If you can't get garlic scapes, use scallions and add another garlic clove.

In a small bowl, combine water with sugar and yeast and let rest for 5 minutes, until yeast is foamy.

In a large bowl, combine flour with yeast mixture, beer, 1 tbsp olive oil, salt, oregano, and pepper. Mix until a shaggy dough forms, then knead for 8 minutes or until dough is smooth and stretchy. Form dough into a ball. Place into a greased bowl, cover with greased plastic wrap and a dishtowel, and let rest in a warm, draft-free place until doubled in size, about 2 hours.

In a small bowl, mix 2 tbsp olive oil with sambal oelek and garlic.

Once dough has risen, spread out over a clean, floured surface. Using a rolling pin, roll it to about 10 x 14 in (25 x 35 cm). Paint oil-sambal mixture over dough, leaving about ½ in (1 cm) around edges. Sprinkle with garlic scapes and scatter with cheese cubes. Form as tight and firm a roll as you can.

Fold edges of roll under, then place into a greased 9 x 5-in (2-L) loaf pan. Cover again, and let rise another 1 to 1½ hours.

Preheat oven to 350°F (180°C).

Using a sharp knife, cut slits into top of loaf. Paint top of loaf with remainder of olive oil, and sprinkle with additional coarse salt. Bake for 45 to 50 minutes. Check bread halfway through baking—turn pan, and if loaf is browning too quickly, cover with foil.

Remove loaf from pan and cool on a rack for at least 1 hour before serving.

Rice & Blueberry Muffins
(page 221)

1
LOAF

FOCACCIA BREAD

1 ½ lb (750 g) Yukon Gold potatoes,
   peeled and quartered

½ tsp sugar

2 ¼ tsp active dry yeast (or 1 packet)

4 cups (1 L) + ¼ cup (60 mL) flour,
   divided

1 tbsp + 1 tsp dried basil

1 tsp ground black pepper

1 tbsp + ¼ tsp coarse salt, divided

½ cup (125 mL) extra-virgin olive oil,
   divided

4 garlic cloves, roughly chopped

½ cup (125 mL) finely grated
   Parmesan cheese

This was one of the first recipes I ever wrote, and I was so pleased with myself at how it turned out. It's a very basic focaccia bread, and you can tweak the recipe with different herbs or cheese or by topping with tomatoes, grapes, plums—anything you've got that goes well with garlic and cheese. I guess you could sub out the garlic, but that would be no way to live.

In a small pot of salted water on medium-high, simmer potatoes, uncovered, until just tender, about 10 minutes. Drain 1 cup (250 mL) cooking water into a measuring cup and set aside. Cool potatoes slightly, then mash until smooth.

Once potato cooking water has cooled to lukewarm, add sugar. Sprinkle yeast over mixture and let stand until foamy, about 5 minutes.

Measure out 4 cups (1 L) flour into a large bowl. Add 1 tbsp basil, pepper, and 1 tbsp salt. Add mashed potatoes and oil, then pour in yeast mixture. Mix until dough is very soft and sticky.

Drop dough onto a floured surface to begin the awesome task of kneading. This is my favorite part of bread-making, and it's particularly delightful with this bread because of the aroma of basil and olive oil. Knead until dough is quite elastic, about 8 to 10 minutes. If you have a stand mixer with a dough hook, you can probably get away with 5 minutes in the mixer, maybe less, depending on the machine.

Scrape dough into a lightly oiled large bowl and cover bowl with oiled plastic wrap. Let dough rise in a draft-free place at warm room temperature until doubled, 2 to 2 ½ hours.

Generously oil a 9 x 13-in (3.5-L) baking pan.

Punch down dough (do not knead) and transfer to baking pan, then gently stretch to cover as much of bottom as possible (dough may not fit exactly). Cover dough with oiled plastic wrap and a kitchen towel and let rise in a draft-free place at warm room temperature until doubled, 1 to 1½ hours.

Preheat oven to 375°F (190°C).

Sprinkle dough with remainder of basil, chopped garlic, cheese, and ¼ tsp salt, and drizzle with ¼ cup (60 mL) oil.

Bake until center is firm and top and underside golden (lift to check), 25 to 30 minutes. Loosen focaccia from pan with a spatula and slide onto a rack to cool. This bread is best when cooled completely and re-warmed for 10 minutes in oven before serving. Cut into pieces, and serve with olive oil and vinegar, for dipping.

GRANDPA'S RADIO PUDDING

Grandpa, my dad's father, was a war vet, a proud Canadian, and probably the only good dancer in the gene pool—when we visited him in the hospital after his hip replacement, he was already eager to get back to dancing at the Legion. When Grandpa poured the drinks, the Coke was just for color. He enjoyed food as much as he enjoyed a good drink, and this was his signature dessert. It's called Radio Pudding because he heard the recipe on the radio. No further details were ever given, so the recipe is as good as his.

Preheat oven to 350°F (180°C).

In a 1½ qt/L casserole or baking dish, whisk together flour, salt, cocoa, baking powder, sugar, and nuts or chocolate chips. Stir in milk, butter, and vanilla.

In a separate bowl, mix cocoa, brown sugar, and 1¾ cups (375 mL) boiling water. Pour over cake mixture. Do not stir.

Bake for 1 hour. Serve hot with ice cream or whipped cream.

4 SERVINGS

CAKE

1 cup (250 mL) all-purpose flour

½ tsp salt

1 tbsp cocoa powder

2 tsp baking powder

½ cup (125 mL) granulated sugar

½ cup (125 mL) chopped nuts (or chocolate chips)

½ cup (125 mL) milk

2 tsp melted butter

1 tsp vanilla extract

SAUCE

4 tbsp cocoa powder

½ cup (125 mL) brown sugar

HORSES' ARSES

12 BUNS

I am not sure where this recipe originated—I don't know how far back it goes. Cuddles used to make these, and Grandpa called them Horses' Arses because, well, I guess if you've seen the back end of a horse, this is kind of what they look like. I don't know. Horses are terrifying, and I don't like getting too close to them. These simple cinnamon buns are fantastic served at breakfast or brunch. I like them on Christmas morning, with a lot of Bailey's in my tea.

2 cups (500 mL) all-purpose flour

½ tsp salt

4 tsp baking powder

½ tsp cream of tartar

2 tbsp granulated sugar

½ cup (125 mL) cold butter

⅔ cup (160 mL) milk

¼ cup (60 mL) butter, melted

1 cup (250 mL) brown sugar

1 tbsp ground cinnamon

Preheat oven to 425°F (220°C). Grease a 9x9-in (2.5-L) baking dish.

In a large bowl, whisk together flour, salt, baking powder, cream of tartar, and sugar. Drop butter into mix in hunks, and gently work it into dry ingredients. Like many doughs, it's best if butter isn't thoroughly combined—you want mixture to resemble coarse crumbs with a few chickpea-sized pieces of butter.

Stir in milk. Turn out onto a floured surface and gently knead dough for about 30 seconds, until it's soft and no longer falls apart or is sticky. Using a rolling pin, roll to about ¼ in (6 mm) thick.

Brush melted butter over rolled dough, leaving about ½ in (1 cm) around edges. Sprinkle brown sugar over dough and press it down so it's not loose. Sprinkle with cinnamon.

Roll dough tightly lengthwise, like a jelly roll. Cut into slices about 1 in (2.5 cm) thick to make 12 buns. Place close together in a prepared baking dish. It's okay if they touch.

Bake for 15 to 20 minutes, until golden and melty and fluffy. Serve fresh from pan with cold milk or hot tea or coffee.

NATHAN'S ROLLKUCHEN

- 2–4 cups (500 mL–1 L) canola oil
- 3¾ cups (925 mL) all-purpose flour, divided
- 1 tsp baking powder
- 1 tsp salt
- 3 eggs, beaten
- 1 cup (250 mL) heavy cream
- 1 large watermelon

Rollkuchen is my brother-in-law Nathan's signature dish. Made from his family's recipe, it's basically a meal of fried dough and watermelon. I know it sounds kind of weird, but it's surprisingly cohesive and sort of genius. We usually luck out and get to have this once each year, usually around pickling season (we pickle together); there's no more refreshing lunch on a sweltering hot day. I bet it would be even better eaten outside. Serve with a dry apple cider or light, cold beer.

In a large, heavy pan, such as a cast-iron frying pan, heat ½ in (1 cm) oil to 375°F (190°C).

In a large bowl, whisk together 3½ cups (830 mL) flour, baking powder, and salt. Add eggs and cream, and stir to form a soft dough.

Spread remainder of flour on work surface. Roll dough out to about ¼ in (6 mm) thick. Cut into strips about 2 in (5 cm) wide by 4 in (10 cm) long, and stab a slit into each slice.

In hot oil, fry each slice until golden on one side, about 2 minutes, then flip and achieve goldenness on the other side. Drain on paper towels, then serve hot with thick slices of cold watermelon.

PEANUT BUTTER BACON FAT COOKIES

2 DOZEN

Never discard your bacon fat—the slightly smoky, porky taste of the fat makes peanut butter taste peanut-butterier. Bacon fat is not substantially different, calorically, from butter, though if you have high cholesterol or are trying to cut back on your sodium, make this a special-occasion cookie.

½ cup (125 mL) bacon fat

½ cup (125 mL) peanut butter

1 cup (250 mL) light brown sugar

1 egg

1½ (375 mL) cups whole wheat pastry flour

1 tsp baking soda

pinch salt

Preheat oven to 350°F (180°C).

In a large bowl, cream bacon fat, peanut butter, and sugar so that color of mixture lightens and texture becomes creamy. Once it's there, add egg, and keep beating.

In a separate bowl, combine flour, baking soda, and salt. Mix to combine well, then slowly add to peanut butter mixture, beating until all ingredients are combined well.

Roll dough into balls about 1 in (2.5 cm) in diameter. Place about 1 in apart on a cookie sheet, and press tops down with a fork dipped in granulated sugar.

Bake for 8 to 10 minutes, and cool for at least 10 minutes on a wire rack before eating.

Why whole wheat pastry flour?

PASTRY FLOUR PRODUCES CAKES AND MUFFINS WITH A MORE TENDER CRUMB THAN ALL-PURPOSE FLOUR BECAUSE IT CONTAINS LESS PROTEIN, WHICH PRODUCES LESS GLUTEN IN THE DOUGH OR BATTER. SINCE ORDINARY WHOLE WHEAT FLOUR CAN MAKE BAKED GOODS HEAVY AND DENSE, SUBSTITUTING WHOLE WHEAT *PASTRY* FLOUR GIVES YOU THE HEALTH AND FLAVOR BENEFITS OF WHEAT BRAN WITH THE BETTER TEXTURE THAT YOU GET FROM PASTRY FLOUR.

12
MUFFINS

1 ½ cups (375 mL) whole wheat pastry
   flour

1 tsp baking soda

1 tsp baking powder

½ tsp salt

1 cup (250 mL) mashed ripe bananas
   (2 or 3 medium)

½ cup (125 mL) peanut butter

½ cup (125 mL) brown sugar

3 tbsp cocoa powder

1 tsp vanilla extract

1 egg

¼ cup (60 mL) canola oil

1 cup (250 mL) semi-sweet chocolate
   chips

½ cup (125 mL) sunflower seeds

1 tbsp ground flax seeds

PEANUT BUTTER CHOCOLATE CHIP BANANA MUFFINS

With his top three flavors represented, these are Hunter's favorite muffins. They're an easy way to use up any bananas going brown on the counter; whatever you lack in bananas, feel free to make up for with applesauce. You may find grabby little paws swiping them off the counter as they cool.

Preheat oven to 375°F (190°C). Grease a muffin tin, or fill with 12 paper liners.

In a large bowl, combine flour, baking soda, baking powder, and salt. Set aside.

In another larger bowl, mix bananas, peanut butter, sugar, cocoa powder, vanilla extract, egg, and oil until thoroughly combined. Stir in chocolate chips, sunflower seeds, and flax seeds. Mix well.

Stir dry ingredients into wet ingredients and mix until just combined.

Spoon into prepared muffin tin. Bake for 15 to 20 minutes, until a toothpick inserted into center of muffin comes out clean.

Remove from oven and cool in pan for 5 minutes before turning muffins out onto a wire rack to cool.

RICE & BLUEBERRY MUFFINS

12 MUFFINS

When you end up with an annoying, not dinnerable amount of leftover rice, do not throw it out! Fold it into some muffin batter and squeeze every last drop of usefulness out of it. These muffins are sweet and bright-tasting and, mercifully, Toddler-approved.

Preheat oven to 400°F (200°C).

In a large bowl, combine flours, baking powder, salt, and sugar. Stir until combined. Add berries, rice and orange zest and juice and mix well.

In a measuring cup, add oil and yogurt, and if cup is big enough, milk.

In a small bowl, beat eggs. Add both to dry ingredients, one after the other, and stir to combine well. It makes a thick, dense batter, so if you're hand-mixing this, as I did, be vigorous. You don't want to find floury bits at the bottom of bowl.

Grease a muffin pan or line pan with paper liners. Fill cups with batter to top.

Bake for 20 to 25 minutes, until a toothpick inserted into the center of a muffin comes out clean. Let sit for 5 minutes before turning out onto a cooling rack.

1 ½ cups (375 mL) all-purpose flour

½ cup (125 mL) whole wheat flour

1 tbsp baking powder

½ tsp salt

⅓ cup (80 mL) packed dark brown sugar

1 cup (250 mL) fresh or frozen blueberries

1 cup (250 mL) cooked rice or other grains

1 small navel orange, zest and juice

¼ cup (60 mL) canola oil

1 ½ cups (375 mL) yogurt

½ cup (125 mL) milk

2 eggs, beaten

4-6 SERVINGS

SKILLET CORN BREAD ~WITH~ BLUEBERRIES

⅔ cup (80 mL) all-purpose flour

⅔ cup (80 mL) cornmeal

½ tsp baking soda

½ tsp coarse salt

½ tsp ground black pepper

1 cup (250 mL) buttermilk

2 tbsp canola oil

2 tbsp honey

1 egg, beaten

1 cup (250 mL) frozen blueberries

Corn bread is different things to different meals, and while I love it with a bowl of chili (p. 96), it's also pretty great on its own for breakfast, with butter and honey. The recipe calls for blueberries, but it works well with blackberries too. Serve with barbecued meats, chili, or anything that's a little smoky and a little sweet.

Preheat oven to 375°F (190°C). Place a 9-in (23-cm) cast-iron pan in oven to heat.

In a medium bowl, whisk together flour, cornmeal, baking soda, salt, and pepper.

In another bowl, whisk together buttermilk, oil, honey, and egg.

When oven reaches temperature, pull out pan and spray with oil to lightly grease. Quickly whisk together wet and dry ingredients. Fold in blueberries, then pour mixture into pan.

Bake for 20 to 25 minutes, until a toothpick inserted into center comes out clean. Let cool for 15 minutes before cutting into slices.

SPAGHETTI SQUASH MUFFINS

2
DOZEN

Hunter is picky, but he'll eat muffins. So I bake muffins every two weeks and load them up with nutritious stuff and send them off with him to daycare, where I am assured that he eats them very happily. These make use of the abundance of spaghetti squash I find myself saddled with each year. If you don't have quite enough squash, you can make up the difference with applesauce. These muffins freeze well.

Preheat oven to 350°F (180°C). If you have 2 muffin pans, you are very lucky—grease them both, or line cups with whatever kind of liner you like.

In a large bowl, combine flours, oats, sugars, flax seeds, baking soda, spices, and salt to mix well.

In another bowl, mix squash, oil, eggs, and vanilla extract. Fold into dry ingredients until just moistened. Add walnuts and fold again.

Spoon batter into muffin tins until each muffin cup is about ¾ full.

Bake for 18 to 20 minutes, until a toothpick inserted in center comes out clean. Let cool for 5 minutes in pan before turning out onto a wire rack to cool completely.

2 cups (500 mL) whole wheat pastry flour

1 cup (250 mL) all-purpose flour

1 cup (250 mL) rolled oats (not instant or quick-cooking)

1 cup (250 mL) granulated sugar

1 cup (250 mL) dark brown sugar

1 tbsp ground flax seeds

2 tsp baking soda

2 tsp ground cinnamon

½ tsp ground ginger

½ tsp ground cloves

¼ tsp ground nutmeg

½ tsp salt

1½ cups (375 mL) cooked and drained spaghetti squash

1 cup (250 mL) canola oil

4 large eggs, beaten

1 tsp vanilla extract

1 cup (250 mL) chopped walnuts

YOU CAN COOK THE SQUASH WHOLE IN A 400°F (200°C) OVEN UNTIL IT'S SOFT, ABOUT 40 TO 50 MINUTES. OR, YOU CAN MICROWAVE IT, WHICH IS FASTER—CUT IT IN HALF, PLACE IN A DISH CUT-SIDE DOWN, AND ZAP FOR 6 TO 8 MINUTES ON HIGH, THEN LET IT COOL FOR A MOMENT. SCOOP OUT AND DISCARD SEEDS. WITH A FORK, SCRAPE FLESH INTO A COLANDER SET IN SINK; DRAIN FOR ABOUT 15 MINUTES, UNTIL COOL ENOUGH TO WORK WITH.

16
SCONES

4 cups (1 L) all-purpose flour

½ cup (125 mL) granulated sugar

1 tbsp baking powder

½ tsp salt

¾ cup (175 mL) cold butter, cubed into whatever size you can squeeze comfortably with fingers

2 large eggs

1 cup (250 mL) cold milk

1 tsp pure vanilla extract

GLAZE

1 cup (250 mL) confectioner's sugar

3–4 tbsp milk

½ vanilla bean or ½ tsp vanilla extract

VANILLA SCONES

These scones are the result of a tantrum I keep having, wherein I have no other options, am starving, and have to buy a pastry from Starbucks to get me through the morning. *Starbucks, why are your pastries always so stale?* Like, every single time. Every single one. Also, they cost way too much. And because I can't abide a stale or overpriced scone, I made these. They're good with tea or strong coffee, and maybe jam, preferably on a weekend morning.

Preheat oven to 400°F (200°C).

In a large bowl, combine flour, sugar, baking powder, and salt. Squish in cubes of butter, the way you would if you were making pie crust. You don't want to crumble the butter into nothing—think of peas, and let butter hunks remain about that size, no smaller. The texture depends on it.

In a separate bowl, beat eggs. Add milk and vanilla. Stir liquid into butter-flour mix, and press gently to form a dough. When dough is a single mass that holds together well, turn out onto a floured surface and cut into 4 equal pieces. Form rounds and cut each quarter further into 4 pieces, making 16 scones in total.

Bake on an ungreased cookie sheet for 15 to 18 minutes. If using 2 pans to bake, rotate them at halfway point. Cool scones on wire racks before glazing.

Meanwhile, combine sugar, milk, and vanilla bean. (You can use entire bean, but scones won't be as pretty a color.)

With a basting brush, paint cooled scones with glaze, which should form a runny, spreadable paste, like Elmer's school glue (and did you know that stuff used to have a minty sort of flavor? It doesn't anymore). Let glaze dry for about 1 hour before serving.

SUGAR

Is there any ingredient more maligned than sugar? We're cautioned to avoid it, and yet it's insidious—try buying a snack food or packaged meal that's not brimming with sugar or mutant high-fructose sweeteners. Even the sugar-free stuff is terrible; it's loaded with artificial sweeteners, which have been shown to negatively affect insulin levels and have metabolic side effects as well. Some artificial sweeteners even have undesirable digestive drawbacks—let's just say it's not very romantic how every year Nick forgets that his sugar-free Valentine's Day chocolate is sweetened with maltitol and then eats too much of it. Oh, how we laugh. Well, I laugh.

The problem with sugar is not its mere existence, but the amount of it that we eat. Sugar exists naturally in many foods, including fruit, vegetables, grains, and milk, and we need sugar in our blood in order to fuel our bodies. Sugar is a problem when we consume too much of it. It's most obvious side effect is weight gain, and studies have shown that in high schools, the availability of sugar-sweetened beverages such as pop and juice improved students' odds of being obese. A diet filled with sugary foods is calorically dense but nutritionally lacking—by replacing whole, healthy foods with sugary processed foods, we can deprive our bodies of essential vitamins and nutrients. In other words, if you fill up on junk, you'll have no room for, like, salad. While sugar isn't the culprit in diseases such as cancer, heart disease, or autoimmune disorders, it may be an accomplice—a tasty one, but definitely something to watch out for.

Of course, if you want to avoid excess sugar (or salt, or anything, really), you need to avoid processed, packaged foods. Cooking for yourself is the best way to monitor your sugar intake.

Recently, many people have been looking to alternative sweeteners to provide the sweetness they crave without having to rely on refined sugars. When Nick was first diagnosed with type 1 diabetes in 2010, I spent a small fortune on things like stevia—a natural calorie-free sweetener with an aftertaste like too much baking soda—and low-glycemic index (low-GI) sweeteners like maple syrup, coconut sugar, raw agave syrup, and brown rice syrup. In hindsight, I realized that anytime you have to buy something sold exclusively at Whole Foods, you should maybe consider whether that's something your budget can sustain long-term.

According to the Canadian Diabetes Association, "the glycemic index is a scale that ranks carbohydrate-rich foods by how much they raise blood glucose (sugar) levels compared to a standard food." A low-GI sweetener is one that will raise blood sugar levels more slowly, without the sharp rise and drop that accompanies cane (or beet) sugar. For people with diabetes, prolonged or frequent bouts of high blood sugar are problematic because glucose sticks to red blood cells, which causes problems with the circulatory system, resulting in damage to the eyes, kidneys, and feet. In extreme cases, this can result in blindness, kidney disease, and ulcers and infections of the feet, which can necessitate amputation.

Unfortunately, the trouble with low-GI sweeteners is that they are still sweeteners, and the way that we use sweeteners tends to be in conjunction with carbohydrate-rich foods. So, it's not the sweetener that's the issue; your stomach can't tell the difference between a cinnamon bun sweetened with coconut sugar versus one sweetened with regular sugar. Your body treats a cinnamon bun the same no matter how expensive or trendy the ingredients. It's a bit of a bummer, but also tremendously freeing—it's one less thing to have to think about, you know?

Alternative sweeteners can contain more nutrients than regular old white sugar, so if you still want to use them there's no nutrition-based reason not to. As with all sweeteners, either use them sparingly or abundantly but less often. And remember:

just because you sweeten it with maple syrup or coconut sugar or whatever does not mean it's sugar free. You can't fool your belly. Trust me. (Sigh.)

Sugar has other problems aside from being a pain in the ass for those of us feeding diabetics and/or trying not to gain quite so much weight, and these are, I think, far more relevant to most people.

The market value of sugar can fluctuate wildly, especially when faced with decreased consumer demand. Increasing global preferences for sugar alternatives such as corn-based sweeteners like high-fructose corn syrup and sugar-free sweeteners has had a detrimental effect on the global value of sugar crops. Sugarcane tends to grow in places where the economy does not favor people who work in agriculture. As a result, sugarcane farmers can have a difficult time earning a living wage from their crops. This means that they, in turn, cannot afford to pay a living wage to the people they employ, and so cheap labor becomes the means through which sugarcane is harvested. In many places, cheap labor means child labor.

Sugar production falls under World Vision Canada's 3D jobs—work that is dirty, dangerous, or degrading. Children as young as six years old are employed in agricultural jobs that include sugarcane farming and harvesting. Sugarcane can grow up to seven yards (or meters) in height, and is harvested via machete, but not before the fields are set ablaze in order to make it easier to chop the stalks down. In El Salvador, I heard stories of kids and families getting trapped in the sugarcane fields, with no warning that the fields would soon be on fire. It's hard, horrible work; it's dangerous, keeps young

kids out of school, and doesn't pay enough to lift anyone out of the cycle of poverty. Families working in low-paying jobs with intense demands on their time, health, and fitness find themselves trapped, generation after generation, in a system of poverty from which they cannot easily escape.

One solution is to always buy Fairtrade sugar. According to the Fairtrade Canada website (*fairtrade.ca*, and see p. 245), farmers who produce Fairtrade certified sugar are guaranteed a minimum price that covers the costs of sustainable production, as well as a premium to invest in social and economic initiatives in their communities. Fairtrade products will cost you a little more, but you can often save a few dollars if you buy them online.

Another option is to find out where domestically packaged sugar comes from. In Canada, most of our sugar comes from Lantic (Rogers) Sugar. While the Vancouver plant packages cane sugar, most of the other sites in Canada package Canadian-grown sugar from beets. Sugar that comes from cane and beets is pretty much the same once it's been refined down into its most commonly used forms. Sugar beets are grown primarily in Alberta. Check the product packaging to determine where sugar comes from and whether it's from sugarcane or beets.

The drawback to using North American beet sugar is that sugar beets are a GMO (genetically modified organism) crop developed to be pesticide-resistant. There are well-reasoned arguments on both sides of the GMO debate, and depending upon your position on the issue, choosing beet over cane sugar can be either a no-brainer, or the lesser of two evils. My position on this continues to evolve, but for now I'm hesitant to accept GMO ingredients if there's a non-GMO alternative in another product.

My preference is for Fairtrade sugar whenever possible, and organic in a pinch. I'll use Canadian beet sugar on occasion as well, because while my ethics around human rights tend to trump price, occasionally price trumps my position on GMOs. That said, I don't have to spend too much on sugar as we don't use much of it—Nick has type 1 diabetes so he can't eat sugary stuff anyway, and I'm not baking a ton just to have to eat it all myself. (Not that I wouldn't, of course … but I shouldn't.) I also use honey, maple syrup, and fruit purées to sweeten some recipes, especially when sugar does not play a critical role in the structural integrity of the finished product.

I love dessert and sugar and carbs (and glazing carbs with sugar), but in the interest of saving money and preserving Nick's feet, I don't make a lot of sweets. So when I do, it's special. Most of the time, I make dessert because we're having company, so many of the recipes in this chapter will be designed to be shared between four or more people. There's something wonderful about finishing a homemade meal for friends with a simple, elegant little sweet. Love is all about a little sweetness, after all.

4-6
SERVINGS

½ cup (125 mL) brown sugar

2 tbsp tapioca starch

2 cups (500 mL) heavy cream

½ cup (125 mL) whole milk

2 tsp rum (preferably dark)

1 tsp vanilla extract

⅛ tsp salt

1½ cups (375 mL) pitted, chopped
    fresh cherries

½ cup (125 mL) semi-sweet chocolate
    chips, finely chopped

BLACK FOREST ICE CREAM

On a budget, a rich, custard-based ice cream can be a bit daunting—it uses up a lot of eggs. Which is why when Mark Bittman's recipe for cornstarch ice cream showed up in the *New York Times* in 2007, frugal home cooks everywhere embraced the idea wholeheartedly. The concept worked well, but there was room for improvement. My friend Grace figured out that the texture could be richer if she used tapioca starch instead of cornstarch. This adaptation has a nicer mouthfeel, a bit more reminiscent of an egg-custard version. Another benefit of tapioca starch? It's about a third of the price of cornstarch—check the international section of the supermarket.

In a heavy-bottomed saucepan on medium heat, whisk together sugar and tapioca starch until well-combined. Add cream, milk, and rum and cook, whisking frequently, until it comes to a boil. Reduce heat to low and cook, continuing to whisk, until thickened, about 7 minutes. Add vanilla extract and salt, whisk again, and pour into a bowl to chill in refrigerator until cool, about 60 minutes.

Prepare ice cream maker. Put tapioca mixture, cherries, and chocolate chips into basin of machine, and churn according to manufacturer's instructions. Spoon into a container, cover, and freeze for at least 4 hours. Let ice cream rest at room temperature for about 10 minutes after removing from freezer and before serving.

BLUEBERRY CRISP

4-6
SERVINGS

I feel very strongly that a dessert should not contain things like oats if at all possible. It's dessert, and dessert is no time to be thinking about soluble fiber. (If you're like me, you're already thinking of it most of the time anyway!) You can use fresh or frozen blueberries with this—it's a great, fast, and easy year-round dessert. I use whole wheat flour; all-purpose is fine, but I like the deeper flavor that whole wheat gives. Serve warm with ice cream topping.

1 tbsp cornstarch

½ tsp salt, divided

2 tbsp maple syrup

zest of 1 lemon + 2 tsp juice

4–5 cups (1–1.25 L) fresh or frozen
   blueberries

1 cup (250 mL) whole wheat flour

1 cup (250 mL) brown sugar

½ cup (125 mL) room temperature
   butter

½ tsp ground cinnamon

Lightly grease a 1½ qt/L baking dish. Preheat oven to 375°F (190°C).

In a small bowl, create a slurry out of cornstarch, ¼ tsp salt, maple syrup, and lemon zest and juice, then pour over blueberries and toss to coat. Put blueberries in baking dish.

In a medium bowl, combine flour, sugar, ¼ tsp salt, butter, and cinnamon, and crumble with your fingers to create a lumpy, streusel-looking mixture. Cover blueberries with flour mixture, pressing down gently to ensure crumble stays put.

Bake for 35 to 40 minutes, or until top is crisp and golden and blueberry goo is bubbling up sides.

4 SERVINGS

1½ lb (750 g) Coronation or concord grapes

½ cup (125 mL) brown sugar

½ cup (125 mL) white granulated sugar

1 lemon, zest and juice

CORONATION GRAPE GRANITA

This is a dish we make in September when Coronation grapes, related to concord grapes, make their brief appearance in our local markets. They are delicate and fleeting, and when they arrive, it is too hot to make jam of them, but this captures their essence simply and efficiently.

Pluck grapes from stems, and plop them into a pot on stove. Add sugars and 1½ cups (375 mL) water, and simmer on medium-high heat until grapes are soft and liquid is purple and dark, about 10 minutes. Add lemon zest and juice.

Remove from heat and mash grape mixture with a potato masher. Squeeze through a fine-mesh sieve into a 9 x 13-in (3.5-L) glass baking dish, and put into freezer.

Every hour for the first 3 hours, pull juice out of freezer and scrape with a fork to move ice crystals around, fluffing them up a bit. After 3 hours, just check in every so often, scraping and fluffing ice as needed. Freeze for about 4 hours in total. Remove from freezer about 10 minutes before serving, and scrape with a spoon into serving dishes. Serve as is or topped with whipped cream.

Grandpa's Radio Pudding
(page 214); left: Cuddles'
Brown Sugar Shortbread
(page 234)

4 DOZEN

CUDDLES' BROWN SUGAR SHORTBREAD

1 lb (500 g) room temperature butter

1 cup (250 mL) brown sugar

4 cups (1 L) all-purpose flour

This shortbread is pure and simple, and it achieves that sandy, perfect shortbread texture without cheats like rice flour or cornstarch. To make these, it's best to have a good, strong mixer, as you're going to need to beat the hell out of them. They are best served with cold granita (p. 232 and p. 239) and warm orange pekoe tea.

Preheat oven to 325°F (160°C).

In bowl of a stand mixer on medium speed, beat butter and brown sugar together until fluffy. Scrape down sides of bowl, then turn up speed to medium-high and beat mixture for 30 minutes, scraping sides of bowl down occasionally.

Add flour and beat until just combined.

On a lightly floured surface, roll dough to about ¼ in (6 mm) thick. Cut dough into rectangles about 2½ in (6.35 cm) long, and poke each slice twice with the tines of a fork.

Place on a baking sheet about 1 in (2.5 cm) apart. Bake for 18 to 20 minutes, until cookies have only just begun to brown and are firm and crumbly but pale.

Cool completely on a wire rack before eating.

I called my grandmother Cuddles, a name she chose for herself because she didn't see herself as "Grandma." Everything about her was colorful, and while "cuddly" wasn't a word you could use to accurately describe her, she was right—she wasn't "Grandma." She transcended Grandma. She was something else.

For reasons I'm not sure I'll ever really understand, the women in my family can be a bit proprietary about their recipes—a recipe is something you own, that you hold onto and keep to yourself and take to your grave. Maybe it's generational or it's just nice to have something that's all yours, a secret, a domain you can be the master of. I'm an over-sharer with a food blog, so this is something I don't really understand.

Everyone who tasted Cuddles' shortbread knew it was the best. The magic was in the method, and it didn't matter if you knew that it was just butter, sugar, and flour; that alone wouldn't get you where you needed to go. Good shortbread is all technique.

My mom wanted to know how to make it, and Cuddles would lead her on: "We'll make it next time you come over," she'd say, and when my mom would show up with the ingredients, it would already be made, or it wouldn't be the right time. One curious thing about this proprietorship over recipes is that it was inconsistent; my mom couldn't have the short-bread recipe, but I could. Maybe Cuddles thought her secret was safe with me. Maybe she just thought she was funny.

And she was funny, with a dark sense of humor and a sharp wit. She was my elder, but she never felt like an authority figure. She was wise, and I would listen to her, but I never felt like she spoke down to me. When I'd say something stupid or show up wearing whatever was stylishly inap-propriate at the time, all she'd say was "Oh, Emily...no."

I'd visit her on Fridays after class, and we'd sit at her table drinking fruity cocktails and eating cheezies, talking and gossiping long into the night. And she would let me in on things, because a secret is only really fun if you can share it with someone; a secret for two is a conspiracy, and much more glamorous. For most of her years with my grandfather, she'd written her recipes down in a book, she said. And oh, when she died— they'd want it, my mom and my aunt. Whoever ended up with it would try to make the recipes in it, but nothing would work because she wrote the recipes down wrong on purpose. While I personally could never be organized or committed enough to have the last laugh, I think it's sort of fantastic that she was, and that she did.

4 SERVINGS

1 cup (250 mL) granulated sugar, divided

¼ cup (60 mL) all-purpose flour

zest of 1 lemon

¼ cup (60 mL) butter, melted

⅓ cup (80 mL) fresh-squeezed lemon juice

½ tsp vanilla extract

3 eggs, whites and yolks separated

1½ cups (375 mL) buttermilk

LEMON PUDDING

This was my grandmother's dog's birthday dessert. There's no way for that to sound anything but weird, but it's true. It's a delicate dish with a bold lemon flavor that tastes like lemon slice, lemon meringue pie (sans meringue), and all those treats most of us rarely make anymore. Riley, a not-thin Black Lab, favored it following a dinner of Toad in the Hole (p. 148). People like it too, which is great because, even if they didn't, my grandma would have made it anyway. Serve warm with whipped cream. Possibly be transported back to your grandmother's messy kitchen table.

Preheat oven to 350°F (180°C). Butter or grease a 1½ qt/L casserole or baking dish.

In a mixing bowl, whisk together ¾ cup (175 mL) sugar, flour, and lemon zest. Add melted butter, lemon juice, vanilla extract, and egg yolks, and whisk to form a batter. Slowly whisk in buttermilk.

In a separate bowl, whisk remaining sugar with egg whites until they form soft peaks. They should be sturdy but malleable—if you overdo it, you can almost "chunk" pieces off. It won't be the end of the world if that happens, but try not to get to there. Fold egg whites into buttermilk mixture and pour into prepared baking dish. Place dish into a larger baking pan with high sides, and fill outside pan with water to halfway up sides of dish.

Bake for 40 to 45 minutes, until top is cake-like and lightly browned. Cool for at least 30 minutes before diving in.

ORANGE GRANITA

4 SERVINGS

When summer's too hot and you're just a ball of sweat but you still for some reason have people coming over, granitas are a great approach to dessert. They come together at a leisurely pace, and you don't have to pay all that much attention to them. They're also not something you see often, so they retain an aura of elegance despite being so, so simple to prepare. This one tastes like Creamsicles.

zest of 1 large navel orange

1 lemon, zest and juice

1 cup (250 mL) freshly squeezed orange juice

1 cup (250 mL) granulated sugar

pinch salt

1 tsp vanilla

½ cup (125 mL) heavy cream

In a pot on medium-high heat, combine citrus zest and juices, sugar, and salt. Whisk until sugar has completely dissolved, 2 to 3 minutes.

Remove from heat. Whisk in vanilla and cream, and pour into a glass pan or pie plate. Place in the freezer.

Every hour for the first 3 hours after that, pull out of freezer and scrape mixture with a fork to move ice crystals around, which keeps them from becoming a solid mass. After that, just check every once in a while to be sure that all is well, scraping as needed. Freeze for about 4 hours in total. Remove from the freezer about 10 minutes before serving, and scrape with a spoon into serving dishes. Serve as is or topped with whipped cream.

ORANGE UPSIDE-DOWN CAKE

6 SERVINGS

Somewhere around the second week of December each year, I inevitably Google "too much vitamin C side effects" and try to convince myself that despite the absurdity of it, eating a 5-lb (2.2-kg) box of Mandarin oranges every other day is a healthy thing to do. By February, I'm oranged-out, but they're still all that's in season, fruit-wise. This recipe comes out of coping with that reality while still very much wanting dessert. It's best made in a 9-in (23-cm) cast-iron pan, but will work fine in a pie plate if that's your option.

Preheat oven to 375°F (190°C).

Using a knife, peel oranges. Cut slightly on the diagonal, running blade along flesh of orange, removing bitter white pith. Slice oranges horizontally to about ¼-in (6-mm) thick. Test to be sure they fit into bottom of a 9-in (23-cm) cast-iron pan with a bit of overlapping. Set aside.

Place cast-iron pan on medium-high heat and melt butter, sugar, and salt until bubbling. Remove from heat, and carefully place orange slices evenly across bottom of pan. If you don't have a cast iron-pan, grease a 9-in (23-cm) pie plate, lay orange slices along bottom, and pour caramel on top.

In a bowl, combine orange and lemon zests, cornmeal, flour, baking soda, and salt. In a separate bowl, whisk together lemon juice, oil, honey, buttermilk, egg, and vanilla. Whisk wet ingredients into dry ingredients, and pour into pan on top of butter-sugar-orange mixture.

Bake for 25 to 30 minutes, until top is golden, edges appear crisp, and caramel has bubbled through in places. Let stand for 5 minutes, then carefully turn out onto a serving plate. Let cool for 15 minutes before serving.

CARAMEL TOPPING

3 to 4 small oranges, such as navel or blood oranges (or a combination)

4 tbsp butter, cubed

¾ cup (175 mL) brown sugar

pinch salt

CAKE

zest of 1 orange

1 lemon, zest and juice

⅔ cup (160 mL) yellow cornmeal

⅔ cup (160 mL) all-purpose flour

½ tsp baking soda

½ tsp salt

2 tbsp canola oil

3 tbsp honey

1 cup (250 mL) buttermilk

1 egg

1 tsp vanilla extract

4 CUPS (1 L)

PLUM & BROWN SUGAR SORBET

2 lb (900 g) Italian prune plums, halved and pitted

¾ cup (175 mL) packed brown sugar

½ tsp ground cardamom

¼ tsp coarse salt

½ tsp vanilla extract

You know those blue, oblong little prune plums that show up in market stalls in the fall? They are a little sour, and ordinarily I think people turn them into jam. This is my favorite thing to do with them, as it means I get to extend summer a little longer. They produce a tart, sort of musky sorbet that you can eat in cones on your balcony while you comment on how it's hard to believe it's fall already, and wonder where the time goes.

In a pot on medium-high heat, bring plums, 2 cups (500 mL) water, sugar, cardamom, and salt to a boil. Reduce heat to medium, and simmer until plums have softened but not broken apart, 7 to 10 minutes.

Add vanilla. Purée contents of pot using an immersion blender; if using a regular blender, be careful—blend in batches, as hot stuff in blenders is a splattery, burning combination.

Strain mixture through a fine-mesh sieve into a bowl, and chill in the refrigerator until cold, about 2 hours. Process in ice cream maker according to manufacturer's instructions, then freeze for at least 4 hours before serving.

ROASTED PEACH SORBET

4 CUPS (1 L)

When I went to France with my friend Grace in 2011, we ended up in Lyon for the weekend. Our first meal was at a bouchon, a type of restaurant that serves traditional Lyonnaise cuisine. The sorbet they served was delicate and smooth and perfectly bright, like they'd taken the best essence of the fruit and distilled it. It was topped with about a tablespoon of Amontillado sherry, and the effect was a bit of warm in the back of your throat with every cool bite. It was magic. If you can swing it, pick up a little bit of sherry or fruit liqueur to serve with this.

2 lb (900 g) fresh peaches, halved, stones removed

¾ cup (175 mL) maple syrup

1 large lemon, zest and juice

Preheat oven to 400°F (200°C). Lightly grease a 9x13-in (3.5-L) baking dish with neutral-tasting oil such as canola.

Place peaches cut side down in dish, and bake for 20 to 25 minutes until fleshy sides have turned golden. Remove from oven, cover with aluminum foil, and let rest for 10 minutes.

Remove foil, and peel skins off peaches. Discard skins. Place peaches in a blender with remaining ingredients and ⅔ cup (160 mL) water. Pulse until smooth, then strain into a bowl. Cover with plastic and refrigerate until cool.

Pour mixture into an ice cream maker and churn according to manufacturer's instructions.

Serve on its own, with assorted other fresh fruits, or with a touch of your favorite liqueur.

If you have any left over, serve in a glass with sparkling wine—it makes a lovely Bellini!

RESOURCES ✳

Food is joy and love and pain and guilt and magic and math, and it's deeply personal and intensely political and frivolous and important. To some, it's a fun diversion, a bit of entertainment, a source of comfort and release. To others, it is everything—survival and culture and economy. It is worth paying attention to.

Pay attention to what you're eating—how it's made and who has been involved in its production, whether it's your partner or your mother or your waiter or some factory somewhere. Know, at least to some extent, where your food has come from.

Pay attention to the seasons, to the backs of packaging, to the stickers on apples, and the stamps on eggs. Ask questions. Visit farms, if you are able, and find out what grows there, and why, and if it's profitable. Notice who is working in the fields.

Pay attention to other people, especially the ones who aren't getting enough. Help them. We have enough food to go around, but it doesn't always reach everyone, and when it doesn't we need to intervene. Support your food bank, local soup kitchen, and neighbors.

When you're buying food, watch for deals. Even if you just pick up a can here and there, or a box or two of cereal every now and again, buy it and donate it. The benefit to watching prices so meticulously, for me, has been that giving is easy; if beans are seventy-seven cents a can, I'll buy as many as I need and a few more to spare; when peanut butter or tuna are on sale, I'll buy extra and just drop it in the donation bin on my way out of the supermarket. Do this throughout the year, not just during the holidays!

Food Banks

United States: *feedingamerica.org*
Canada: *foodbankscanada.ca*
Australia: *foodbank.org.au*
UK: *trusselltrust.org/foodbank-projects*

SUSTAINABILITY & HUMAN RIGHTS ORGANIZATIONS

World Vision

worldvision.org/our-impact/food-agriculture
Information on industries where children are exploited, particularly in agriculture (coffee, chocolate, sugar, fishing, and more) in easy-to-read infographic, video, and short article formats. A good introduction to what you can do to avoid products that employ children in dangerous, dirty, and degrading work, with ways to get involved.

Fairtrade International

fairtrade.net
Fairtrade is a global non-profit that works to improve transactions between farmers and the marketplace for better livelihoods, working conditions, and human rights. Look for the Fairtrade logo on everything from coffee to wine. If you can't find products in your area, look for them online through the Fairtrade site.

Rainforest Alliance

rainforest-alliance.org

The Rainforest Alliance works to conserve biodiversity, curb climate change, and help those in poverty to break the cycle by promoting, evaluating, and certifying sustainability standards in several industries, including agriculture.

Fairfood International

fairfood.org

Fairfood is a global non-profit whose aim is to improve the socio-economic conditions of the most vulnerable people in the global food system, promote the sustainable use of natural resources, and preserve the environment. Identifies and highlights areas, industries, and specific food commodities—such as tomatoes, shrimp, and livestock—to inform consumers. They also work to empower vulnerable and impoverished workers to raise their voices and demand their rights in their home countries.

The Conservation Alliance for Seafood Solutions

solutionsforseafood.org

Eighteen North American alliance members, including OceanWise, the Monterrey Bay Aquarium, and the World Wildlife Federation, bring conservation expertise to seafood businesses and consumers so ocean and freshwater seafood stocks and environments they depend on can thrive. They also work to address some of the biggest barriers to seafood sustainability.

Food and Agriculture Organization of the United Nations: Fisheries and Aquaculture Department

fao.org/fishery/about/en

The UN's fisheries branch produces an annual report, *The State of World Fisheries and Aquaculture* (SOFIA), detailing current issues in seafood stocks, environmental threats, labor, trade, and consumption. It's fairly comprehensive, and a great resource for understanding the state of the oceans and the people who work in and profit from them.

NUTRITION INFORMATION

Canadian Diabetes Association

diabetes.ca/diabetes-and-you/
healthy-living-resources/diet-nutrition

The Canadian Diabetes Association has some great information and resources for maintaining a healthy lifestyle for those with type 1 and type 2 diabetes, but much of it applies to everyone, including those with other illnesses, including heart disease, hypertension, and high cholesterol.

Meatless Monday

meatlessmonday.com

Meatless Monday is a non-profit initiative of The Monday Campaigns, which works in collaboration with the Center for a Livable Future (CLF) at the Johns Hopkins Bloomberg School of Public Health. The goal of the Meatless Monday program is to encourage everyone, everywhere to go meatless once a week in order to reduce meat consumption by fifteen percent, for our personal health, and to benefit the environment. The site offers resources, recipes, and news related to nutrition, specifically around environmental issues, meat consumption, and vegetarianism.

NIH's Human Nutrition Research Information Management Database

hnrim.nih.gov

This site details past and current/ongoing studies in human nutrition from a wide variety of academic and hospital sites across North America. You can filter your searches by category and read abstracts, other publications from principal investigators involved in research, and whether or not there are pending or ongoing clinical trials involved.

Centers for Disease Control and Prevention: Nutrition for Everyone

cdc.gov/nutrition/everyone/basics/index.html

A fairly straightforward site with basic information on simple health topics, including nutrition (food groups, dietary fat, carbohydrates, protein, etc.), chronic diseases, and more.

Seafood Nutrition Partnership

seafoodnutrition.org

An American non-profit group whose sole purpose is education around the benefits of seafood consumption, particularly as it relates to heart health and brain development. They're a partner of FishWatch, a program of the United States' National Oceanic and Atmospheric Administration's National Marine Fisheries Service.

ACKNOWLEDGMENTS ✳

Thanks to everyone who helped with the research for this book: Kelly Mulder and Crystal Karakochuk, Registered Dietitians and PhD candidates in human nutrition at the University of British Columbia; Sharon Leung, Registered Dietitian and Certified Diabetes Educator at the Diabetes Centre at Vancouver General Hospital; Ray Bucknell, Head Butcher and Production Manager at Two Rivers Specialty Meats; Teddie Geach, Ocean Wise Representative at the Vancouver Aquarium; Cheryl Hotchkiss, Senior Manager, Public Engagement and Brand Development; Britt Hamilton, Advocacy Communications Officer; and Ryan Mulligan, Policy Advisor, Food Security and Nutrition at World Vision Canada.

Thank you to Susan Safyan at Arsenal Pulp Press, who I wish could edit every word that comes off my keyboard and out of my mouth. There is no good writing without skilled editing.

Thank you to my friend Grace Yaginuma, who has tested many of the recipes contained herein (and been constructive in her feedback), and who continues to teach me important things about cooking, grammar, and karaoke. Thanks to my loyal team of eaters and food critics: Theresa Connor, Paul Bell, Tracy Stefanucci, Greg and Missy Rinsma, Chris Gerber, Laura Klompas, Aimee Taylor, Corinne Leroux, James Kim, Justyna Krol, Dan O'Brien, and Dennis Wee: I can always count on you to try something new, weird, or deep-fried.

Thank you to Nick's family, especially Sid and Candy VanderWoud and Nathan and Sharon Page, who introduced me to Dutch food, wild meat, and how weird people can be about birds.

Thank you to Lynn Newman and George Saunders for broadening my culinary horizons, and whose support has been unwaveringly enthusiastic and much appreciated.

Thank you to John and AJ Wight, who provided me with a solid foundation, a wealth of material (for this book, future books, and therapy), and all that free babysitting. Thanks to Hudson Wight for hanging out/putting up with Hunter for so many long hours while the book got written.

And thank you to Nick and Hunter, who have been very noisy and distracting through all of this, and who I ultimately do all this cooking and writing for.

INDEX

EMILY WIGHT is a writer, blogger, and home cook. A graduate of the Creative Writing program at the University of British Columbia, she's spent the past six years blogging at Well Fed, Flat Broke, a site that chronicles her forays in the kitchen as she tries to balance a career and parenthood, which includes a picky-eating toddler and a neurotic cat. Everything in her life is sticky.

wellfedflatbroke.com